Exquisite Love

Heart-Centered Reflections
on the Nārada Bhakti Sūtra

Exquisite Love

Heart-Centered Reflections
on the Nārada Bhakti Sūtra

William K. Mahony

Anusara Press

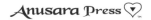

Anusara Press™
9400 Grogan's Mill Road, Suite 240
The Woodlands, TX 77380
(888)398-9642
(281)367-2744 (fax)
www.anusara.com

EXQUISITE LOVE
Heart-Centered Reflections on the *Nārada Bhakti Sūtra*

First Edition
9 8 7 6 5 4 3 2

Library of Congress Control Number: 2010912672
Mahony, William K.
Exquisite Love: Heart-Centered Reflections on the *Nārada Bhakti Sūtra*

ISBN 978-0-9823884-5-7
Printed in the United States of America

Mixed Sources
Product group from well-managed forests and other controlled sources
www.fsc.org Cert no. SW-COC-002888
© 1996 Forest Stewardship Council
FSC

Printed on FSC-Certified paper that includes a minimum of 10% post-consumer recovered fiber. The FSC trademark identifies products which contain fiber from well-managed forests certified by SmartWood in accordance with the rules of the Forest Stewardship Council.

Printed with Low-VOC vegetable based inks including Linseed, Soya and other natural oils.

Contents

Foreword by John Friend ... vii
Acknowledgements ... xi
Pronunciation Guide for Sanskrit Words ... xiii
Introduction ... 1

Part I

What is Bhakti?

1 Initial Comments and Reflections ... 23
2 The Highest Love, the Love for the Highest ... 35

Part II

Components of Bhakti as a Yogic Practice

3 Grace and Self-Effort in Spiritual Love ... 53
4 Foundations of Bhakti as a Yogic Discipline ... 69
5 Devotional Practices in the Yogic Life ... 91

Part III

Inner Transformations brought through Bhakti as a Spiritual Practice

6 Ecstasy, Enstasy and Delight ... 123
7 Brighter Splendor in One's Love ... 139
8 Refinement of the Emotions and Deepening of Devotional States ... 163

9 Equanimity, Mindfulness and the Calming of Harmful Desire 189
10 Inner Freedom, Expansiveness, Constancy, Sublimity, Serenity, Joy... 207
11 Communion with the Divine 225

Part IV

Fulfillment in Love

12 In Love, the Path and the Goal are One 237
13 In Love, All is Love 247

Translation of the Nārada Bhakti Sūtra *259*
List of Tables *275*
Notes *276*
Index *283*

Foreword by John Friend

Even before I was in kindergarten I felt a desire burning within me to penetrate the deepest mysteries of existence. This was more than a profound inquisitiveness. It was a deep, insatiable longing to know the purpose of life, to enter my heart and to merge with the Supreme. When I was just 8 years old I would write, "I Love God," with my finger on the frosted windows of my mother's car as she drove me to church. It was the outpouring of a surging fountain of ecstatic emotion that would arise within me as I contemplated the unlimited vastness of the creative intelligence at the Source of everything.

When I was thirteen years old, I bought my first copy of the classic Indian scripture, the *Bhagavad Gītā.* This little book opened me to a whole new world of devotional love for God, a love called *bhakti* in Sanskrit. As my studies in Indian philosophy and yoga expanded while I was in college, I learned about the *Bhakti Sūtra,* a set of teachings on bhakti said to be composed by a sage named Nārada. In just 84 terse aphorisms, this 10th century Sanskrit text provides comprehensive and sparkling wisdom on the nature of spiritual love and devotion. For over thirty years now I have referred to this splendid work as a guide to cultivate ever-expanding levels of love throughout every activity of my life.

Now it is my great honor to present *Exquisite Love* by Bill Mahony, which brings extraordinary elucidation to the great subject of divine Love for the modern yoga student. Bill Mahony is not only an outstanding

Sanskritist and preeminent scholar of Indian philosophy; he is a long-time bhakti yogī, a lover of God. I first met Bill in 1993 at an ashram in upstate New York and since then we have become dear friends. The first impression people usually have of Bill is of his radiant and gentle kindness. In addition to his intellectual brilliance, his being exudes great tenderness and love.

To be an effective and accurate scholar of the *Bhakti Sūtra*, I believe that one not only needs to be highly knowledgeable about the vast subject of South Asian philosophy, but one needs to have practiced devotional yoga for many years. Certainly one needs to have embodied bhakti in every aspect of life to authoritatively comment on this text. As an ardent practitioner of yoga for decades, Bill constantly orients himself with wonder and gratitude toward the complex mystery and splendor of life. Most importantly, Bill seeks always to turn toward Love as the basis of every element of his sādhana, his own spiritual practice. This is why Bill Mahony is a perfect commentator on the *Bhakti Sūtra* for the modern yoga student.

In *Exquisite Love*, Bill Mahony translates and explains 20 key sutras from the larger work. It is important to note that he also includes a translation of the entire text at the end of the book. Based on his extensive yogic experiences and his immense scholarly knowledge, Bill insightfully offers his personal reflections on the path of bhakti as deep devotion to God and how this profound spiritual practice can be applied in one's daily life. Bill defines bhakti in a very accessible way for any earnest spiritual seeker. It is a spiritual love that is both unconditional and without ego, yet expressed in a uniquely personal way. In bhakti there is a juicy emotional quality associated with each loving offering to Spirit.

Although bhakti can encompass a passionate offering to Spirit, it arises from an intoxicated state of desirelessness and fullness of love. Readers of *Exquisite Love* will clearly understand that the path of bhakti is not one of dry detachment related to the seeking of spiritual liberation from the entanglements of the physical world, but rather as a path of deep affirmation of life in this world. Bill's lucid reflections on bhakti provide students of yoga philosophy a great source of information to study, contemplate and incorporate into their lives. These cogent insights exhibit a finely-tuned appreciation of the nature of love in its many forms and how the different ways that we experience love variously reflect the universal light of divine Love. *Exquisite Love* emphasizes the value of bhakti as a profoundly transformative and fulfilling sādhana that affirms the wonder of life for any level of yoga student.

The central image and theme that Bill Mahony uses throughout *Exquisite Love* is that of the Heart and of a Heart-centered yogic practice. He speaks of the Heart as the divine core of existence, the presence of Divinity within all beings. As the foundation of divine Love, the Heart is the ultimate affirmation of existence that finds various expressions of giving and receiving love throughout human experience. Bill characterizes yoga as the practice of aligning with and immersing in the Heart. This perspective is consistent both with the teachings of the *Bhakti Sūtra* and with Anusara yoga's philosophy of Shiva-Shakti Tantra. It is the path of beneficial attitudes, alignments and disciplined actions attuned to the Goodness found within all life. By attuning to the Heart we allow Love to guide all our relationships, while also leading to deeper self-understanding. The deeper we abide in the Heart, the more fully we open to the graceful, affirming power of Divinity at the very essence of life.

Exquisite Love is not only a clear exposition of the Heart, but it is a luminous guide to help people skillfully connect to the graceful, loving Presence at the very center of their Being. In addition to wonderfully presenting a set of reflections on how we can become more immersed in the Heart through yogic sādhana, *Exquisite Love* inspires us to deepen and refine the experience of Love within our lives. This spiritual process of alignment through devotional love is never-ending and ever expanding for the rest of our lives – for the Heart always yearns to connect with others and to offer Love as its naturally creative expression.

Composed 1000 years ago, the *Nārada Bhakti Sūtra* contains spiritual teachings that people today can contemplate, assimilate and repeatedly integrate into their modern lives, bringing them more happiness and love.

May Bill Mahony's radiant reflections on this important yogic text help you gain invaluable insights into the full spectrum of the experiences of love throughout your life. May you find the teachings within *Exquisite Love* to be informative, illuminating, and so inspiring that Love for God becomes the ever-expanding basis of your life.

January 11, 2011 (1.11.11)
The Woodlands, Texas

Acknowledgements

This set of reflections on the spiritual life responds in part to the graceful inspiration I have received through the years from Swami Chidvilasananda, the current head of the Siddha Yoga path, whose teachings embody qualities of what the *Nārada Bhakti Sūtra* calls *paramapreman*: the highest love. I offer my gratitude to her for the love through which she guides the unfolding of the spiritual heart.

Preparation of this book has taken me through a number of drafts. Harold Ferrar and Jonathan Shimkin read separate earlier versions and gave me structural and stylistic suggestions that I subsequently incorporated. Angela Rudert diligently and thoughtfully read more recent drafts and shared with me her perceptive, insightful and wise responses to them.

It has been a true pleasure to work with Anusara Press. John Friend steadfastly encouraged me to publish the book and kindly agreed to write the Foreword. Christy Nones skillfully undertook the final line editing with a gracious intuition into the book's topic, helped with the Tables at the ends of chapters and prepared the Index. Anh Phan artfully designed the cover, fashioned the internal format and oversaw the printing process. Kara Fox, Stacey Millner-Collins and Jessica Cristen Pruitt read the work before it was published. Dana Shamas supervised the whole project. To them and to all on the publication team at Anusara Press I express my appreciation.

Unless otherwise noted, all translations in this book are my own. The following publishers gave me permission to quote from their publications: Penguin Books for quotations from *Bihārī: The Satasaī*, translated from the Hindi and with an introduction by Krishna P. Bahadur; State University of New York Press for passages from *Shaiva Devotional Songs of Kashmir: A Translation and Study of Utpaladeva's Shivastotravali*, by Constantina Rhodes Bailly; SYDA Foundation for quotations from Swami Chidvilasananda's published works and for passages from *Jñaneshwar's Gita* by Swami Kripananda.

My wife Pamela has been constant throughout the years in her encouragement, patience, friendship and emotional support. Our daughters Abigael and Olivia are for me wondrous embodiments of the mystery that is divine Love. To my family I offer all my heart.

William K. Mahony

Pronunciation Guide for Sanskrit Words

This book makes use of conventionally established diacritical marks to help in the pronunciation of Sanskrit words. Here is a chart of ways in which Sanskrit sounds are represented in Roman transliteration. Letters with dots under them generally represent sounds made with the tongue arching toward the roof of the mouth. English tends not to have these sounds, so it is somewhat difficult to find equivalents. The letters in this chart are organized according to the English alphabet.

Letter	Equivalent sound in English
a	b<u>u</u>t
ā	f<u>a</u>ther
ai	<u>ai</u>sle
au	c<u>ow</u>
b	<u>b</u>utter
bh	cra<u>b-h</u>ouse
c	always pronounced as in <u>ch</u>erish, not as in re<u>c</u>eive
ch	chur<u>ch-h</u>ouse
dh	ma<u>d-h</u>ouse
ḍ	<u>d</u>oor
ḍh	square<u>d-h</u>ouse
e	g<u>a</u>te
g	<u>g</u>o

Letter	Equivalent sound in English
gh	always pronounced as in dog-house, not as in enough
h	hut
ḥ	adds a slight breath to the preceding vowel; when at the end of a sentence, adds a brief echo of the preceding vowel
i	still
ī	machine
j	jump
jh	sledge-hammer
k	kitchen
kh	back-hoe
l	lower
ḷ	little
m	mother
ṁ	nasalizes the preceding vowel
ñ	onion
ṅ	sing
ṇ	happened
o	boat
p	push
ph	always as in up-hill, not as in telephone
r	ray
ṛ	rich
s	sun
ś	shoe
ṣ	shun
t	towel
ṭ	flute
th	goat-herder
ṭh	dentist
u	smooth
ū	lute
v	halfway between value and way
y	yes, never as in silly

Introduction

The thoughts and reflections offered in this book arise from the experiential intuition that the source, foundation and fulfillment of life stand in the affirming power of Love. I capitalize the word here to signify the ultimate nature of this Love, which supports and cherishes each and all of us at the core of our being as the graceful power that enlivens all of existence itself. In this book I will refer to this Love in other similarly capitalized ways, too: it is the Source, the Highest, the Mystery, the Sublime, the divine Beloved, Divinity itself. At times I will refer to the ground of this Love as the universal Self that dwells within our particular selves. It is the divine Heart that stands within, inspires and gives movement to all our experiences of our own spiritual hearts. I will frequently associate the Heart's love with God. I will say more about my use of the word God shortly.

The Love that stands within all of existence is the ultimate source of our own human sentiments of love in all of its forms. Immersing more fully into this Love, we can more fully strengthen and refine our own particular expressions of love in our lives.

Yet, we do not always experience Love. One reason this is so is because there is much in the world that distorts and constricts the expansive dynamics of Love. There is pettiness, apathy, closed-mindedness, greed, malevolence and hatred. As we all know, at times this degradation of the inherent beauty and dignity of the human spirit can be profound.

Another reason we may not experience Love is because we ourselves can become less aware of its presence within us and therefore less attentive to it. When our hearts are closed to Love we are less able to align ourselves with its grace or to allow it to express itself through us. It becomes hidden, cloaked, obscured. When we turn from Love we thereby turn from the deepest foundation and ultimate source of our being. When we neglect our own love, we diminish the highest possibilities of our own true nature, and the extent to which we do this is the extent to which we feel incomplete, alienated and unfulfilled.

On the other hand, to live our lives moved by love, to any degree, is to live our lives illumined by the light of Love within us to that same degree and thus to more fully fulfill the promise of our birth. This is why our profoundest and most human yearning, our most compelling longing, is to turn toward Love.

To turn toward Love — to return to Love — is to open our hearts to its presence within us and within others, and then to live our lives in steadier alignment with it. The turn toward Love thus implies a movement of sorts, a transformation of our existence. It begins within us when we feel various human sentiments associated with wanting, receiving and giving love.

That there is the possibility of such movement toward higher love implies that there are levels of love, some more elevated than others. Our longing to know and experience higher forms of love will lead us to elevate the quality of our love, to refine our coarser expectations and expressions of love, and to cultivate and nourish love in our lives. As we do so — as we enter more fully into experiences of our love and give ourselves more fully to the expression of our love — we come to know that divine Love itself has always been with and within us, and our feelings of incompletion, alienation or unfulfillment can dissolve. The turn toward Love is a turn toward a full and appreciative affirmation of existence.

This movement, this transformation, begins with and is supported throughout by our openness to the benevolent grace that is the nature of divine Love. Then, it takes conscious, intentional commitment and practice on our parts to refine, strengthen and purify our hearts. This is to say, it takes spiritual discipline to elevate our love.

Such a life becomes increasingly infused with gratitude, contentment and devotion. It is a life that leads us to fuller and fuller immersion into the Love that shares itself with us, cherishes us and affirms our existence at the deepest levels of our being.

In this book I offer thoughts on the nature of Love and our response to it. I will give some attention to ways in which we can turn toward Love and note some of the transformations that can take place within us as we expand our immersion into Love. My sources for these reflections lie in the religious traditions of India, although we could of course find inspiration in teachings presented by other religious traditions, too, particularly in their devotional and mystical dimensions.

As a way to anchor my reflections, I will refer specifically to a Sanskrit text on devotional love known as the *Nārada Bhakti Sūtra*. This text is often referred to more simply as the *Bhakti Sūtra*, and this is what I will also at times do in this book. In addition, I will refer to a number of other works from the spiritual traditions in India — sacred texts, poems, songs, philosophical musings, contemporary teachings — that support, illumine and expand the points being made as I offer those reflections.

I will say more about the *Nārada Bhakti Sūtra* itself in a subsequent section of this Introduction. Before doing so, I would like to offer some initial comments regarding some foundational concepts and perspectives that will find repeated expression throughout this book.

Love as the Divine Heart of Existence

The sense that Love gives rise to all things can be found in visionary insights and sacred teachings first presented in India as far back as the ancient period. In a song from the *Ṛg Veda* dating to roughly 1500 BCE we hear sentiments of wonder in view of the otherwise incomprehensible fact that the universe actually exists. We ourselves can share the same wonder. What a mystery existence is! By what force is existence pulled from the depths of nonexistence? Why does existence exist? How can we, as human beings, come to understand this? The song expresses an appreciation of this compelling, profound mystery in the form of a creation narrative:

> There was neither nonbeing nor being then.
> There was no region of air nor sky beyond it.
> What moved? Where? Under whose protection?
> Was there water, deep and unfathomable?
> There was neither death nor immortality then.
> There was no distinction between night and day.
> By its own inner power that One breathed, windless. . . .
> Love-yearning entered that One, in the beginning:
> That was the first seed of thought.
> Searching within their hearts with wisdom,
> Sages found the bond of being within nonbeing.[1]

We can join the visionaries who first sang this song by envisioning a state of absolute potential, an encompassing field of unbounded, infinite possibility that precedes emergence of any dualities whatsoever. There was "no distinction between night and day," no "region of air nor sky beyond it." This field of potential is beyond even the duality that is death and immortality — beyond even the duality of nonbeing and being themselves. Our song refers to this absolute potential simply as "that One."

What then is said to happen, "in the beginning"? Our song suggests that a movement of sorts stirred within the One: "By its own inner power that One breathed, windless." It was this power that drew the foundational Mystery from a state of pure potential into the actuality of manifold existence.

What was this power? What was the nature of that "first seed of thought" that impelled being out of nonbeing?

It was the power of that One's own yearning-to-be that brought the world into existence. This motion-toward-being did not seek gratification in any object or the fulfillment of any conditions, for objects and conditions did not yet exist. Rather, it expressed an unconditional affirmation of existence itself.

When I reflect on this song of creation, I sometimes picture in my mind a vast, unbounded ocean of undifferentiated Consciousness. It is an ocean of pure light. Then, a pulse — Love itself — moves within this infinite field of potential. Rays of Love spread outward from this center, taking countless different forms as individual waves rise into existence, each refracting the light of Consciousness in their own particular ways and conditioned by various forces. The One becomes the Many, all of which also hold within them the essence of the One. You and I are instances of such waves in this ocean of Consciousness, at the center of which is Love.

We can think of this creative Center of all existence, this essential Core of all being, as the divine Heart. Just as the light of the Center shines within all the particular waves emanating from it, so too the Heart stands within each of us in our own particularity, as the foundational essence of life itself. Transcendent, unlimited divine Love expresses itself in our own relative, human lives in the form of our particular experiences of love. By entering into our own love — by entering our own hearts and by honoring the hearts of others — we turn toward the divine Heart that supports all of those experiences of love. We can be like the ancient sages who, "searching their hearts with wisdom," found within themselves reverberations of the same yearning that, at its most profound level, brought the world itself into being. As a verse from the *Atharva Veda*, a sacred text from India dating to about 1000 BCE, declares,

> Through Love, love has come to me;
> from Heart, to heart.
> The thought of distant others:
> may that thought come to me, here.[2]

Initial Comments regarding God as Love

What is that divine Source in which or in whom Love stirs? What is the Heart that holds this Love and from which our own feelings of love emerge?

In this book, I will refer frequently in this regard to God. I am of course aware that this word will carry different connotations for different people. Some may feel uncomfortable with the word. This is understandable. Some people have been injured by others' concepts of God. Reference to God has been used by some people in a divisive, judgmental manner and expressed with a sense of superiority over others. As we know, this has sometimes led even to war. Some people may find the idea of God a rather obsolete notion in the context of various scientific and social scientific trends.

Accordingly, it might be helpful if I were to say a few initial words about what, in part, I mean in these reflections when I refer to God.

- I would begin by saying: *God is Love.*
- Accordingly, also: *love is of the nature of God.*
- And thus: *to love is to share in the divine nature.*

Of course, it would take some time to explore the implications of this stance that identifies God with love. For now, I ask you to think of your own experience of love, at any level. Whether you love music, love to gaze at the stars, or love children, you experience in that state to some degree an affirmation of existence. It is good that music, the stars, and children exist and it is good that you are here to enjoy them. Loving them, you may well feel the tendency to respond to them by saying "Yes" to them in return, in some manner and at some level.

To experience and express love in any way and to any degree is therefore similarly to experience and express an affirmation of existence. Just as there are relatively superficial ways of affirming the goodness of life, so too there are relatively superficial ways of living in love. When we move deeper into the affirmation of existence we move deeper into that auspicious power or principle by which anything and everything exists — and indeed by which all of existence itself exists.

The more we move into the ultimate power and affirmation of being, the more we move into God, as I will be using the term. As the ultimate affirmation of being, God is the exuberant force by which the world and all things in it come into being, through which all things are sustained, and by which all things move toward their completion. God is Love. Understood from this perspective, without Love there would be nothing, nothing at all.

Love dances within the emergence and movements of the immense galaxies soaring through space-time, just as it does at the most minute levels of the subatomic realms. Your own being has its own unique existence — its particular nature, its meaning, its value — in the embrace of that Love. This Love for you does not end with your death, for the wondrous truth that is you remains real in Love's eternal memory.

To experience God as Love invites and supports a response. The heart yearns to offer love in return. It is with this longing in mind that I rather frequently refer to God as the divine Beloved. By speaking of God in this way, I mean to imply, in part, that whenever we love anything we are actually to that degree recognizing and responding to the presence of the Divine within it.

This is true perhaps most immediately in our love for others. As the divine Source that gives rise to and supports the existence of all things, God cherishes all people. To love another person is thereby also to love God. Accordingly, you will notice in the following reflections that I often refer to ways in which we can love people as well as God.

So, too, God's love is revealed when we open ourselves to the divine Presence deep within our own hearts. Indeed, we are able to love another person in the first place because God, the ultimate Source and Object of all love, in some way already moves within us. At the deepest level, or the highest level, the loving heart shares this essence with the true Beloved. By cultivating, strengthening and refining our love, we thereby turn toward the divine Heart.

The *Bhakti Sūtra* speaks of God as Bhagavān, which is not a name but rather a title. It means "possessing *bhaga*," the latter term by the time of this text meaning "goodness, wellbeing, prosperity, dignity, excellence, majesty, beauty." Both words, bhaga and Bhagavān, come from a verbal root (*bhaj*) meaning to "portion out, dispense, share, participate in, be part of." The title Bhagavān as the possessor of bhaga can thus be said to refer to God as the majestic, ultimate source of Love who distributes that love to the world. As a word, Bhagavān is sometimes therefore translated in Indian texts as "the Lord, the Munificent One, the Blessed One, the Loving One." So, too, Bhagavān is the one who draws and receives the lover's own share of love, the lover's adoration, in return; the title therefore is also variously translated as "the Adorable One, the Venerable One, the Holy One" and, understandably, "the Beloved One."

God Dwells in the Heart of All Beings

The understanding that all of existence is held in the embrace of Divinity turns in part on the mystical intuition that within all the world of multiplicity is a single, pervasive, eternal and abiding foundation, a ground of all being, that supports, envelops and sustains all things. Indian thought describes this as *sat*: the truth that existence exists, the very Beingness of being itself. The *Bṛhadāraṇyaka Upaniṣad*, a sacred text dating to around 700 BCE, speaks of this as "The real within the real."[3] Without the fact of Being, there can be none of the many beings that populate the world, just as without an ocean there can be no waves. Similar texts speak of a universal power and essence that stands hidden within the many objects of the universe. The *Śvetāśvatara Upaniṣad*, which dates to around 500 BCE, describes this divine essence as residing within all things "like oil in sesame seeds, butter in cream, or fire in wood."[4]

This single, fine, vital and powerful Reality inwardly supports the existence of each person, too, as the very ground of his or her own particular being. Within the diversity of the many stands the One.

According to this understanding, ultimately there is only one Self in the world of multiplicity, for this universal Foundation of all things dwells within all things. A later Upaniṣad uses an effective simile to make this point:

> There is only a single Being-Self.
> It lives in each and every being.
> Uniform, yet multiform,
> it appears like the [reflections of the single] moon
> in [the many ripples of] a pond.[5]

In recognition of this way of thinking, in this book I will capitalize the word "Self" when referring to this universal Foundation within all things. Said differently: the Self is the Heart, and the Heart is the Self.

The understanding that a single divine Self exists within all particular selves stands at the core of some of India's most abiding of religious and philosophical sensibilities. As the ancient sage Uddālaka is remembered in the *Chāndogya Upaniṣad* to have taught his son Śvetaketu, a "subtle fineness" exists within all manifest form and that "this whole world has that as its soul. That is Reality. That is the Self. Thou art That."[6] The *thou* here refers to the foundation of Śvetaketu's being, and the *that* refers to the Foundation of all things. Uddālaka is telling Śvetaketu here that the essence of his true self is identical to the essence of the universal Self.

My reflections and comments in this book are based, in considerable part, on a similar understanding regarding the divine Self. The Self dwells in the innermost heart of each of us as embodied beings, and yet also extends, infinite and unbounded, through all of existence. As the *Chāndogya Upaniṣad* says elsewhere,

> This is the Self within my heart: smaller than a grain of rice, or a corn of barley, or a mustard seed, or a grain of millet, or the kernel of a grain of millet. This is the Self within my heart: more vast than the earth, more vast than the atmosphere, more vast than the heavens, more vast than all the worlds . . . This is the Self within my heart.[7]

According to a number of lines of Indian thought with which I will align my comments specifically on the *Bhakti Sūtra*, the single, true Self that dwells within all beings is none other than God. The *Śvetāśvatara Upaniṣad* expresses this view when it refers to "God, the creator of all things, the great Self, ever seated in the heart of creatures."[8] That text notes the place of loving adoration of God in response to that universal Presence:

> It is the greatness of God in the world,
> by which this whole universe is eternally embraced.
> The Supreme, the great Lord of lords, the Transcendent one:
> may we know him as God,
> the Lord of the world, the Adorable one.[9]

To experience the One who draws our love is to experience the Ground of all existence itself, and to experience the divine Self within others as well as oneself is to experience profound joy. As the *Śvetāśvatara Upaniṣad* says:

> The wise who perceive the one God —
> hidden in all things, all-pervading,
> the inner Self of all beings —
> as abiding within their self:
> to them belongs eternal happiness.[10]

The *Bhagavad Gītā*, a text dating to around the second century BCE to which I will refer frequently in these reflections, makes use of another simile to express the understanding that, while remaining transcendent and supreme, God is present in all things. At one point, the Blessed One declares:

> There is nothing superior to me . . .
> this whole universe is strung on me,
> like pearls on a string.[11]

Transcendent yet also fully imminent — dwelling within all beings, holding all beings — God is present to the soul at the very center of one's own being. In that same text, God teaches a beloved disciple that,

> The Lord of all beings
> dwells in the region of the heart.[12]

Those who expand and deepen their reverence for God's inner presence thereby see and honor the light of Divinity within all things. When we ourselves turn toward our true hearts we also turn toward the divine Heart; and when we do this, we open our hearts to Divinity wherever we may be. As the *Īśā Upaniṣad* says,

> This whole world is to be enfolded into the Lord,
> everything that lives in this world. . . .
> Seeing oneself within all beings and all beings within oneself,
> one never turns from the Lord.[13]

Yoga, Yogas and the Yogic Life

My thoughts in this book are directed toward the place of Love in the spiritual life. I am aware of the ambiguity of the word "spiritual" and that, accordingly, the phrase "spiritual life" can be understood in various ways. Here, I use it to refer to what might otherwise be called the yogic life. The word "yogic" itself is of course an English neologism. The Sanskrit term *yoga* from which it is constructed carries a number of related meanings. For some readers, this word will bring immediately to mind the practice of *haṭha yoga* or of *āsana* practice, that is to say, of placing the body in beneficial positions, often coordinated with *prāṇāyāma*, which is the conscious engagement with the breath. Yet, yoga includes much more than these practices.

In a broad sense, the word *yoga* itself refers to a harnessing of some sort. It is related to the English word *yoke*, as when two bullocks are yoked to each other to pull a plow. From this sense of harnessing for an effective purpose the word also comes to refer to an application of a skill or cultivation of an effective technique at completing an endeavor. Ancient texts in India speak, for example, about a yoga of lighting a fire, a yoga of making tools, a yoga of cooking food: anything that benefits from the use of an effective technique.

More to our purposes, the term *yoga* has come through the centuries to refer to techniques, attitudes and disciplines associated with what can broadly be called the spiritual life. A person who practices yoga is a *yogī* (masculine) or *yoginī* (feminine). Such disciplines involve, arise from, and lead to some sort of union or bringing together — a yoking, if you will — of various states or qualities. So, accordingly, even as it denotes a set of spiritual practices, the word *yoga* also refers to a state of unity or integration toward which such practices lead.

We can think of several components of such a coming together in unity: breath and body, body and mind, mind and heart, individual self with the larger human community, human community with the natural world — the possible modes of such a joining or coming together are many.

In this book I am most interested in yoga in a large and encompassing sense. As I will use the term for our current purposes, I will define "yoga" and characterize "the yogic life" in this way:

- At the highest level, yoga is the communion of the human spirit with God.
- So, too, yoga is a means by which this communion takes place.
- Accordingly, at the highest level, the yogic life is a life that is oriented toward communion with God.

There are many and various ways in which one can become aligned with or immersed in the presence of Divinity. Accordingly, there are many spiritual practices that serve this purpose. This is to say that, within the larger sense of yoga itself, there are various yogas. There is the yoga of sacred knowledge, the yoga of responsible and engaged activity in the world, the yoga of meditation, the yoga of absorption into divine consciousness, and so on. In their various ways, all of these methods — all of these yogas — are understood to serve as various ways to be open to, turn toward and commune more fully with God.

In these reflections I will direct my thoughts specifically to a yogic life that is oriented toward communion with God as Love, a communion that is facilitated and empowered by grace and refined through a host of spiritual practices. A yogic life illumined by devotional love requires conscious, diligent discipline on the yogī's or yoginī's part. It involves contemplation, meditation, study, service, attention to harmonious living, care for the body, mindfulness and other intentional practices. It is also a life infused with increasing joy, spontaneity and wonder lived in the warmth and boundlessness of the divine Heart. In a larger sense, the yogic life of love and devotion is the spiritual life in all its fullness.

The *Nārada Bhakti Sūtra*

Dating to the tenth to eleventh centuries, the *Nārada Bhakti Sūtra* is a set of 84 short teachings and aphorisms (*sūtras*) on spiritual love and devotion (*bhakti*) composed in Sanskrit and attributed to the sage, Nārada. The fuller title, with its reference to Nārada, can be used to distinguish it from another text from roughly the same period, the *Śāṇḍilya Bhakti Sūtra*. The latter is considerably longer than the *Nārada Bhakti Sūtra* and, being more focused on philosophical issues, is perhaps of rather less interest to nonspecialists. The *Nārada Bhakti Sūtra* will fit our current purposes well.

Even though there are many sūtras in the *Nārada Bhakti Sūtra*, the collection as a whole can be understood to be a single presentation on the nature of this form of love. The word *sūtra* literally means "thread." So, here we have 84 short threads that, taken together, constitute a large thread that presents a systematic whole. Accordingly, we can speak of the collection itself as a sūtra, as we do, for example, of Patañjali's *Yoga Sūtra*. In this book I will capitalize the word *Sūtra* in reference to the entire text and use the lower case *sūtra* when referring to an individual teaching within it. While it would be good to include commentary on all 84 of the sūtras, to do so in the manner I envisioned for these reflections would not have been possible in a book of this length. Therefore, I have chosen to reflect on aspects of the spiritual life grounded in spiritual love as represented by twenty particular sūtras. Readers who would like access to the whole text will find my translation of it toward the end of this book.

I say that this text is attributed to Nārada because "Nārada" is a composite of many different literary figures through several centuries. These sūtras were most likely composed by an anonymous sage or perhaps group of teachers, whom tradition then associated with this figure. There is reference to Nārada in other sacred texts, too, some of which predate these sūtras considerably. For example, some hymns from the *Ṛg Veda* dating to the second millennium BCE are traditionally attributed to a poet-singer named Nārada.[14] So, too, there is reference in the *Bhagavad Gītā*, from roughly the second century BCE, to a divine seer (*devarṣi*) named Nārada.[15] Among other works, the name is also associated with the *Nārada Smṛti*, a collection of instructions and guidelines for proper living (*dharma*) dating to roughly the second century CE, and in the *Nārada* (or *Nāradīya*) *Purāṇa*, a collection in verse form of sacred stories and theological stances dating to the mid to latter part of the first millennium CE. The figure of Nārada appears, too, in the important *Bhāgavata Purāṇa*, another of such major collections of religious narrative dating from about the fourth to sixth centuries CE but that includes material that is considerably earlier. Indeed, tradition holds that it was Nārada's words to the sage Vyāsa that inspired the latter to compose the *Bhāgavata Purāṇa* itself as an expression of the realization that love is the highest goal of human knowledge and the fruit of all sacred learning.[16] The thirteenth century poet-saint Jñāneśvar has said that "the sayings of Nārada are like rivers of devotion."[17]

The composite image of Nārada in these literatures is of a visionary poet and wandering spiritual seeker who travels across the earth and in the heavens while meeting various people and celestial beings in many different circumstances. He often is depicted as singing songs of devotion to God and playing his *vīnā*, a stringed lute-like instrument that produces a beautiful, golden sound. In some of these texts he is represented as a rather mischievous prankster who sees and often enjoys peoples' foibles as well as exhibits a number of his own. At times he plays the part of a holy fool. Some traditions imply that his experiences and conversations give him understanding of people in their various stages of the spiritual life and that this enables him to serve as a spiritual teacher who brings goodness to the world, particularly during difficult times. This latter image of him is consistent with the Nārada of the *Bhakti Sūtra.*

For the sake of simplicity, in this book I will refer to Nārada as if he were a particular person, but for our current purposes we can think of the words that form our text as those of a timeless, almost archetypal sage who has gained his wisdom after a long spiritual search of his own, a search undertaken over a life lived to its fullest.

The *Nārada Bhakti Sūtra* is generally associated with theological perspective in India that regards Bhagavān as Viṣṇu, the All-Pervader, often in the beautiful and compelling form of Kṛṣṇa. As has also been said by others, however,[18] the fact that the text does not address God with a particular name allows the possibility for people to call on God by any name. In this way, we can understand the lessons these sūtras teach regarding love for God to be available to all people, including those from cultures other than India's.

The Sūtra-Style of Spiritual Teaching and Study

The short statements that form Nārada's *Bhakti Sūtra* are most likely lessons originally used by teachers to guide the spiritual development of small groups of students and by philosophers pondering the nature of spiritual love. As I have said, the word *sūtra* itself means "thread." We can think of a *sūtra* as a small but strong string or cord of some sort that holds larger things together. (It is related to the English word *suture.*) A *sūtra* is a statement that in just a few words holds within it ideas, perspectives and realizations that otherwise might take many more words to express.

Sūtra-style texts often serve as succinct encapsulations of much larger bodies of wisdom and collections of teachings pertaining to the topic at hand. In the context of spiritual study and learning, the markedly concise nature of this genre serves several purposes.

First, a sūtra is understood to be a crystalization of a deep and extensive knowledge or wisdom. Therefore, each sūtra is understood to hold a significance that extends beyond its surface meaning. As a text, the *Bhakti Sūtra* is typical in this regard, for it condenses into its few short statements the key ideas, values, views and intentions of a large number of devotional stories and teachings in India up to its time.

A second reason why these teachings may be in the form of sūtras is that this style allows students to memorize them. The *Bhakti Sūtra* as a collection of teachings was composed long before the development of book publishing. Students could not go to a library or bookstore to get access to them. So, the very brevity of the sūtras allowed them to carry their lessons wherever they went. Holding the wisdom of the sūtras within their minds and hearts, students were more able to let the light of that inner guidance illumine their own way on the spiritual path.

Because we now have books and other ways of keeping information we may no longer need to memorize texts. However, it is still just as important for those on a spiritual path to enter deeply into sacred texts as one of the foundations of their spiritual study. Indeed, in sūtra 76 of our text, Nārada makes the point that the study of teachings on loving God is one of the components of the spiritual path of love itself. When we get to that sūtra, I will note a process in which students assimilate and apply the knowledge, insight and wisdom they gain from such study.

A third and important reason is related to the second, and this is that each phrase in a sūtra, and indeed every word in each phrase, can serve as an illuminating source of spiritual reflection. The meaning of the sūtra may not be readily apparent because it is so concise. It is necessary to ponder them, think about them, allow them to reveal their meaning, internalize them. This invites and supports the practice of contemplation.

In this same spirit, I will reflect here on our selected sūtras phrase by phrase, and even word by word and will encourage you to do the same. This gives us the setting in which we can undertake a form of spiritual contemplation in which seekers on a spiritual path read or listen attentively to short lines of sacred texts. Having heard or read them, students reflect deeply and in a sustained manner on their meaning and search within themselves for ways to apply those lessons in their own lives. This is a process that invites inspiration, allows for guidance, leads to fuller understanding and nourishes the soul.

A Note on Perspective

The *Nārada Bhakti Sūtra* is not a philosophical treatise. It is a succinct set of teachings on the nature of devotional love. However, its phrasing does reflect the background influence of various Indian philosophical stances. Accordingly, the interpretive frame that supports my reflections on this text is rather syncretistic in nature. Readers who are familiar with Indian philosophy will recognize the influence of the Vedānta in my comments, particularly in my frequent reference to the divine Self. Such readers will recognize Bhāgavata ideas regarding the supreme Self as God. So, too, they will see Sāṁkhya views, especially in reference to the qualities and characteristics of various physical, mental and emotional states of being.

Some of my comments also express perspectives with which the sūtras may not historically have been directly aligned but with which I feel can be fruitfully applied to them. I am thinking here of some Tantric views, particularly those that affirm the beauty and value of human embodiment and the sacred nature of existence at its many levels.

Since this is not a book on these particular philosophies, *per se*, readers who are not familiar with them need not worry. I hope I have composed these reflections in such a way that they are accessible to all who read them. There is fairly extensive use of Sanskrit vocabulary in these comments. I do this as a way to help those who wish for some degree of specificity in their familiarity with relevant concepts, practices and terms. As a way to help such readers, at the end of each chapter I have placed vocabulary lists that define words appearing in that chapter and occasionally included tables that organize some ideas associated with that chapter's topic.

My larger purpose throughout this book is to reflect on a spiritual life oriented toward love in our own contemporary lives. I do so, in part, because of my sense that we as people really *can* turn ever more fully toward Love. Aligning ourselves with Love's grace, we honor the divine Power that supports us throughout our lives. Opening to Love, we live more expansively in our own love: for others, for the world, for life itself. The more fully we return to Love, the more we fulfill the promise of our births and the more our highest and most splendid of yearnings are fulfilled.

Terms appearing in the Introduction

āsana Literally, a sitting position. In *haṭha yoga*, a particular body posture or pose.

bhaga Originally "share, portion," *bhaga* also thereby means "benevolence, graciousness, goodness, worthiness, dignity, beauty, loveliness."

Bhagavān One of several Sanskrit words referring to God. Literally, "the one who possesses *bhaga*" (see above) and thus, "the one who shares" divine care, affection and love for the human soul. This is a term of address that can also be translated as "the Lord, the Majestic One, the Blessed One, the Generous One, the Beloved One" and so on. The title can also suggest the idea that God holds and supports all human hearts, which are particular "portions" of his divine Love. The title Bhagavān is also at times used in devotional traditions in reference to revered spiritual masters.

Bhāgavata Literally "pertaining to Bhagavān" (see above), refers to the religious and philosophical tradition that calls on God as Bhagavān. While the title Bhagavān can be applied to various deities, the Bhāgavata tradition, as a tradition, is most often associated with the praise of God as Viṣṇu, often in the form of Kṛṣṇa.

bhakti The "sharing a portion" or "participating in" divine Love; often translated as "devotion." For more definitions, see the discussion in Chapter 1 and throughout subsequent chapters.

devarṣi Literally, "seer of divinity" or "divine seer," the word is one way of describing and referring to revered, ancient sages.

dharma Derived from a root meaning "support, uphold," *dharma* refers to the encompassing and particular set of truths, actions, responsibilities and so on that supports the well-being and integrity of the world.

haṭha yoga Technique of yoga (see below) characterized by disciplined practice of placing and holding the body in particular positions and postures known generally as *āsanas* (see above).

Kṛṣṇa One of the names and incarnations of God, according to the Vaiṣṇava tradition (see below) and especially in the Bhāgavata tradition (see above) within Vaiṣṇava thought. Kṛṣṇa is revered and adored for both his transcendent power and majesty and his loving, familiar intimacy with the human spirit.

prāṇāyāma Literally "restraint of the breath," a yogic practice involving exercises in controlled breathing and conscious engagement with one's breath.

Sāṁkhya One of the six classical schools of orthodox Hindu philosophy. The word means "enumeration" or "numbering" and applies to the system of thought that discerns and enumerates twenty-five stages or levels (*tattvas*) of successive material embodiment of all existing things.

sat Reality, truth, true existence, that which truly is. *Sat* is the reality of existence itself. It is Being or absolute Beingness as the foundation and ground of all beings.

sūtra A short phrase that holds within it or reveals a large body of knowledge and wisdom; also, a sacred text in a genre characterized by concision and brevity.

Vaiṣṇava Literally "pertaining to Viṣṇu," (see below) refers to the religious and philosophical tradition that recognizes God as Viṣṇu.

vīṇā A stringed, lute-like musical instrument.

Viṣṇu Literally, "the Pervasive One." One of the names of God and, according to Vaiṣṇava thought (see above), the Absolute itself.

yoga The process of yoking, joining, harnessing; in the religious context, a set of spiritual disciplines leading to the discernment of and alignment or union with the divine Self.

yogī/yoginī One who practices yoga or is in a state of yoga (see above). A yogī is male, a yoginī is female.

PART I

What is Bhakti?

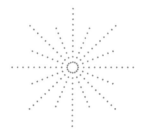

Chapter 1

Initial Comments and Reflections

In traditional modes of yogic study and reflection, students will often open their endeavor by intoning an invocation. This is often directed to God, whom in this book we will describe as absolute Love. God is called on to be with the students as they seek to know and experience that holy presence more clearly and fully. The yogic study of texts involves the active, productive use of the intellect. It requires concentration, clarity of thought, commitment, and an openness of mind that allows for new ways of thinking and understanding. Yogic study also benefits from an open heart, for the heart can and does bring vitality and warmth to students' intellectual understanding. The elevation of the human spirit through spiritual reflection comes through use of both the mind and the heart, and both the mind and heart are illumined by graceful divine wisdom. Yogic study can give a context in which this wisdom can speak to the student through the words of a text. An invocation thereby calls on a sacred, supportive, transforming Power that opens the yogī or yoginī to a revelatory process that can take place through the discipline of yogic study itself.

Accordingly, I would like to begin with the following traditional invocation:

हरिः ॐ

Hariḥ Oṁ

We might note the first word in this particular invocation. It is Hari, which is one of the names of God. In yogic thought, a name of God holds within it the essence of some aspect of God's nature. To speak a divine name is to make a sacred truth manifest in sound. Indian spiritual tradition holds that when one pronounces a divine name one brings God into one's awareness and thereby allows God to reveal an aspect of the divine nature more clearly, fully, powerfully. Pronouncing a name such as Hari before saying anything else, one opens oneself to God and turns one's praise and longing toward the affectionate and loving deity who brings seekers ever further into the reality of God's own love.

The name Hari itself literally means "the one who carries away." We can think of it in this context as referring to God as the divine Beloved who steals the heart, as it were, and carries from it whatever may otherwise keep it closed. Hari's enchanting call refreshes and renews the human spirit. Hearing and responding to it, we turn from constrictions of narrow self-concern. By stealing our hearts, God as Hari frees us to experience an inherent joy and releases from within us expressions of loving benevolent kindness to others and to the world.

The next word is *oṁ*. This syllable is sometimes described as the *praṇava*, literally the "moving forth," for the syllable *oṁ* is the sacred universal impulse, the Word from which all things in the inner and outer worlds emerge. The sound of *oṁ* thus gives voice to the universal power of creativity, transformation and completion. Reverentially pronouncing the syllable, *oṁ*, we as spiritual aspirants, yogīs and yoginīs, bring our minds and hearts into that Presence that is the ground and fulfillment of our being.

The text of the *Nārada Bhakti Sūtra* begins with this opening line:

अथातो भक्तिं व्याख्यास्यामः ॥१॥

athāto bhaktiṁ vyākhyāsyāmaḥ

"Now, therefore, we will speak of bhakti."

— Sūtra 1

This looks like quite a straightforward statement of intention; and it is certainly that. Yet, there is more to these otherwise simple words than might at first appear. We should remember that, in the sūtra style of literature, each word is significant to the lesson as a whole. Accordingly, we will look separately and at some length at the different phrases of this first sūtra. I will do so by starting with the key word in the phrase.

"Bhakti"

The Sanskrit word *bhakti* can be translated as "devotional love," "spiritual devotion," "spiritual love," "loving devotion," "sharing in divine love," and other similar ways.

In referring to bhakti in this opening sūtra, Nārada joins saints, spiritual masters and wise teachers from around the world who have long taught that the most direct way to know and serve God is through the power of love. How do they know this? It is because — illumined and refined through their own lives of spiritual discipline, warmed through the cultivation of compassion, and enlivened by divine grace — their own hearts have come to experience divine Love. Listening to them, inspired by their wisdom, and refining our own experience of love in its various forms, we too can come to a similar intuition that our own feelings of love themselves ultimately have their source in God. Awakened to any degree to that Love, we can to a similar degree reflect its nature in our lives. We do so by entering into the delights, joys, poignancies and commitments of our human love. We can share it with God in return by acknowledging and appreciating our feelings of love, by offering ourselves to others and the world in the service of Love, by honoring and revering the Source of our love through adoration and worship, by listening to Love through prayer and immersing in Love through meditation, by singing forth our love for the divine Beloved in the songs of our hearts. As we will see in subsequent sections of this book, there are many ways we can participate in Love.

Such sensibilities have long found expression in Indian sacred texts. Perhaps the most well known of such texts is the *Bhagavad Gītā*, the "Song of Bhagavān." A primary text in the Bhāgavata devotional tradition of which the *Bhakti Sūtra* is also a part, the *Bhagavad Gītā* consists of a conversation between God as Bhagavān — the Lord, the Beloved One — personified here as Kṛṣṇa, and his disciple, Arjuna. In it, Kṛṣṇa teaches Arjuna many things, including the nature of God, the nature of soul, and the way in which the soul becomes at one with God. In one verse Kṛṣṇa says that,

> In truth, it is through bhakti that one knows me,
> who I am and what I am;
> and when one knows me in truth,
> one enters into me.[19]

The message here is as profound as it is simple. It is through love that one knows God, for God is Love. Similarly, when one enters into love, then one enters into God's own nature. As Tirumūlar, an eighth century devotional philosopher from India, has said:

> Those who do not yet understand
> think that love and God are two.
> They do not understand that love is God.
> After truly knowing that love is God,
> they remain in the love that is God.[20]

Since God is Love, God lives in the heart of one who loves. Accordingly, when we feel love we are actually experiencing God. Further, when we offer genuine love we are not only seeing and honoring God's presence in that which we love, but also aligning ourselves with God's self-expression as love through our own words, intentions and actions. To love is therefore to share in God's nature.

This reverential turn toward God, this sharing in God's nature as Love, this communion with God: this is bhakti. As a contemporary Indian theologian has defined it, bhakti is "the felt participation of the soul in the total being of God."[21]

The opening into Love itself takes place in different ways and at different times for different people. It may happen seemingly countless times in various moments when one's heart is moved. It may happen very suddenly, even unexpectedly. It may take place slowly, perhaps over many years. It may be like the sudden opening of a thundercloud followed by the rush of rain, or it may open gently, like a sprouting seed. This is because this transforming act of opening to Love takes place deep within our own souls, so deep that it may either dramatically alter our entire being or take place so quietly that we may not see or appreciate it.

Awakened to the reality of the Love that supports and sustains our lives, as it does all others, we may find ourselves spontaneously responding with gratitude. We become less attracted to those ideas and patterns of behavior that distort or veil the light of Love within us. We turn our minds and hearts away from those selfish forces that separate us from Love and direct them increasingly to those ways of living that anchor and strengthen our gratitude for it. Here, we both dwell in Love and offer ourselves to it. This immersion into the fullness of the divine Love and the giving of oneself in love to it, this participating in Love: this, too, is bhakti.

One who experiences and expresses bhakti is known as a *bhakta.* To be a bhakta is to share one's being with God through the experiences, expressions and responsibilities of love. There are, of course, many different kinds of people; accordingly, there are various ways bhaktas feel and express devotion to God. According to the *Bhagavad Gītā*, God welcomes loving hearts from whatever direction they come; in that text Kṛṣṇa is said to affirm, "In whatever ways people approach me, I receive them with love."[22]

Indian tradition draws on the fullness of the human experience of relationship to represent a number of these different forms of bhakti. I will mention some of them here. I do so not merely to list them but to help make a point, namely, that love for God takes different forms. A single Love shines within the many human experiences of love, like the light of a single sun is reflected in multiform ways by differently colored crystals. These various human responses to and expressions of Love become the different modes of bhakti.

So, for example, the devotional tradition of which our sūtras are a part speaks of a mode of spiritual love wherein, once one opens into Love, one yearns to serve that Love. Here, one enters into *dāsya bhakti*, which is similar to the devotion a willing servant feels for a kind and just master. There is also *sākhya bhakti*, which is devotion that is like the steadfast love one feels for a true friend. So, too, there is *vātsalya bhakti*, which is selfless affectionate love that is similar to the devotion a parent feels for a child. There is *mādhurya bhakti*, or devotion turning on sentiments that are similar to the deep and abiding connection one has for one's cherished life partner. There is *viraha bhakti*, the intense sentiments of love one feels when one is separate from one's beloved. There is *śānta bhakti*, peaceful devotion, in which one knows from one's own experience that God is of the nature of Love and thus is not disturbed by doubt in that divine nature.[23]

Spiritual devotion can be nascent and emerging and thus described as *bhāva bhakti*, and it can be infused with mature love and therefore known as *prema-bhakti*. Immersion into love can become so deep and embracing that one realizes the ultimate unity of lover and divine Beloved. This state of unity in devotional love is known in Indian tradition as *parābhakti*: the highest bhakti.

These are just some of the types of bhakti recognized in Indian devotional traditions. We will have occasion in the following pages to mention more. Those traditions generally hold that, through divine grace and through their own personal effort, the love that has arisen in bhaktas can and eventually will find expression in all dimensions of their being. This love redirects a bhakta's thoughts, purifies a bhakta's emotions and grounds a bhakta's actions toward others in the recognition of the inherent value of their lives. It dissolves the constricting bonds of narrow egotism and allows us to see the larger grandeur and majesty of life and breaks the bondage to self-centeredness that leads to many forms of suffering in the world. In responding with love to the Power that supports, enlivens, honors, guides, and fulfills all beings, the bhakta thereby shares and participates in the love that is that Power's nature. It really cannot be otherwise. God's love brings forth our own love; but, truly speaking, our own love is nothing but God's love expressed through us. All love is God's love, for God is Love.

"We will speak"

At the time the *Bhakti Sūtra* was composed, teachers did not write books as much as they shared their knowledge and directed their students' spiritual lives through the medium of speech. Students listened closely to their teachers and then reflected deeply and at length on their words. So, when Nārada says here that "we will speak," he invites students to take part in this contemplative process by which they clarify and anchor their understanding.

Now, of course, we have books we can read. Nonetheless, the process need not be so different from hearing the teacher speak. As we contemplate the teachings given by these sūtras, we inwardly share conversation with an eternal teacher, for in a sense the figure of Nārada here represents a teacher who speaks to us with the wisdom of the ages.

When Nārada says *we* will speak of bhakti, he involves his students themselves in the process. Similarly, if we think of ourselves as students on a spiritual path, then with this phrase he brings *us* into the conversation. As we study and contemplate these sūtras, we can bring insight from our own experiences of love and devotion into our study. We can be a fellowship, a *saṁgha*, a *kula*. With this encouragement, we can follow the illumined guidance given to us by all the teachers Nārada represents, and we can turn to each other for insight, help, and joyful affirmation as we do so.

"Now, therefore"

Let us turn now to the opening of this first sūtra. It begins with two short words: *atha* ("now") and *atas*[24] ("therefore"). It may seem on first reading that these are rather insignificant words. However, they carry implications that are worth our noting, for they help place us within the long history of disciplined spiritual inquiry and give us encouragement as we undertake our study.

The word *atas*, "therefore," suggests that there is a previous conversation of sorts that has taken place between Nārada and his students. He seems to be saying that he is familiar with the contours of their search and appreciates their openness to learn. He also seems to understand that those who yearn to know and serve God have not come to this longing out of nowhere. They have been seeking more understanding of their love for the divine Beloved, and they have opened themselves to God. Some may have spent virtually their entire lives in this search, filled with yearning, ever-looking, ever-seeking. For some, the number of years may not have been as important as the intensity with which they now feel the fire of love burning in their hearts. They want to experience God and to share their love with God.

The wisdom represented by the figure of the Nārada of these sūtras knows this. By saying "Now, therefore," Nārada shows that he is aware of his students' search; he knows that they have prepared themselves to learn, and in a sense he is declaring, "Good. You are ready." He knows they are serious in their longing to delve further into their inquiry into the nature of bhakti. So, Nārada says, now is the time to speak of spiritual love.

In beginning this way, Nārada's sūtras are like other influential and long-respected collections of sūtras associated with various schools of religious and philosophical thought in India. The first sūtra of Patañjali's *Yoga Sūtra* is "Now, the teaching regarding yoga." Similarly, the first sūtra of Bādārāyāna's *Brahma Sūtra* opens with "Now, therefore, the desire to know Brahman," which is the term Bādārāyana uses to refer to ultimate Reality. Classical and contemporary commentators have noted the importance of these opening sūtras. Over the many centuries, influential philosophers have said that the opening words of the *Brahma Sūtra* indicate that the students who were to study the text possessed a yearning to do so and that they had prepared themselves for such study.[25] The twentieth-century Indian scholar-contemplatives, Swami Tyagisananda and Swami Prabhavananda, have commented on the significance of this initial phrase of the *Nārada Bhakti Sūtra* in a similar manner.[26]

If we, too, think of ourselves as spiritual students, then we can think of our own preparation for study to consist of our longing to understand the nature of spiritual love and thus to know and love God more fully, to purify and strengthen our hearts with that love, and to share it with others for the betterment of the world. Whether our interest in spiritual love is only now emerging or whether we have sought understanding for many years with intense yearning, everything in our lives has come together at this moment in a way that we are now ready to study devotion, to deepen our knowledge, to move beyond the surface of our experience. So, Nārada says that *atha* — *now*, not later — is the time to do this. Life is already so short! There is no point in delaying. We are ready. Let us now begin.

Terms appearing in Chapter 1

Bhagavad Gītā The "Song of Bhagavān" (for a brief definition of "Bhagavān," see the list of terms following the Introduction), thus the "Song of the Blessed One, Song of the Majestic One, Song of the Beloved One" and so on. Taking the form of a dialogue between God as Kṛṣṇa and his disciple Arjuna, the *Bhagavad Gītā* is one of the most influential of sacred texts from the Indian spiritual tradition.

bhakta One who feels and expresses devotional love (*bhakti*: see below), a devotee.

bhakti Spiritual love, spiritual devotion, devotional love, loving devotion, sharing in divine love, participating in the Beloved's nature as love. For an initial list of some forms of bhakti, see Table I, below.

Hari One of the divine names; a name of God, especially from a devotional perspective. Literally meaning, "one who carries," it can be understood as "one who carries my heart away," the "captivating one," "the one who takes away impurities," and so on.

kula A spiritual community, often one that is gathered around a teacher for purpose of study. (It is related to the English word *school*.) It thus also implies a close and supportive connection between teacher and student and between students themselves. At the mystical level, *kula* also refers to the Heart that is shared by loving teachers and disciples and by the divine Beloved and those who love the Beloved. See also *saṁgha*, below.

oṁ A sacred syllable that is said to hold all sacred truths within its sound; the divine word that creates, sustains and brings all things to fulfillment.

praṇava Literally, the "moving forth," a reference to the creative power of the syllable *oṁ* (see above).

saṁgha Literally, a "coming together," this refers to a community of spiritual practitioners and seekers who gather together to study and learn together, to undertake spiritual practices together, and to support each other in doing so. See also *kula*, above.

Table I

Some Types of Bhakti

(See also Tables IV and X)

bhāva* *bhakti	New, emergent devotion. The word *bhāva* in this setting means "coming into existence" and thus connotes a fresh, innocent, uncomplicated feeling of devotional love.
dāsya* *bhakti	Devotion that is similar to that a devoted servant feels for a kind and just master. The similar term *dāsya bhāva* refers to the devotional feeling of being a servant of a master; similarly, *dāsya āsakti* is the state of holding this kind of devotion dear to one's heart.
mādhurya* *bhakti	Devotion that is like the sweet, intense feelings one holds for one's cherished lover.
prema-bhakti	Mature, affectionate, unconditional devotion that includes, affirms and embraces the complexities of love. The hyphen here indicates that this is a compound word consisting of *preman* (love) and *bhakti.*
sākhya* *bhakti	Steadfast devotional love that is shared by two trusting, good friends. The similar term *sākhya bhāva* refers to the devotional feeling associated with this love that is of the nature of friendship and *sākhya āsakti* is the cherishing of this devotional relationship.
śānta* *bhakti	Devotion that is characterized by a state of peacefulness. A calm, quiet, strong, unpretentious, welcoming devotion grounded in confidence and trust. The word *śānta,* "peaceful," is related to the word *śānti*, "peace."
vātsalya* *bhakti	Selfless affectionate love for God that is similar to the love a mother feels for her child; kind, tender, gentle, embracing love. The word *vātsalya* derives from *vatsala*, and thus literally also to a cow longing to feed her calf.
viraha* *bhakti	The word *viraha* means "separation, parting." This is the intense, yearning-filled devotional love associated with the feeling of being separated or parted from one's Beloved. It is the devotional longing one feels in the Beloved's seeming absence.

Chapter 2

The Highest Love, the Love for the Highest

To be a bhakta is to know and adore God through the sentiments, acts and responsibilities of love. It is also to be immersed in the divine Heart's abiding and powerful presence within one's own heart. Again, bhakti is both the offering of love and the state of love from which this offering comes.

What is the nature of that adoration itself? It will take us some time to reflect on this question. Nārada gives us initial entry into our discussion by characterizing bhakti in these succinct statements:

सा त्वस्मिन् परमप्रेमरूपा ॥२॥

sā tvasmin paramapremarūpā

"It, truly, is of the nature of the highest form of love in this."

— Sūtra 2

अमृतस्वरूपा च ॥३॥

amṛtasvarūpā ca

"And its essential nature is ambrosia."

— Sūtra 3

The reference in each of these sūtras is of course to bhakti, as mentioned in the first sūtra. We will turn shortly to the reference to the highest form of love and to its essential nature as ambrosia. Before doing so, however, I would like to share some thoughts arising from the part of sūtra 2 translated as "in this" (*asmin*).

"In this"

This short phrase may at first seem rather unremarkable. Yet, we are to remember that all words and phrases in sūtra literatures can be used for extended and focused contemplation.

We are not explicitly supplied the reference to the "this" here. However, given the topic of the *Bhakti Sūtra* in its entirety, we might justly say that Nārada is speaking of God. To enter into "this" is therefore to enter into the Source, Foundation and Power that supports and stands within all existence, which is also to say, to enter into Love. Replacing the pronouns "it" and "this" with these references, a translation of this sūtra would thus read: "Bhakti is of the nature of supreme love in God."

Something holds my attention in the use of the word *asmin*, "in this." It suggests to me the experience or state of being drawn into God, or of being immersed in God, or of living within God's encompassing presence. The deeper we are pulled into "this," the deeper we are pulled into Love. This suggestion has then led me to the following reflections.

At the center of all existence stands a deep mystery, and this is the mystery of existence itself. The fact that there is *something* rather than infinite nothingness reflects and gives form to a profound truth. The universe *exists* and we are alive in it.

How simple it would be if there were to be nothing at all. Yet, wondrously, there remains the inexplicable fact: there *is* being; and being continues to *be* from moment to moment, year to year, eon to eon. At the arrival of each new moment from within the deep mystery of being, the universe itself in a sense proclaims "Yes!" to the miracle of existence.

A profound affirmation resounds in this proclamation. In their own unique ways, the daffodil reaching through the late winter snow, the baby bird breaking through its shell, trees reaching for the sky, the river running to the sea, the stars blinking in the vast night, all in a sense proclaim "I am!," and in so doing, take part in the mystery that is existence itself.

Who is it who hears this universal proclamation, "I am!"? We ourselves hear it, and we ourselves are moved by it, when our hearts are open to it. The effect such an open heart has on us is unmistakable. The experience is so powerful, or perhaps so subtle, or so inexplicable, that we often feel it cannot be expressed in words; and in its very ineffability resides one of the elements of its deep mystery. Try to describe the feelings you experience as you truly look into the eyes of a newborn child, sit quietly with your life partner or closest and deepest friend, or gently stroke the cheek of a person you cherish who is dying.

One word comes back to us again and again, and that is *love*. What do we feel when we open our hearts to the wonder of existence? We feel love.

Whom is it we love? Do we love the child, the friend, the dying person? Yes, of course we do, for it is the light in *this* person's face, *this* one's unique personality, that we find so beautiful, so compelling, so poignant. Yet, as we allow ourselves to move ever deeper into the love we feel, we move ever deeper into a sublime and wondrous mystery that lies behind that face — a Mystery that gives rise to, supports, fulfills, and sparkles within this particular person's existence, as it does within each being in the entire universe.

To say this differently, we are touched and moved by others, we love others, because in a mysterious and compelling way we see in them lovely intimations of the divine Self. In their eyes we see the light of the universal "I am." The person's outward situation does not affect or determine this inward loveliness. The one we love may be strikingly handsome or pretty, or perhaps in some ways rather homely. He or she may be full of good health or suffering from illness, wealthy or holding few material possessions, young or old. We love particular people not simply for what they look like or what they do for us, but rather for who they truly are, and in truth they are lovely expressions of the Self.

In love, the particular embodies and reveals the Absolute. To paraphrase the *Bṛhadāraṇyaka Upaniṣad*, a text from ancient India:

> It is not for the love of a husband that a husband is dear; it is for the love of the Self [within a husband] that a husband is dear. It is not for the love of a wife that a wife is dear; it is for the love of the Self that a wife is dear. It is not for the love of children that children are dear; it is for the love of the Self that children are dear.[27]

Revelation of the Self can take place in any circumstance. I remember one time, many years ago, I was sitting near a small tree at the edge of a desert in India in the midday heat. This was a time when India was at war with Pakistan. Some of the fighting was going on quite near where I was. I knew there was tension in the air. Yet, where I was sitting everything was perfectly still. There was nobody around, perhaps for miles. I hadn't spoken with anybody for many days.

At one point, a small and rather plain looking bird landed on a low branch in the tree, just a few feet from me. It did not make a sound. I fixed my eyes on it and watched it for some time. It looked at me, too, then away, then at me again. Then, it focused its attention on me. What might otherwise have appeared as its rather bland feathers struck me as quite beautiful in their own shimmering way. The bird shifted its head back and forth as it looked at me, seemingly getting different perspectives of me. I felt a warm sense of fondness for the bird. Actually, it was more than that: it was a recognition of sorts. By this, I mean that I both noticed the bird's presence and at the same time was aware of my own presence in that moment I shared with it. I felt a soft upwelling of my own soul as the bird and I briefly lived our lives together.

That the bird and I existed at all was for me, in that moment, a wondrous fact. There we were: sitting near each other in the compelling mystery of existence itself. I shifted my eyes from the bird and looked around me. I saw that the tree was part of that same wondrous universe, as were the desert sand, the small cliffs and hills that rose out of the sand, and the deep blue sky that stretched above them. Everything seemed alive with and embraced by a quiet yet powerful presence that I experienced as a single Consciousness that infused and supported all things in all of their vast multiplicity.

I sensed that this Consciousness was of the nature of pure affirmation of life and that in fact there was no difference between this Consciousness and Love. No word came to my mind to name this Presence — yet, if one had come, it probably would have been *God*. All that I could see, everywhere I looked around me, was an expression of God's benevolent wishes for the world. Everything I saw was set in Love. The bird was an expression of Love, the tree was Love, even the blanket I sat on was Love. All was Love.

All of this happened within just a few minutes, but I seemed to enter into the infinite depths of eternity within that moment. Boundaries of time and space dissolved into a unity of being pulsating with Consciousness that is itself Love. This sacred Presence was transcendental and powerful beyond all imagining, for I understood it to be the force that creates and sustains the whole universe. At the same time, it was soft, gentle, and closer to me than my own heartbeat. All-embracing, it was at once both majestic and intimate and, in that moment, I experienced it as benevolent.

I knew that nearby there was much hostility between people, as there had been in so many different contexts throughout history. I could not forget that there is much suffering, sorrow and pain in so many peoples' lives. Yet, I sensed that the Power and Presence I experienced as Love and identified as God continued nevertheless to shimmer and move within the fact of existence itself. I felt it to be immeasurably patient, for certainly people have not always responded to the wonder of life with their own love and have sometimes mistreated each other and themselves in the most grievous ways. And yet, I knew that, even though I may not always experience it, Love is nevertheless real and it is constantly here. I felt that Love to be infinitely compassionate, even in a world torn by forces to the contrary. My response was to put my hands together in a prayerful position at the level of my heart and quietly to say, "Thank you" to this embracing, affirming, sacred presence — God, Love — that supports and infuses all life. I then spontaneously and gently closed my eyes and entered into quiet meditation, immersed in God's love. Some time later, as I came out of meditation, words of prayer moved through my heart: "May all people know God's love for them and for all others."

This all occurred as I shared a brief moment with a small bird. The experience of the divine Self within all things can happen in any context, even an otherwise seemingly insignificant one such as this. It reaches profound depth when it comes through the face of a person you truly love. Yet, even then, the experience of love takes you beyond the surface of the person who draws it from you and into the Self reflected in the light of his or her soul. The ultimate object of your love remains that divine Self.

My time with the bird is far from unique. I am confident that most readers will have had many similar moments in their lives. Simple as it may have been, experiences like these can give us entry, at least to some degree, into sensibilities represented by these lines from the *Bhagavad Gītā*, in which Arjuna expresses his recognition of God's presence and his reverential response to it:

> The entire universe is pervaded by you,
> you of infinite form. . . .
> Homage to you from in front and from behind.
> Homage to you from all sides.[28]

As our spirits open to the wonder and appreciation of the divine Self within all things, we sense, perhaps imperfectly at first, that the same Self abides deep within us, too. Spiritual love, bhakti, turns toward this indwelling divine essence within us. As Swami Tyagisananda has put it, "The object of Bhakti is the Soul of our own souls."[29] Drawing on the language of Nārada's sūtra 3, it is "in this" Soul where supreme Love dwells.

There is one more point I would like to make regarding our phrase *in this*, inspired in part by both Swami Tyagisananda's and Swami Prabhavananda's commentaries on this sūtra.[30] The Sanskrit pronoun used here is grammatically neuter in gender. If it had been masculine, then we might assume that God is to be understood as male. If the pronoun were feminine, then we might think Nārada was speaking of God as female. That the pronoun here is neuter suggests a linguistic way of representing the realization that God transcends all limitations and particular categories. Similarly, as the divine Power and Presence that sustains the whole universe, God is available to and embraces all things. Love for God is therefore not constricted by sectarian or theological exclusivism. Accordingly, God's love cannot be claimed by one religion over another religion, one sect over another sect, or one person over another person. God loves all beings, for all beings are in God and God is Love.

"Of the nature of the highest love"

Nārada characterizes bhakti here as *paramapremarūpa*. This term can be broken into three components: *parama-prema-rūpa*. The word *rūpa* refers to the unique "form" of something and thereby also to its essential nature. The Sanskrit word *preman* can be translated as "love." (It appears as *prema* here for linguistic reasons. Also the Sanskrit *preman* has come, in modern Indian languages, to take the form *prema*.) The prefix *parama* means "highest" or "supreme."

What does it mean to speak of "the highest love?" This whole book is directed toward discerning some answers to this question. We might begin by noting that, as we know, there are different levels or "forms" of love. Think of our own use in English of the word *love* itself. People love chocolate. They love it when it rains after a hot day. They love their job, their country, their pets, their families.

In these various states, we feel to varying degrees a sense of delight in something, fondness for something, affection for something, care and concern for something, sense of satisfaction or fulfillment in something, or a strong emotional attachment to something. But the various forms of love we experience in our lives are not necessarily equivalent to each other. There are varieties in the several sentiments we generally call love. To use the metaphor of height suggested by Nārada's vocabulary: some types of love are higher than others.

Let's reflect for a moment on some of those differences. An obvious one lies in the degree of intensity in the emotions and desires we associate with love. I may love various kinds of music, but the intensity with which I do so does not, of course, compare to that with which I love my children. Higher love is more intense love.

Another difference can be identified by the various degrees of clarity in our emotions and feelings. Some are purer than others. I do not mean this in a puritanical way, but rather in the sense that quite often an experience of what we might identify as love is actually a mixture of several different emotions, desires and projections. For instance, what we interpret as love for another may be more an expression of fear of being alone. We may desire another's attention out of a sense of inferiority, or of superiority. We may think we love others for some quality they possess when in fact we are projecting our own ideas, expectations and hopes onto them.

We may not be aware of these different forces and patterns working within us, for they may express residual memory traces of events or relationships that happened in the past. We may not even consciously remember these events, yet they nevertheless form psychological templates through which we experience and interpret the present. These templates are patterns of thought and emotion that are pressed into our minds, affecting our understanding of ourselves, of others and of the world. They are psychological lenses that bend and distort our ability to see things clearly and accurately, and can be so deeply impressed in our minds that we may not even be conscious of them.

Yogic thought identifies two related types of memory traces that influence our perceptions and our expectations as well as our experience of ourselves and others. A *vāsanā* is a patterned way of thinking or feeling that has its origins in a memory of an experience from an earlier part of our lives or of an idea we have held in the past. A *saṁskāra*, according to Classical yogic thought, is an effect of a pattern or template that comes as a result of experiences in former lives, that is to say, in experiences we may not remember or have suppressed. A yogic way of thinking holds that, while we may be consciously aware of a vāsanā and of its affect on our understanding, a saṁskāra functions at a subconscious or unconscious level.

The effect of vāsanās, and especially of saṁskāras, is generally understood in negative terms. They distort the clarity of one's awareness and keep one trapped in constricting habitual patterns of thought and emotion. Lower forms of love are textured to varying degrees by the effect of the vāsanas and saṁskāras. Higher forms of love are less distorted by those effects. We can dissolve vāsanās through diligent self-inquiry and yogic spiritual discipline. Release from a saṁskāra comes primarily through divine grace, although that graceful release can be supported through our own effort toward spiritual growth.

Still another difference between different types, levels or forms of love centers on the motivations or intentions behind them. In the lower forms our feelings are motivated to various degrees by the gratification of desires, satisfaction of our predispositions, sense of control over another, or the meeting of our demands. In such instances, we turn to an object of some sort in hopes that it will give us pleasure. What we call love can therefore actually be a form of self-centered exploitation of something or someone so that we ourselves may experience some sort of happiness. In this case, our love is conditional love, since it is based on the presence of particular conditions. Higher forms of love, on the other hand, are those that do not turn on manipulative intentions. They express purer and more selfless delight in something for being what it is, in its own integrity, not for how it can satisfy us. Higher love is unconditional love.

Other differences between lower and higher forms of love turn on the nature of its immediate object. In lower forms of love, the object of one's attention is more specifically defined by physical characteristics whereas the higher forms of love are directed to more subtle or more essential qualities or states of being. Few people would equate their love for chocolate with the love they feel for their children, life partner, or closest friends. Why is this? Well, isn't there something mysterious, wonderful, and beautiful about the child, partner or friend that is not defined by his or her physical qualities? Isn't there something at the level of a living presence in the person you cherish that you don't find in the chocolate? I make this admittedly rather silly comparison to suggest a point: the object of higher forms of love is not so much a physical object as it is a subtle essence, namely, the Self shimmering within it. Higher forms of love express the recognition of and entry into this sacred divine Self within the object. This Presence is the presence of God within the one you love.

Yet another difference between lower and higher forms of love is that, in the former, the object of desire is by nature more impermanent whereas, in the latter, it is longer lasting. When one desires satisfaction from something that is impermanent, then the gratification gained from it is similarly fleeting. The chocolate you love to eat is eventually gone and it can no longer satisfy you. Desire for satisfaction by that which is impermanent is therefore bound to lead to dissatisfaction and disappointment. But if you look deeply into the eyes of a person you truly love, you see beyond the temporary object and perceive within that person something eternal, something incomparably valuable. In higher forms of love, the object itself may change, go away, and even die, but this does not change your love, for your love is not, in a sense, objective. Indeed, this is one of the distinctions between lust and higher love. Lust is the conditional desire for an object. Love, on the other hand, is the unconditional appreciation for the subject, the Self, within the object.

Thus, there are lower forms of love, and there are higher forms of love. Summarizing the last few paragraphs, I might venture to say that, among many other possible descriptions, higher forms of love are increasingly:

- All-encompassing of one's being;
- Refined and pure more than they are coarse and mixed;
- Intense more than vague;
- Focused on one's beloved rather than driven by selfish motivations;
- Unconditional rather than conditional;
- Appreciative of intangible essences rather than only of physical characteristics;
- Directed toward that which is abiding more than that which is temporary;
- Experienced and expressed continually rather than sporadically; and
- Grounded within one's own being rather than derived outwardly only.

These, then, are some of the qualities of higher love. I am confident you could list some more. In our sūtra, Nārada speaks of a *highest* level of love. Accordingly, the highest love is that in which all of these characteristics apply in their highest form.

Now, let's note once again that our sūtra says that bhakti is of the nature of supreme love "in this." It is this highest form of love that arises from, dwells in and is directed toward *God*. The love that Nārada is going to speak about in these sūtras is not really the love one might feel for chocolate, as it were. It is love for God. When the highest love with all of its characteristics — refined, intense, unconditional, essential, abiding, inward — pulsates within the soul's immersion in God, then this is true bhakti.

At the same time, all of the various forms of love we may experience can and do contain some elements that, when refined, can be elevated in the direction of this supreme form. It is almost as if the different types of love exist on a continuum. To return to the perhaps rather silly example, the love of chocolate is, to its own small degree, an affirmation of existence. Accordingly, it is to that same degree the love of God. This is because God is the source of all affirmation at any level of existence. Without that foundation, there would be no such delight, even at the level of tasting chocolate. That love is of course immeasurably more powerful when it centers on the beauty and dignity of the human spirit.

A yogic life oriented toward communion with Divinity turns on the openness to and cultivation of those qualities of love that shift toward the highest levels. This means that we can use all of our experiences of love, even those that are in some way lower than others, to turn toward God. Accordingly, as we move toward the highest level of spiritual love we do not need to renounce our lower forms of love as much as transmute or transform them into more refined, elevated and pure forms.

By deepening, strengthening and purifying our love for all we hold dear in our lives we can deepen our love for God. In that highest love all other kinds of love therefore find their purest expression.

Accordingly, just as bhakti is the highest love, so too it is love for the Highest. It is love for the transcendent Source and ultimate Object of all of our other feelings of love. Entering into the Heart and aligning our lives with its grace, we more fully open ourselves to the Highest within our own hearts.

"And its essential nature is ambrosia"

In this phrase, which constitutes sūtra 3, Nārada characterizes the highest level of love as *amṛtasvarūpa*. You recall from discussion of sūtra 2 that *rūpa* means "form" or "characteristic." The *sva* here, in this context, means "own." So the word *svarūpa* means "own particular form" or, as I have translated it, "essential nature."

Nārada says here that bhakti's essential nature is *amṛta*. This word can be translated in different ways, two of which are relevant here. The literal meaning of amṛta is "not-dead" (*a-mṛta*) and thus "immortal." (Perhaps you can see the similarity between the words *amṛta* and *immortal*.) The word also means "nectar" or "ambrosia," which is the translation I prefer in this context. Yet, both ways of interpreting the word here give us entry into deeper understanding of the nature of spiritual love.

First, what might it mean to say that this love is of the nature of immortality? Is Nārada speaking literally of a physical state in which the body never dies? I suspect not. It seems relevant here to distinguish between physical immortality, on the one hand, and what Nārada would refer to as the "essential nature of immortality," on the other hand. The latter phrase would refer to the characteristic of immortality, namely, to a state of being that is not constrained or bound by the passage of time. Understood in this way, there is no time in which it is not real. In this sense, the highest form of love does not die. As such, it exists in the eternal now, and therefore it is real in the present moment. Love's "immortal" nature allows it to be ever-present, ever-available and ever-effective in one's experience of life.

Again, I am confident that you know what I mean. Look deep into the eyes of one you truly love, and you see in those beautiful depths the presence of a divine Mystery. That person is sustained by God's love, just as you are. When you love another, your heart opens to God's inner, affirming presence within your loved one. It is within this opening of the heart that you recognize, appreciate and remember that person's particularity. Love for the special uniqueness that is this person does not dissipate over time. This is why we continue to love our loved ones even after they are no longer physically alive.

So, it is of course not that we gain literal deathlessness when we enter into love. Rather, when we love, we enter into that which does not die. This "immortality" is present within the moments of our love. We can taste it in each moment, in any moment, in every moment.

This sense of tasting immortality is thus consonant with the translation of *amṛta* as "ambrosia," the way I have done so here. In its original sense, ambrosia was understood to be a divine nectar, the sipping of which is said to bring immortality. The Sanskrit word *amṛta* similarly connotes a pure and refined nectar that, when tasted, opens one to sublime states of being.

As an ambrosial essence, *amṛta* is similar in some ways to what is known in Indian thought as *rasa*, the latter of which we can translate as a "delectable sublimity." I will say more about rasa in Chapter 8. For the moment, it may be enough to know that the term *rasa* originally refers to the purest, most refined single essence of something in the context of multiplicity, like honey is an essence refined from many flowers' sweet juices. One of the Upaniṣads uses the term *rasa* to describe the single, universal, divine Self within all things.[31] Following this line of thought, to taste the essence of the true Self is to taste ambrosia.

How would Nārada have us relish this ambrosial Essence? Our sūtras suggest that we can do so by entering into higher forms of love, for the degree to which we enter into Love is the degree to which we taste the nectar of immortality itself.

Terms appearing in Chapter 2

amṛta Ambrosia, nectar, an essence of immortality. The word consists of two parts: *a*, "not, without,“ + *mṛta*, "mortality, mortal." *Amṛta* is nectarean, ambrosial essence of an eternal, immortal state. As "ambrosia" and "nectar," *amṛta* also means "sweet, pure, beautiful, beloved."

paramapremarūpa Literally, "the form (*rūpa*) of supreme (*parama*) unconditional, mature love (*preman*: see below)."

preman Love that is mature, unconditional, abiding, selfless, tender, fond, kind, affectionate and respectful. In modern Indian languages, the Sanskrit word *preman* has become *prema*.

rasa Sap, juice, flavor, nectar; thus, pure essence.

rūpa Literally, "form" or "appearance," can also mean "of the nature of" something. Thus, for example, *paramaparema-rūpa* (see above) can be translated as "the form of supreme love" or "of the nature of supreme love"

svarūpa The essential nature of something, literally "own-form" (*sva-rūpa*).

saṁskāra Unconscious pattern of thought or subliminal memory that distorts one's perception, experience and understanding. In Indian yogic thought, a saṁskāra is said to have been pressed into one's subtle body in previous existences.

vāsanā Derived from *vāsana*, "dwelling in, residing in," this term refers to a residual effect or trace in one's subtle being from a past experience or set of experiences. The difference between a vāsanā and a saṁskāra (see above) is that whereas a vāsanā is formed in one's current life, a saṁskāra has been pressed into the subtle body in a previous life.

PART II

Components of Bhakti as a Yogic Practice

Chapter 3

Grace and Self-Effort in Spiritual Love

In the chapters of Part I we have seen some initial definitions of bhakti and have noted in an initial manner some of the characteristics of lower and higher levels of love. Throughout this book, and particularly in Parts III and IV, we will look more closely at these various types of love and how, through yogic discipline, we may move from lower to higher levels. Before doing that, though, in this next section, Part II, we turn our attention to some of the foundational attitudes and practices on which a yogic life of devotional love is grounded. In yogic terms, these spiritual disciplines constitute the yogī's or yoginī's *sādhana*, a word literally meaning "leading to the goal" and frequently used to refer to one's spiritual practice or set of practices.

We might ask: why do we even begin the undertaking of such a sādhana? Why do we experience longing? Why cultivate and refine our love? Is the state toward which it leads really real?

A number of stories from India suggest that, whether consciously aware of it or not, spiritual seekers in their various ways sense that divine love *is* real, and that this intuition is the reason there is so much yearning to experience it. It is as if in some way they already have known this Love, but then may seem to have lost it. Love's compelling memory drives their longing to know it again.

One such story tells of the sage Parikṣit, whose name in Sanskrit means "one who looks everywhere." Here is a shortened version.[32]

In the wonderfully imaginative style of Indian sacred narratives, while still in his mother's womb Parikṣit is said to have had a vision of God as Kṛṣṇa, who stood with him at his side as a friend and protector who cared for and loved him. But after Parikṣit was born he lost this vision of his Lord, for all he then could see were the various objects of the external world. Yet, deep in his heart he longed to find Kṛṣṇa again and spent his life looking throughout the wide land for him. Parikṣit looked into the face of each person he met to see if he or she were the Kṛṣṇa from the depths of his memory. "Are you Kṛṣṇa?" he would silently ask. Then, of the next person, he would again ask: "Are you Kṛṣṇa?" His entire life took the form of a spiritual search, filled with his yearning to see Kṛṣṇa again.

If we in some way identify with this story, it may be because in some way it narrates our own experience. Perhaps it is because somewhere deep in our souls we too sense that we once saw God, as it were, and knew that God's love for us was real, but that somehow we seem to have lost that experience and we yearn to see God again. This yearning is in part what fuels our search. Our very longing demonstrates the existence of that for which we yearn — for if we did not already know the reality of God's love, then why else would we even look for it?

To say this in a different way, when each of us first came into the world, the universe celebrated through us the joy of existence itself. Yet, having taken birth, we can feel small, incomplete, and insignificant. We forget that a splendid force of affirmation moves within us, and the expansive light of Love that shines within us becomes dimmed. According to various schools of Indian philosophy, this darkened and constricted awareness is a form of ignorance, *avidyā*. This nescience, this not-knowing, leads to a sense of separation from the Self, and this leads to a sense of spiritual brokenness, alienation and incompletion. The sense of separation comes to be so strong, so pervasive, that it seems to have been true since before time itself. Our souls become trapped by the weight of what the *Bhāgavata Purāṇa* describes as a "beginningless ignorance," *anādyavidyā*, of God's love for the soul.[33] Our perspective having been distorted by this ignorance, we act in ways that are not consistent with the affirming power of Love that is a characteristic of the true Heart's nature.

A yogic life oriented toward love is based, in part, on the understanding that this is not the divine Beloved's wish for us. God, whose nature is Love and who dwells within us in the joy of our being, wants us to know and bathe in the light of the Love that is the Self's nature. Our hearts warmed and illumined by that love, we can share it with others so that they, too, may know and experience love in their lives.

How, then, from the devotional perspective, do we regain the remembrance of the affirmation of existence when our misunderstanding of ourselves can be so deep, so pervasive, so determinative, that we cannot free ourselves from its grasp? How can we be free of ignorance, when our very ignorance keeps us from experiencing this affirmation? Nārada gives us words to contemplate in sūtra 38:

मुख्यतस्तु महत्कृपयैव भगवद्कृपालेशाद्वा ॥३८॥

mukhyatastu mahatkṛpayaiva bhagavadkṛpāleśād vā

Indeed, it is primarily through the compassionate
grace of a great one, or through a portion
of the compassionate grace of God.

— Sūtra 38

The reference here is to what sūtra 2 earlier described as *parama-preman*, supreme love. As this sūtra implies, it is difficult to experience this state on our own. This is due to the darkening, constricting effect of our forgetfulness of the Heart. Our awareness of the expansive Love that is our Source fades to the point that it can seem that this Love does not really exist.

The Love that is the Heart's nature is real, though, and it is powerful, even though it may be hidden. So, it needs to be uncovered, enlivened and expressed. This recovery of our own deepest, human love takes place through the gift of what Nārada in this sūtra identifies as *kṛpā*, translated here as "compassionate grace." In other contexts, *kṛpā* can refer to such sentiments as tenderness, sympathy, pity or concern for another. By translating it here as compassionate grace I want to imply a positive, revelatory, purifying, active quality, the effect of which brings about spiritually transforming results.

The Power of Grace

What is grace? We can define it as the effective, supportive, affirming, transforming power of divine benevolence, given freely and unconditionally. It is the mysterious creative and supportive power by which we come into existence as living beings and through which we continue to exist from moment to moment. Grace expresses the divine intention that we be free of the ignorance that leads us to feel separate from the Self and thus to be free from the suffering such forgetfulness brings. The power of this graceful compassion reveals the nature of the Self as Love. So, grace is the transforming divine force that opens our eyes and hearts to the divine Presence itself. So, too, grace is the power that allows us and impels us to move forward in our spiritual lives toward higher levels of love and into fuller communion with Divinity.

What if you do not feel this grace? How do you know if you have received it? In such moments, remember that you are a living, embodied being. The power of life itself moves through you. This power is an expression of God's love for you. The fact that you continue to live from moment to moment reveals the fact that grace is constantly given to you by its divine Source. Without it — without the power of life itself — you simply would not continue to exist. Once you understand this, you then can realize that this grace is never absent from you. Furthermore, this Source of grace continues to cherish you in the depths of the divine Heart even when you no longer live.

In this sūtra, our text speaks of the compassionate grace of God, *bhagavad-kṛpā*, and of the compassionate grace of a great one, *mahat-kṛpā*. It says that it is "primarily" through the grace of a great one that supreme love is revealed to us. Who is a great one of which Nārada speaks? How is the grace of a great one related to the grace of God? Let's reflect, then, on what Nārada might mean when he speaks of these two sources of compassionate grace.

"It is primarily through the grace of a great one"

The phrasing here leads me to a set of reflections on the help we may receive from a compassionate spiritual master in our spiritual awakening and growth. Such great ones are teachers in the highest sense of the word. Through word and example, they teach us the true nature of the Self that dwells within them, as it does within all people. Doing so, these great ones can lead us from our forgetfulness of the divine Heart and free us from the misunderstanding that the Heart is not present within us. As remembrance of Love within us grows, we are less likely to act in unloving ways toward others. Remembering the Heart — returning to Love — we turn from acts arising out of forgetfulness of Love and are more able to bring our own compassionate love more fully into a world so much in need of healing.

Indian spiritual thought has long recognized the importance of such spiritual teachers. As the *Chāndogya Upaniṣad* says, a seeker without a teacher is like a person who has been blindfolded and led into the wilderness without being given directions out of those wilds. But the person who has such a teacher "becomes conscious" and finds the way revealed.[34]

There are different kinds of such masters. Some may be widely known as such. Some may live quietly in the world, sharing the power of Love in inconspicuous ways. Some may live like hermits who seem to turn from the world yet whose love affects and moves those who come to them. Whatever form they take, they have the power to open people's hearts to the reality of Love within them. Of such great ones, the ninth-century philosopher, Śaṅkara, has said:

> There are pure souls, peaceful and great,
> who bring good to others, like the coming of spring.
> They help others without any selfish motivation.
> It is the nature of these great ones to work of their own accord
> to remove the troubles of others,
> like the moon of its own accord
> soothes the earth scorched by the blazing rays of the sun.[35]

For our purposes, in my comments on this sūtra I am going to interpret the reference to a great one as being to a genuine *guru*, a word often translated as "teacher." In common parlance, there are different kinds of teachers, depending on the subject matter and the relationship between the teacher and the student. We ourselves know that there are teachers who instruct others regarding various particular topics: cooking, literature, music, history, law, science, sacred ritual, and so on. Whether or not the teacher cares much for the pupil's inner life is not always relevant. In Indian tradition, a guru is a teacher who not only is adept at the subject being taught but who also cares for the student and who stands as one whom the student deeply admires, respects and emulates.

In Indian sensibilities, all such teachers are worthy of appreciation and respect. However, although there may be many gurus guiding students toward knowledge in different skills or aspects of life, it is not just any guru who can open the seeker's mind and heart to the ultimate object of knowledge, namely, the true Self. The *Kaṭha Upaniṣad* notes that,

> Unless taught by one who is not-different [*ananya*] from it,
> there is no access there,
> For — being more subtle than the subtle —
> [the Self] is inconceivable.[36]

This passage makes the point that access to the Self — in other words, experience of the Heart — can be taught only by a teacher who is himself or herself "not-different," *ananya*, from the Self, this is to say, a teacher who has realized his or her own unity with the Self. Immersed in the Love that is the Heart's nature, such a person inspires people and reveals in their own hearts the reality of that same Love. This compassionate revelation brings light to one's inner darkness, illuminating the soul by dissolving the bonds of one's seemingly beginningless ignorance of the Self and of the Love that is its nature.

A teacher who is completely absorbed in the Self's nature is at one with that nature. Accordingly, I capitalize the word *Guru* when referring to such a special teacher, in part, because the Guru teaches from the knowledge that comes from the experience of the Self.

One important implication of this is that, understood in this way, the Guru is actually not so much a physical person as a state of awareness — namely the awareness of the Self — in which such a teacher continually dwells. So, too, the Guru is the power of grace that this awareness holds. When there is the continuing, unbroken awareness of the Self, then the Self is also said to reveal Itself within that awareness. This Self-revelatory power — which is the Guru — has the power to awaken, illumine and transform other peoples' awareness, too.

Further, the Guru is not only the awareness of the Self; the true Guru *is* the Self, the Ground of all awareness, just as it is the Source of all love. This being the case, the divine Self is therefore also the true Guru.

As the Self, the Guru is the universal divine Presence within the particularity of each person's soul. Swami Chidvilasananda has said that, "There is no difference between the Guru and the inner Self. The Guru is your own Self." The true Guru is therefore the inward presence of God's affirming Love. Accordingly, to experience the Guru is to experience Love itself. Perhaps this is why Swami Chidvilasananda, who is also known as Gurumayi ("absorbed in the Guru"), equates the experience of the inner Guru with the act of devotion: "When you experience the Guru in this way you have experienced devotion. When you experience devotion in this way you have seen the Guru."[37]

Viewed from this perspective, we can say that the "great one" to which our sūtra refers is the true Guru, whose sustaining and transforming grace supports the soul and leads it to its inherent perfection. Understood in this way, the grace of a great one, *mahat-kṛpā*, is the same as the grace of the Guru, or what in Indian devotional sensibilities is known as *guru-kṛpā*; and the grace of the Guru is identical to the grace of the Self, or what is known as *ātma-kṛpā.*

"Or through a portion of the grace of God"

The first part of our sūtra held that it is "primarily," *mukhyatā*, through the compassion of a great one that a person comes to experience what Nārada earlier described as supreme love, *paramapreman*. The latter part of the sūtra then refers to God's compassionate grace, *bhagavad-kṛpā*, as having what may at first reading seem to be of secondary importance relative to the grace of a great one.

The issue turns on the meaning of the Sanskrit particle *vā*, translated here as "or." While *vā* can mean "or" in the sense of an opposition, such as in "either ... or," it can also serve to intensify the meaning of the phrase in which it appears. In this sense, *vā* means, "in other words," or "indeed," or "which is really the same as." This is the case in this sūtra. The *vā* makes the point that the phrase *bhagavad-kṛpā*, "the grace of God," augments, expands or intensifies the phrase that precedes it, namely, *mahat-kṛpā*, "the grace of a great one."

This is to say that the grace of the great one is in some way the grace of God. God's love is the source and power of all spiritual transformations. As Nārada says elsewhere, in sūtra 41, "there is no difference" between God's grace and "those arising from it," the latter referring to those great ones who share that Love with others.

Let's take a moment to reflect more on what it might mean to say that there is no difference between God's grace and the grace of those arising from it. Looking further at sūtra 38 we see that Nārada refers to a portion, *leśa*, of God's grace. In other words, the grace of a great one is a portion of the grace of God. In terms of its essential nature, a portion of something is no different from the larger whole. You can taste the same essential sweetness of sugar from a spoonful of it as from a bucketful. In fact, you may find that you taste it more powerfully when it is a portion rather than when it is everything at once. As human beings with particular bodies, minds, experiences, relationships and so on, we are of course not able in our relative existence to hold the infinitely vast power of the transcendent Absolute. Part of God's gracefulness is to share that Power in portions that we can receive.

The grace of the great one, *mahat-kṛpā*, is ultimately grounded in and expresses God's own grace, *bhagavad-kṛpā* — for all that exists does so, finally, through the efficacy of that same power. As we become more fully aware of and grateful for that grace, our love for God as the ultimate Source of grace becomes stronger, purer and more pervasive. It is through this graceful power that we have the capability to turn toward the divine Heart to begin with.

God's grace sustains each and everything in the whole universe in the way that is suitable to it in its particularity. We each receive our own portion of it. Though God's love is and always remains absolute, grace is available to us in our own unique individuality. The compassionate Heart gives us that unbounded power in stepped-down quantities, the way an electrical transformer reduces high-voltage electricity to low-voltage power so that it can be used to turn on household lights. In this way, God's powerful Love, which supports the infinite immensity of existence, is thereby available to us in our own particular lives. Our portion of God's grace contains in it everything that we need to live a life infused by Love.

The Importance of Self-Effort

The discovery or recovery of Love softens and opens one's hardened heart and releases the power of compassion within us. But the transformation does not stop here. Once plants have started to grow in a farmer's field, the farmer makes sure that they receive water and sunlight and other nourishment and that they are protected against harmful insects. The farmer does not allow them to be smothered by weeds. Similarly, once the seed of Love has sprouted in our hearts, then it is important that we cultivate it. We need to care for it, protect it, and nourish it. This is to say that we put in our own effort in living a life infused by love at various levels of our existence. This is bhakti sādhana. We will return at some length to various aspects of this sādhana later in this book, particularity in Part III.

For now, let us note that devotion exists not only in our feelings of love for God but also, significantly, transforms the way we act in the world. This, in part, is what Nārada means in sūtra 19, to which we now turn:

> **नारदस्तु तदर्पिताखिलाचारता तद्विस्मरणे परमव्याकुलतेति ॥१९॥**
>
> ***nāradastu tadarpitākhilācāratā tadvismaraṇe paramavyākulateti***
>
> "According to Nārada, however, it is when all of one's manner of action is of a consecrated nature and when there is supreme sense of being lost upon forgetting."
>
> — Sūtra 19

This sūtra appears at the end of a series of four sūtras in which Nārada summarizes a number of ways other figures in the devotional tradition characterize bhakti. (You can read these sūtras in the full translation at the end of this book.) Before it, sūtra 16 had referred to one teacher's definition of bhakti as "the attraction to worship;" sūtra 17 had noted that another sage associated it with telling stories about spiritual matters in an inspiring manner; and sūtra 18 had said that according to still another bhakti is "the constant delight in the Self." Here, in sūtra 19, Nārada then presents his own characterization of spiritual love.

"When all of one's manner of action is consecrated"

The term for "all" here is *akhila,* which literally means "without a gap" and thus connotes the entirety of something. The word for "manner of action," *ācāratā,* could also be translated as "condition of one's conduct," or "established behavior." At the time the *Bhakti Sūtra* was composed in roughly the tenth century, the word may well have referred particularly to sacred rites and rituals that were to be performed at various times in one's life-cycle. We ourselves can also understand this to refer to all the activities in general that one undertakes as one moves through one's life. With the phrase *akhilācāratā* Nārada is therefore speaking of the encompassing or characteristic manner in which one lives in the world.

Our sūtra describes the yogic manner of being in the world with the word *arpita,* translated here as "consecrated." It could also mean "given to," and thus "offered." It is in this latter sense that I have rendered this reference to the nature of the yogic life as a life of consecration. When we consecrate our actions, we bring to them our sense of the sacred expressed through them. In the context of bhakti, all of our actions are to be offered in service of God's love. When we visit an elderly neighbor, when we hold a child's hand, when we prepare food to eat, when we take care of our health: all of this can be done as an offering. When there is love for God, everything we do increasingly becomes an expression of that love. Accordingly, it becomes increasingly difficult to separate our "worldly" from our "devotional" ways of being, for our attitudes and behavior become increasingly driven and textured by our immersion into the encompassing embrace of Love. Illumined and informed by Love, we more clearly sense the divine Heart within all beings; and we honor that Presence by acting in a manner that respects and reveres it. We can honor God not only when we go to a church, temple, synagogue or mosque, or when we pray, or when we sit in meditation; we can also honor God when we treat our children properly, when we are kind to others and when we appreciate and protect the natural world. All that we do can be consecrated by acts of love in service of Love.

"And when there is supreme sense of
being lost upon forgetting"

The term Nārada uses for forgetfulness is *vismaraṇa*. The word generally refers to the act of being unmindful of something or, perhaps more to our point, the fading of remembrance. It is the opposite of the important word *smaraṇa*, which literally means "memory, recollection, remembrance." The word *smaraṇa* is used to refer to the act of remembering God, that is to say, of holding God in one's mind and in one's heart. To remember God is to see God's presence in the moment at hand; to perform all of one's actions in service of that loving Heart; to honor the Beloved One with a sense of humility and reverence at all times.

To be in the state of forgetting, vismaraṇa, on the other hand, is to lose remembrance of the divine Beloved. It is to turn from the Heart. Forgetting God, we separate ourselves from the divine Self within all things. When we do this, we feel alienated from the world, from others, and from ourselves. We lose a sense of celebration and affirmation of the world. In the context of the spiritual or yogic life, this state of vismaraṇa is therefore not only forgetfulness or lack of mindfulness; it is the state of feeling separate, alone, empty, broken.

Our sūtra tells us here that when one is in the state of forgetfulness one feels lost, *vyākula*. This is a strong word to use in this context. It means "disoriented, confused, confounded, troubled." Nārada is saying that when we forget God's presence in our lives we feel a sense of spiritual homelessness, and thereby a feeling of purposelessness and lack of direction, even of deep meaninglessness, and thus even of anguish. Notice, though, that the state of forgetfulness is for Nārada not only *vyākula*; for him it is *paramavyākula*, the supreme and most powerful form of disorientation. Forgetfulness of God is the experience of meaninglessness in its extreme.

Please also note, though, that this sūtra implies that there is also a positive aspect of this experience of feeling lost. It can actually be a mark of spiritual love. Why might this be the case? Nārada implies here that we do not fully recognize or understand the significance of this sense of meaninglessness unless we have already had at least some inkling of what is truly meaningful. There is a subtle yet important point here: In order to forget God we must in some prior way have known the reality that is God. Our very forgetfulness implies a deeper knowledge, for one cannot forget what one does not already know. The same holds for love. One cannot feel the absence of love at any level if there were not already a deeper knowledge of the reality of love at that same level. Accordingly, when we feel forgetfulness of God we may actually or unknowingly be affirming our love for God. In this way, what we experience as forgetfulness can paradoxically be a mark of devotion. Then, when that forgetfulness dissolves through grace and through a yogic life of consecration and recollection, we realize that God's love has always been present and has always been real.

Love is a living, pulsating, vital reality. Because love is alive, it can wither if it is not nourished and thus become weak and ineffective. On the other hand, it can become strong and powerful from the mindful nourishment we give it. We become open to love through God's benevolent, compassionate grace. We strengthen our love by consciously holding and feeding the flame of love in our hearts, allowing it to illumine our view of the world, and expressing its warmth and light with all of our being. Through cultivating our awareness of grace, we deepen our gratitude for that grace, and in deepening our gratitude, we offer our love to God in return.

Terms appearing in Chapter 3

akhila Steady, constant (literally, "unbroken:" *a-khila*).

anādyavidyā Beginningless ignorance; misunderstanding that has trapped the soul in ignorance seemingly since the very beginning of our existence as embodied beings.

ananya Literally, "not other." This can characterize a state of communion, union or a deep state of being identical to something. It can also mean "focused on nothing other than" something and thus "focused on one thing only." Thus, *ananya bhakti* is devotional love for the Divine alone.

avidyā Not-knowing (*a-vidyā*): ignorance, specifically, ignorance of the true Self.

bhakti sādhana Spiritual practice and discipline (*sādhana*) that supports and refines devotional love (*bhakti*).

guru/Guru Literally, "heavy" or "weighty" and thus "important" and "dignified" (the word is related to the Latin *gravitas*), at the conventional level, a *guru* is a valued teacher, especially a spiritual mentor and guide. Some traditions associate the first syllable *gu* with darkness and the second syllable *ru* with light. In mystical yogic traditions, the Guru (capitalized here) is the divine Teacher, identified as the universal, graceful Power of inner transformation and illumination that brings light to all forms of inner darkness.

kṛpā Benevolent grace, loving tenderness. For some different forms of grace, see Table II (below).

leśa A portion or part of a whole.

paramapreman Literally, supreme (*parama*) love (*preman*).

paramavyākula Supreme confusion, highest disorientation (*parama*: supreme + *vyākula*: disorientation).

sādhana	Spiritual discipline, a set of spiritual practices, the yogic life. Literally, "leading to the goal, leading to completion."
smaraṇa	Literally, "remembering." In the spiritual context, refers to the spiritual practice of recollection; remembering God, remembering sacred texts, recalling sacred teachings.
vismaraṇa	Forgetfulness; here, forgetfulness of the Divine.
vyākula	Disoriented, confused, confounded, troubled.

Table II

Some Forms of Grace *(Kṛpā)*

ātma-kṛpā	Grace of the divine Self (*ātman*: the "n" is dropped here for grammatical reasons). (The hyphen here indicates that the two words form a compound word.)
bhagavad-kṛpā	The grace of God (*bhagavān*: the spelling is different in this linguistic setting due to grammatical reasons. The hyphen here indicates a compound word).
guru kṛpā	Grace of the Teacher. (For *Guru*, see above).
mahat-kṛpā	Grace of a "great one" (*mahant*: the spelling is changed in this compound word for grammatical purposes). Grace of a spiritual master. Grace of the Guru (see above).
śāstra kṛpā	Grace of sacred teachings; grace given through sacred words.

Chapter 4

Foundations of Bhakti as a Yogic Discipline

Reflections in the previous chapter were based in part on the understanding that all love has its source in God and that it is the creative, sustaining and transforming power of grace that awakens it. Once our hearts have been opened, we spontaneously want to express the love that moves within us. We want to respond to it. This is to say, we come to a sense of responsibility in our devotion. This responsibility is not an external set of constraints imposed on us, but rather a naturally-arising, inwardly spontaneous expression of love. As we open to grace, we thereby have the opportunity to see that our response to it becomes purer, stronger and more elevated through the sādhana of love. Swami Chidvilasananda has said, "Love is not something you experience only once, and then that's it, there's nothing more to do. Love is something you learn again and again."[38] For those yogīs and yoginīs who sense the divine Heart within all things, the cultivation and strengthening of love for that Presence can become the most important part of life, for everything else finds its source, purpose and fulfillment in the Love that is God.

There are forces that weaken or impede one's emerging love, and there are ways of living one's life that support it. It is therefore important that one's nascent sentiments of our spiritual love be protected and nourished. Then, our love can become so strong that it can transform and redirect even the forces that otherwise obstruct it so that they, too, can be used in service of the highest Love.

Indian tradition speaks of spiritual love as being like a tree sapling.[39] When the young tree is growing, it is good to build a fence around it so that animals do not step on it. But once that sapling has been protected and allowed to grow into its fullness, then the tree gives shelter and shade to those very same animals, who take refuge under it.

In this chapter we will look at two sūtras that articulate some of the foundational components of a yogic life grounded in spiritual love. These perspectives and practices support our yogic life as sādhana. They constitute some of the basic elements of what we might call the *dharma* of bhakti, for they express some of the behavioral, ethical and moral responsibilities and commitments that support and express devotional love. We will look first at a sūtra that will help us reflect on some tendencies that we might well take care to avoid. Then we will turn to a sūtra that brings our attention to some attitudes and values to cultivate.

Sūtra 43 succinctly notes one way to protect one's spiritual love. It says that,

दुःसङ्गः सर्वथैव त्याज्यः ॥४३॥

duḥsaṅgaḥ sarvathaiva tyājyaḥ

Harmful association in every respect is to be given up.

— Sūtra 43

Let's first think about what Nārada might mean when he refers to harmful association. Then we will reflect on what he means when he says that it is to be renounced in every respect.

"Harmful association"

The word *saṅga* literally refers to a bringing together of two or more things and thus means "attachment" and thus also "association." (It is not to be confused with the word *saṁgha*, which in the spiritual context refers to a community of fellow seekers, contemplatives, devotees, and so on.) From a yogic perspective, a person's attachment to something can be beneficial, as in true and genuine devotion or dedication to that which is true, good, healthy, holy. Yet, attachments of various sorts can also be harmful. Nārada here warns of the dangers of harmful association, *duḥsaṅga.*

I interpret the phrase in three ways. One way is that it refers to dangers of harmful clinging of any sort, including emotional addiction. Another is that Nārada is saying that there is need to take care regarding the people with whom we outwardly associate. A third way to understand the phrase would be that we may have some inner company, as it were, who distract us from cultivating our higher forms of love. In terms of the yogic life, these inner associates — perhaps more accurately, these inner enemies — can be more harmful than our outer company. They can block us from the path of love.

Regarding the first interpretation, the understanding that there are forms of harmful clinging is of course not unique to bhakti yoga. Spiritual paths from around the world and across time have in their various ways noted the constricting and debilitating effect of a psychological, ideological, emotional or spiritual grasping that strangles the inherent expansiveness of life. We cling when we are afraid of change, even if that change is necessary or for the better. We grasp when we insist on maintaining control over something that really is not ours to control. We hold onto something even though deep down we know it is detrimental to us to do so or that it is not true. Sometimes what people may think is love may instead be an emotional or psychological attachment to a state of being that actually inhibits or smothers love. The opposite of such constrictive grasping is openness, particularly openness to grace.

Turning now to the second interpretation, let's ask why our sūtra might urge us to renounce outward bad company. It may seem that Nārada is being rather harsh. In urging us to avoid such company, is he being elitist, judgmental or condescending? Are we to think that if we are on a spiritual path we are thereby superior to others?

The answer to these questions is "no." In another sūtra we do not have space to study at this time, sūtra 64, Nārada is firm in saying that arrogance and other forms of self-centeredness are to be relinquished. Nārada thus admonishes us against any tendency toward spiritual haughtiness or self-righteousness. This being so, there is no room on the path of love for close-mindedness, prejudice, or bigotry of any sort, nor for feelings of superiority over people who follow other spiritual paths.

Yet, Nārada does say here that we are to renounce harmful companionship. This may be because we can tend to assume the attitudes and values of those with whom we associate. We are affected by our surroundings. This is why the nature and quality of the company we keep is important. If we spend our time with people who are cynical, fearful, judgmental, distrustful, spiteful or hateful, then we place ourselves in a situation that can bring ice to our own hearts, chilling what otherwise can be so warm and loving.

When one's sentiments of love are emerging, it can be better to keep some distance from the influence of such people, while still honoring the essential Love that dwells within and supports them, though they may not recognize it. I am reminded of a lesson from folk wisdom in India regarding the benefit of not touching charcoal. If the charcoal is hot, it will burn you. If it is cold, it will dirty your hands. So, if you don't want to be burned and if you want clean hands, then don't touch charcoal.

By saying this, I am not saying that you literally should avoid all such people. I am suggesting that you distance yourself from the *influence* of such people. It may well be that actual distance from such company is difficult to establish or maintain, or that your dharmic responsibilities to some people mean that you need to stay in relationship with them. Perhaps you have important people in your life who do not share your vision, hopes and yearnings. Some may feel hostile toward it. Would Nārada say that you should literally abandon such people?

My sense is that the answer would be "not necessarily." Several times in the *Bhakti Sūtra* as a whole, Nārada mentions and stresses the importance of living responsibly in the world and that true devotion to God, in fact, sanctifies all of one's activities. This means that we are to continue to maintain, strengthen and deepen our relationships with those whose lives overlap in important ways with ours.

However, if such people do bring us their negativity, then we should try not to be deflated by it. It depends on how we hear what they say. Sometimes what may seem at first to be negative is actually not. In such instances we need to be attentive to what is being said under the surface. Other times people may say things that are genuinely negative and stand against the flow of love in the world. At such times we need to allow these comments to slide off of us. It may take courage, patience, imagination and a good sense of humor to do so. But it is important that we do not make such voices our bad company, as it were, for the attitudes and perspectives they express can pull us away from the path toward higher love.

The third way of understanding the use of the word *duḥsaṅga* here — namely, that it refers to harmful inner company — comes from a more specifically yogic perspective than the second interpretation. Yogic thought in general holds that the quality of our thoughts and emotions determines our experience of the world. An optimistic person will see a world that is filled with potential, whereas a pessimistic person will see a world that is encumbered by frustration and limitation. The former will be enthusiastic, energetic and expansive, the latter will be distrustful, constricted and fearful. Our ideas, preconceptions and predilections tend to stay with us as we move through our lives.

In a sense, our thoughts and feelings are our inner companions. They are with us wherever we go. That companionship can be harmful if it expresses itself in the form of those sometimes pernicious inner voices that feed our doubts, our fears and our sense of unworthiness or inadequacy. This negative inner company is perhaps much more influential than our outer company, for the perspectives we take from it affect the way we see, experience and understand our outward world. This is why we should not cling to harmful inner associations.

What are some of the constituents of this type of inner company? Our sūtra does not specifically tell us. However, we can get guidance by looking at other works from the spiritual traditions of India. The *Bhagavad Gītā*, for example, mentions such characteristics as hypocrisy, arrogance, pride, anger, insolence and ignorance as being what it calls demoniacal in nature.[40] Similarly, the *Vivekacūḍāmaṇi*, a text from the 8th-9th centuries, notes that "lustful desire, anger, greed, arrogance, malice, egotism, envy, jealousy, and so on" are forces that trap us in bondage.[41]

Spiritual teachers from the Indian tradition sometimes speak of the "inner enemies" that stand in the way of our experience of spiritual love — and thus our experience of the Self — and against whom we therefore need to resist as valiant and courageous warriors. Swami Chidvilasananda uses the phrase in the following passage, where she speaks of six such enemies and of their effect:

> Picture the heart surrounded by a hard thick shell of impurities. Think of it as like a living thing trapped inside a rock. . . . In the same way, the heart is encased by impurities, by the impressions of past actions and the ravages of the six enemies — anger, lust, pride, jealousy, delusion, and greed.[42]

What is the basic force that gives these inner enemies their strength? Each of these enemies is driven by narrow self-centeredness. We feel anger when things do not meet our expectations; lust when we seek self-gratification of some sort at the expense of somebody or something else; arrogant pride when we artificially pump up our sense of worthiness rather than standing confidently yet humbly in the inherent warmth of the Heart; jealousy when we forget both another person's splendor and our own value; delusion when we define the world according to our own limited way of seeing things; and greed when we do not express gratitude for all that God has given us.

The effect of this harmful inner company can drain us of our love. It can eat away at the inner splendor that is our love, the way rust will corrode even the hardest of containers. It can gnaw at our hearts like termites will eat through the foundations of even the most beautiful house. Everything in our spiritual lives can fall apart if this harmful inner company is not vanquished or transformed.

"Should be given up"

The word this phrase translates is *tyājya*, which is related to *tyāga*, the latter often translated as "renunciation." Both words are based on a verbal root that refers to a process of leaving something behind. By using the word *tyājya* our sūtra thereby brings to mind the yogic discipline of renunciation itself. The fact that Nārada uses this kind of language in a set of aphorisms on bhakti means, again, that he sees loving devotion itself to be a sādhana, a disciplined yogic life that leads to the purification, transformation and liberation of the human spirit. The more we practice renunciation of attachment to our harmful inner company, the less hold our harmful habits, attitudes and desires have on us. The culmination of this renunciation takes place when all of our self-centered desires, attitudes, motivations and addictions drop away and we desire, instead, to know and love God.

It may be difficult to leave our inner enemies behind, for they may have been with us for a long, long time and have become, in a sense, our most familiar, if harmful, company. Regarding them, Nārada's remedy is bold: turn from them. Quit them. Give them up. Do not let yourself be pushed by the inner enemies, and do not let them define your world. Be a spiritual warrior.

But, you may ask, aren't there appropriate times for such feelings as anger? The answer here certainly would be "yes." There is an effective and positive place in our world for anger at the social and personal ravages of bigotry, cruelty and injustice. One who loves God turns the energy of that anger into beneficial work to resist and dissipate dehumanizing forces that go against the imperatives of an ethical and just life. Such a yogī or yoginī uses the energy of that anger in a constructive manner in bringing forth what is right and good.

Likewise, isn't desire sometimes helpful, such as our desire to know and love God? The answer again is "yes," as long as we distinguish between self-centered motivations and true yearning for God. I will say more about this in Chapter 8. For now, I would say simply that our longing for God expresses the very essence of our being. It is the Self within our hearts calling out to the Self that is God. So we need to understand that the lover of God does not renounce this special kind of yearning, but rather intensifies it, elevates it, refines it, enriches it and deepens it.

I would want to say, therefore, that there is another way to understand the nature and process of renunciation, one that is just as transforming and purifying as the way of the warrior.

To give something up is also in a sense to give something away. Understood in this sense, the renunciation we are talking about is not only a courageous, active dismissal or refusal of an inner state of being; perhaps more importantly, yogic renunciation is an act of offering. Ancient religious texts from India sometimes use the word *tyāga* when speaking of the performance of a *yajña*, an offertory ritual, in which priests, acting on behalf of the human community, pour seeds, flowers, milk products and other elements of life into a sacred fire. The blazing heat of the fire purifies these offerings and carries their essence to the gods in the heavens, who then return this gift of life by pouring that purified living essence back down to earth in the form of rain. Similarly, in the devotional context, tyāga is not so much the harsh and sharp quitting of something, but rather the sanctifying act of giving oneself to the world in the spirit of service to God.

Renunciation in this sense is not so much a sharp and definitive throwing away of an undesirable characteristic. It is discerning acknowledgment of that negative companion and the resolute offering of it to the fire of God's love, so that God's grace may transform it into a force of good in the world. Nārada's call to renunciation may therefore be regarded as an invitation and encouragement for us to see our lives as the continuing setting in which we offer ourselves to that transforming flame of love and thereby to the world.

We may well feel anger at times. Yet, in the yoga of love, anger can be transformed into a positive energy that can change something that needs to be changed. So, too, we may at times feel pushed by greed, delusion, pride and jealousy. When we do confront these negative companions, however, we thus have two ways of renouncing them.

We can banish them by refusing to be caught up in them, thereby diffusing their energy. If we are angry at a colleague or family member, we can take a deep breath, calm ourselves, unburden ourselves from the weight of that anger, and move forward.

Or, we can transform the energy of a negative companion into forces of benevolence and compassion. If we feel greedy for something, for example, we can be mindful of the energy such greed takes and redirect that energy into doing something that helps others rather than merely satisfies our own selfish desires.

Both ways of renouncing the inner associates work well and each is to be undertaken at various times. Given the fact that we do embody various forms of energy in our lives, it seems to me personally that the second is often more effective in terms of our spiritual growth. In either case, though, it is important that we be open to grace, for our negative companions can cling so close to our souls that we may not be able to be free of them by ourselves.

"In every respect"

The relevant word here, *sarvathā*, can be understood either as an adjective referring to harmful associations or as an adverb describing the act of renouncing them. If interpreted as an adjective, then the lesson to us is to renounce all kinds of harmful association. If it is understood as an adverb, then the lesson is that this association is to be renounced by any means possible.

As it appears in this sūtra, the word may serve in both of these ways at the same time. That is why I have placed the English "in every respect" in the middle of the sentence, for in this way it can modify both the noun and the verb. In understanding the phrase "in every respect" in this way, I see our text to imply that a bhakta is to renounce all forms of negative association, whether this be outward or inward. Our text suggests that this renunciation is to be undertaken both by turning away from that harmful association and by transforming the inner forces on which that association is based.

In either case, how do we turn away from this negative companionship? The answer is: We turn toward selfless love, for love is the antidote for all forms of narrow self-centeredness. Doing so, we protect the vital yet in some ways delicate love that throbs and pulsates deep in the heart. Then, harmful company that supports narrow self-centeredness can be replaced by helpful company, namely, by beneficial feelings of devotion to the benevolent Self that is our deepest and truest Company. These words by Utpaladeva, tenth century lover of God as Śiva, can become our own:

> In speech, in thought,
> In the perceptions of the mind,
> And in the gestures of the body,
> May the sentiment of devotion be my companion
> At all times, in all places.[43]

Utpaladeva's prayerful turn toward bhakti in these verses reflects his realization that love for God is to be cultivated and expressed in all situations and at all levels of one's being and suggests that this can indeed be the case. Nārada's sūtras imply a similar understanding of the nature of this love. They also indicate a number of ways in which these sentiments can become more firmly established. In sūtra 78 Nārada mentions several modes of being that will help the lover of God participate in God's own Love:

अहिँसासत्यशौचदयास्तिक्यादिचारित्र्याणि परिपालनीयानि ॥

ahiṁsā-satya-śauca-dayāstikyādi-cāritryāṇi paripālanīyāni

"Unwillingness to do harm, truthfulness, purity, generous compassion, the affirmation of Divinity and other such beneficial modes of conduct are to be fully protected."

— Sūtra 78

"Modes of conduct are to be fully protected"

Let's begin with the latter part of the sūtra. The word for "beneficial modes of conduct" here is the Sanskrit *cāritrya*, which perhaps more literally means "way of moving" in the world but which more particularly in this setting refers to behavior, attitudes, values and intentions that enhance progress on the spiritual path. The sense of movement implied by the word suggests that there are ideals that are to be actively applied in a life infused with devotional love. Each moment and situation in life can bring new challenges and opportunities. Sometimes we may not know just what to do. When we are grounded in some core values we are more able to respond creatively, effectively, benevolently and lovingly to whatever is at hand.

Various forces — we can think here for example of the harmful associations we just discussed — can erode that ground. They are to be renounced or transformed. On the other hand, there are ways of approaching and living life that support the devotional attitude and enhance our ability to express love. These qualities and characteristics of spiritual love may at first be tender, fragile and easily injured. Even if they are strong, they can become weakened. Therefore, beneficial attitudes of love are continually to be nourished, cared for and strengthened, and this attentiveness is to be encompassing, complete and constant.

Our sūtra leads us to understand that these virtues "should be fully protected." The word here is *paripālanīya*, which could also be translated "should be fully preserved, maintained, observed." It is worth noting that our sūtra does not say simply that these ideals are to be protected: *palanīya*; it says that they are to be fully protected: *paripalanīya*. Remember, in sūtra literature no word is unimportant. The presence of the prefix *pari* — translated here as "fully" — suggests that these attitudes, stances, and ways of conducting oneself are to be applied, not in a partial or halfhearted way, but rather with commitment, resolution and steadfastness.

"Unwillingness to do harm"

The first of such virtues our sūtra lists is *ahiṁsā*. The term is often translated as "nonviolence." It consists of two parts: *a-hiṁsā*. In Sanskrit the prefix *a-* negates whatever word that follows it; it is therefore equivalent of the "non" in "nonviolence." The word *hiṁsā* means "injury" or "harm." In a sense, the word is actually a bit more complicated than such translations might suggest. Linguistically, the word *himsā* has a volitional, desiderative component to it. Accordingly, it connotes not only the doing of harm but, more importantly, the desire to do harm. It is said to be of three types: mental injury, that is to say, the wishing of harm on another; spoken injury in the form of knowingly speaking hurtful words; and outward injury in the case of intentional physical violence.

The opposite of himsā is ahimsā. Accordingly, rather than "nonviolence," I prefer to translate ahimsā as "the unwillingness to do harm," for the latter has a more active component to it. I sense that this understanding of the word is closer to the yogic perspective than is the simpler "nonviolence," for it seems to me to reflect more accurately the realization that all of our actions originate in, and are motivated by, our desires and intentions. Ahiṁsā is a virtue that keeps us from doing harm to another because it cuts off the possibility of those actions before they can happen.

Although semantically the word *ahiṁsā* is negative, the virtue it represents therefore has quite positive connotations and implications. To practice ahiṁsā is not only to avoid harming others but, more positively, to maintain and express a benevolent attitude toward life. Ahiṁsā is an expansive and generous desire for the welfare of all beings. This is an attitude of love.

I also translate *ahiṁsā* as "the unwillingness to do harm" because some people may feel that if they are to practice this virtue then they cannot ever do anything that might bring pain or discomfort to anybody. Sometimes, though, our love for and responsibilities to others may require us to do what we can to help bring an end to certain destructive modes of behavior, either in ourselves or sometimes in others. At such times there may be an experience of pain on somebody's part. The key lies, again, in our intention in causing this discomfort. If it has any element of wishing harm on another, then this is hiṁsā. On the other hand, if there is no such desire but rather there is only the expression of genuine love, then our actions reflect ahiṁsā. When a person maliciously stabs another with a knife, this is hiṁsa. Yet, when a heart surgeon opens a person's chest with a knife in service of the patient's larger health there is no such desire to harm. Similarly, a yogic attitude toward any action in the world is always focused on the quality of the intention behind that action. A yoga of love is directed by the intention of ahiṁsā.

Of course, it should be said, we must be diligent in our self-inquiry. Sometimes what we call selfless concern for another's welfare actually masks our own deeper self-interest; we inflict sorrow, saying "I am only doing this because I love you" when actually there may be other, less loving and more self-centered reasons why we do so.

The true Self, on the other hand, is generous, supportive and creative, and its love is unconditional. Therefore, ahiṁsā is a virtue in the yogic life because to hold a nonviolent attitude toward others is to help make the love that is the Heart's nature manifest through one's values and in one's actions. To live a life grounded in ahiṁsā is therefore to honor the Self within others and within oneself, and to honor the Self in this manner is one way of expressing love for God.

"Truthfulness"

The second quality Nārada lists here is *satya*. Again, we can understand this at different levels of meaning. The most obvious way of being truthful is not to lie. What is the problem in lying? Well, first of all, to lie is to show disrespect for another. It is a manipulative act that dishonors the integrity of the other. Lying is not loving. To love is to respect the integrity of the other, and thus not to lie.

We can also look at the stance of truthfulness from another perspective. When we lie we are *asatya* ("not true"), and by this I mean we are neither true to what is real nor, more importantly, to who we really are. At the deepest or highest level of soul we are of the nature of *sat-cit-ānanda*: being, consciousness and bliss. As we know, the first word in this compound, *sat*, means not only "being" but also "reality" and "truth." To be satya, "truthful," is therefore to experience and express the real presence of the true Self within us. To be *satya* is to be *real*. When we are otherwise, when we are untruthful, we alienate ourselves from the true Self within us, and this means that we alienate ourselves from God.

To be at one with the Self is to be at one with the Love that lies within us. That Love may have been hidden and distorted by ignorance of the Self and thus by false identification with the machinations of pretentious and narrowly egoistic forces. Therefore, if we are to be devoted to God, then we are in a very deep sense to get real with ourselves as much as with others, and certainly with God. In spiritual love there is no room for pretense of any sort, for pretense obscures and veils our true nature. In order to be at one with God, we are therefore to cultivate the virtue of satya, truthfulness, at every level of our being.

"Purity"

A third virtue listed here is *śauca*. This can been understood in two general senses. There is outer purity (*bāhya śauca*) and there is inner purity (*āntara śauca*).[44] Traditionally, outer purity had something to do with bathing and various forms of cleansing before performing sacred rituals. From there, it came to include the attentiveness to maintaining a clean temple or sacred domain, and then to a clean household and living space. Inner purity, on the other hand, refers to the quality of one's mind and heart. There are some states of being that allow the light of Love to shine more clearly and warmly than others. Those states that are purer are those that are less covered by the dusty clouds of self-centeredness.

In the yogic life the outer and the inner aspects of existence are closely related. This holds true for śauca, as it does for other yogic virtues. Yogic discipline in general includes a process of simplification and a move toward cleanliness in all manner of being. At times, that cleanliness begins outwardly. This is why yogis clean their rooms and sweep their floors, as it were. This fosters more inner clarity, supports a greater sense of respect for oneself and others and for one's environment, and leads to a fuller and more refined attentive awareness of whatever is taking place in the moment at hand.

While remaining attentive to the value of outer cleanliness, the yogic life as a whole generally emphasizes the importance of the inner world. The idea, in part, is that just as a cluttered mind leads to a cluttered life, so too a clear mind leads to an uncluttered and thus freer life. Thus, the importance of śauca.

There is more we could say about śauca in the context of the yoga of spiritual love. The word derives from a verbal root that connotes the purifying heat of fire, and thus also a shining, glimmering brightness and clarity. The image here is reminiscent of the offertory flame that burns during the performance of sacred rituals. Accordingly, in cultivating śauca, we not only strive to keep our living spaces clean and our thoughts pure; in the spiritual discipline of love we pour all of our impurities into a blazing fire of sorts. This is the flame of God's own love for us. Just as butter that is heated in a pan gives rise to a clear, sweet essence, so, too, our commitment to a pure heart reveals and brings forth the clarity of the soul's foundation in pure Love. To become more immersed in that Love, we need to rid ourselves of selfish motivations and allow

God's bright, shining and expansive love to burn within us. We develop genuine śauca to the degree that we purify our love in the cleansing, refining and transforming fire of devotion.

"Generous compassion"

The word this sūtra uses here is *dayā*, one of a number of Sanskrit words that could be translated as "compassion." For example, yogic values also stress the importance of cultivating *karuṇā*: a feeling of warmth, empathy, tenderness and caring concern for another. So, too, texts associated with Buddhist traditions similarly speak of *mettā* (from the Sanskrit *maitrī*) as "loving kindness" toward others.

Dayā includes these same sentiments, too, and also what might be called "charity" in that latter word's sense of a generosity of spirit. The noun *dayā* is based on the verb *dā*, which means to "give." Accordingly, it seems to me, our sūtra's use of the word *dayā* here suggests an important point: compassion involves some action on one's part. One can feel sympathy, pity or tenderness for another, yet if one does not in some way express this sentiment in a generosity of spirit, then one has not yet given compassion in the sense of dayā.

Expressions of dayā can include gifts of material and mental well-being: food, clothing, housing, physical and emotional security, education, protection from fear. In the yogic context, this compassionate giving also involves the act of dwelling in the true Self, Ātman — the same Self that resides within the other, too. Charitable communion with the Self is the immersion into and participation in the divine Presence in all beings. Compassionate love thus recognizes and honors the Self — both in the being of the other *and* in one's own being.

When we open ourselves to the Heart, we naturally and spontaneously experience a longing to do what we can to align ourselves with the Beloved's own wish that all people be free of suffering. By doing this, we also free the Self within us to express its true nature as generous, powerful and loving. Yogic compassion therefore not only serves the person toward whom it is directed — it also opens the one who feels compassion to the sustaining and liberating love that is the Self's nature. This is one reason why generous, compassionate love is transforming. It brings both the object of love and the person who feels that love closer to God, who is the Source of all love.

"The affirmation of Divinity"

Our sūtra then refers to *āstikya* as one of virtues associated with the path of bhakti. This word is built on the verb *asti*, which means "there is" or "there exists," and is thereby related to *āstika*, which literally means "one who asserts the existence" of something. Through the history of Indian religious thought, the word *āstika* has referred more specifically to one who has faith in the existence of Divinity and in the power of sacred texts to guide one toward the knowledge and experience of Divinity. The reference to *āstikya* in our sūtra similarly describes one who has faith that God is real. In using it here Nārada is saying that one who loves God has faith in God. Nārada thereby affirms the value of illumined teachings regarding God's nature.

This faith in God comes in part from one's own experience that Love is real. If there were not this experiential knowledge, then one's devotion could possibly be based on a flimsy, hypothetical wish that this love be real. The danger is that such a wish can actually be a veiled desire and, like any other desire, can lead to disappointment, discouragement, even despair if it seems not to be gratified, at least not in the way one expects that desire to be gratified. Our sūtra does not refer to some vague hope that God's love might be real. It is talking about a stance that recognizes that Love is real, even if at times it may not be experienced in ways that one expects. It is real even if we do not seem to experience it at all.

Here, we can draw on our various experiences of human love. They can come to us in ways we did not foresee - a kind gesture from someone, an act of forgiveness, an affirmation of one's inner value, a word of encouragement and hope. Sometimes it is only later that we see that our lives have been touched and supported by others' love, although we did not recognize and appreciate it at the time. God's love is like this, but at the supreme level. It is real all the time. It is always with us, even if we do not knowingly experience it, holding us in the light of the divine Heart.

The affirmation of Divinity is not a static perspective. We should note that sūtra 78 places āstikya in this list of active modes of being that also includes not wishing harm on others, truthfulness and compassion. Like these, the affirmation of Divinity is to be put into action in one's life.

To share oneself in divine Love is one reason why a yogic life oriented around bhakti is important. If we truly affirm the reality of Love, then we are to behave in ways that are in alignment with that Love. We do so by loving God's presence in others, in the world, and in our own truest hearts, and by acting accordingly. To affirm God is to do what we can to bring more love into the world. To bring more love into the world is to participate in God's nature as love. A yogic life oriented toward this participation in God's love, this communion with God's nature, is a life infused with bhakti.

What if we do not always feel this love? This is when both faithful trust in God and dedication to the yogic life come in. In the context of bhakti as a yoga, to affirm Divinity is to trust in the reality of God's love based on one's larger experience beyond the moment. As it has been said by many people, we know the sun continues to exist even when it is a cloudy day because we have experienced the sun at other times. Our experience leads to and supports our trust. The same holds for faith in God as Love. Such faith is not a shallow belief or hypothesis based simply on what one wants to be true or has been told is true by others. It is based in one's own experience of love, at any level of our existence. The more immediate, expansive, generous and unpolluted this experience of love is, the more possibility there is for an elevated devotion to God. This is why the virtue of āstikya is important to devotional sādhana, for it brings clarity, strength, resolution and maturity to one's spiritual life.

"And others"

The last term in this string of virtues is the word *ādi*, which could also be translated as "the rest" or "and so on." Nārada seems to want us to know that there are more virtues for us to cultivate than those he has listed in this short sūtra. We are not told what they are.

We can assume, though, that the students in India to whom the *Bhakti Sūtra* as a whole was first taught would be familiar with other lists of similarly beneficial attitudes, spiritual practices and modes of behavior. The *Bhagavad Gītā*, for example, lists a number of such yogic virtues associated with spiritual love:

> Fearlessness, clarity of essence,
> steadfastness in the yoga of knowledge,
> generosity, self-restraint and sacrifice,
> study of sacred texts, austerity, rectitude,
> not wishing harm, truthfulness, absence of anger,
> renunciation, serenity, aversion to fault-finding,
> compassion for all beings, free of greedy desire,
> gentleness, modesty, not fickle,
> vigor, patience, fortitude, purity,
> without malice, without excessive pride.[45]

We are reminded, too, of the Noble Eight-Fold Path, as taught by the Buddha about 2500 years ago and presented, for example, in the *Dhammacakkapavatanna Sutta* ("Sūtra on the Turning Forth of Truth"). This set of spiritual disciplines consists of cultivating and maintaining the right view, which allows one to see things as they are rather than as one wishes them to be; right intention, characterized by selfless, loving, and nonviolent thoughts toward others; right speech, in which one neither tells untruths, slanders, engages in gossip, nor utters any harsh or unkind words; right action, which precludes killing, taking what is not freely given, and sexual misconduct; right livelihood based on values that recognize the inherent dignity of all beings; right effort to avoid unhealthy states of mind and cultivate beneficial ones; right mindfulness that brings clear attention to the activities of the body, feelings and emotions and ideas flowing through one's mind; and right meditation, in which one enters into deeper and deeper levels of awareness leading finally to the experience of dispassionate and loving bliss.[46] The Buddhist path thus includes practices that broaden one's compassion and deepen one's wisdom, the realization being that compassion and wisdom augment and strengthen each other.

Similarly, Patañjali's *Yoga Sūtra* dating to sometime around the third century CE notes the value and importance of various forms of "restraining" (*yama*) and "controlling" (*niyama*) one's mind and body so that one can be increasingly free of spiritually dissonant or harmful tendencies. For Patañjali, like Nārada, such practices include the turning away from wishing harm on others, from speaking untruths and from uncleanliness. Patañjali also refers to the restraint from stealing, from sexual impropriety and from greed of any kind; he encourages the cultivation and practice of equanimity, austerity, chanting and study of sacred texts, and he notes the importance of holding a reverential attitude toward God.[47]

The more fully we practice such virtues as those mentioned in sūtra 78, the more all of our actions in the world will arise out of love for God and thus be sanctified by that love. This is one reason to perform the sādhana of devotion. A yogic life infused with such sensibilities and disciplines allows us to become more immersed in the Source of life in all of its complexity and thus to relish the Self's presence in the heart of all beings, including our own. Forgetting that Presence, we can experience deep anguish. Remembering it, we express joyous gratitude for it. Accordingly, as Nārada says elsewhere, in sūtra 42, "It alone is to be cultivated; it alone is to be cultivated."

There are many ways in which we can express and nourish our emergent love. In the next chapter we will look at several such ways that come to us from the traditions of devotional yoga.

Terms appearing in Chapter 4

ahiṁsā	Unwillingness to do harm, nonviolent attitude.
āntara śauca	Inner (*āntara*) purity (*śauca*), inner splendor.
āstika/āstikya	The word *āstika* literally means "one who believes there exists" and thus refers to one who believes in the existence of God or is inspired by what are understood to be sacred truths. The related word *āstikya* thus means "belief, faith, faithfulness."
bāhya śauca	Outward (*bāhya*) purity (*śauca*), outward cleanliness.
cāritrya	Beneficial manner of being, good conduct.
dayā	One of a number of words meaning "compassion, sympathy." See also *karuṇā* and *mettā* (below).
dharma	Literally "that which supports" truth and goodness, the word *dharma* has many related connotations: spiritual practice, moral responsibility, proper behavior, duty, ethical truth, established custom and so on.
duḥsaṅga	Literally "harmful association, harmful company."
karuṇā	Compassion. See also, *dayā* (above).
mettā	A Pali word often translated as "loving kindness;" from the Sanskrit *maitrī*, meaning "friendship, friendliness, kindness."
niyama	Literally, "restraining, holding back;" in the yogic context, a particular "observance" or "inner practice" involving the restraint of narrow self-centeredness. Patañjali's *Yoga Sūtra* enumerates five such *niyamas*: equanimity, austerity, chanting and study of sacred texts and honoring Divinity. See also *yama* (below).
Śaiva	Literally, "pertaining to Śiva" (see below), refers to the religious and philosophical tradition that recognizes God as Śiva, the Auspicious One.

saṁgha	Spiritual community, fellowship. (Not the same word as *saṅga*, for which see below).
saṅga	"Association, company," as in *duḥsaṅga*, "harmful association" in sūtra 43. (Not the same word as *saṁgha*, for which see above.)
sat-cit-ānanda	A Vedāntic description of ultimate Reality as of the nature of Being (*sat*), Consciousness (*cit*) and Bliss (*ānanda*), the three aspects being equivalent to each other in the entirety of the Absolute. This is why the phrase is often translated as one word consisting of three parts.
satya	The truth, that which is true; reality, that which is real.
śauca	Physical and mental purity.
Śiva	Literally "the Benevolent One, the Auspicious One. One of the names of God and, according to Śaiva thought (see above), the Absolute itself.
tyāga	Yogic renunciation of narrowly self-centered tendencies.
tyājya	Literally, that which is "to be renounced." See *tyāga* (above).
yajña	A word from ancient Vedic India meaning "offering, sacrifice" and referring to formal ritual actions offered in praise and support of deities to the benefit of the larger world; this offertory sensibility in part stands as a basis of subsequent notions of *dharma* as one's offering of one's actions in support of the world.
yama	Literally, "control, restraint;" in the yogic context this is the disciplined practice of moral and ethical behavior. Patañjali's *Yoga Sūtra* mentions five such yamas — restraint from: wishing harm, speaking untruths, outward and inward uncleanliness, stealing, sexual impropriety and greed.

Chapter 5

Devotional Practices in the Yogic Life

Reference to sūtras 43 and 78 in the previous chapter allowed for reflection on various foundational inner stances, values and attitudes of bhakti as a yoga. We can now turn to some of the more outward practices that will support, enliven and give direction to a yogic life oriented toward spiritual love. To do so we look now to sūtra 76, which reads:

> भक्तिशास्त्राणि मननीयानि
> तद्बोधकर्माणि करणीयानि ॥७६॥
>
> ***bhaktiśāstrāṇi manananīyāni tadudbodhakakarmāṇi karaṇīyāni***
>
> Teachings on bhakti should be reflected on;
> practices that awaken it should be undertaken.
>
> — Sūtra 76

Three points in the phrasing of the sūtra initially strike me as worth noting. The first is that it stresses the importance of thoughtful contemplation and study in the yogic life. Sometimes people may think that there is no need for such study in the yoga of devotion. They might say, "My love will illumine the way for me. There is no need for anything else. Besides, isn't textual study for the jñāna yogīs, those whose sacred path pursues the way of knowledge?"

It is true that dry intellectual knowledge alone does not guarantee the experience of the Heart. It is also true that one's love for God brings a certain kind of knowledge, namely, the knowledge that God is of the nature of love itself, and that this knowledge is not necessarily found simply through textual study. But this does not mean that lovers of the holy One are not to seek deeper understanding, insight, wisdom and guidance from sacred texts on devotional love. As we will see, yogic study illumines, refines and elevates our understanding of the nature of spiritual love; when undertaken fully, such study helps us make that love effective and real in our lives.

The second point I find interesting is that the sūtra refers to study before it refers to the performing of devotional practices. By this I do not think it means that one must necessarily undertake textual study before one can undertake these practices. Devotion arises spontaneously in a heart that has opened to God's love. However, in putting this phrase first, Nārada signals that he is speaking to those who listen to him as genuine students. They are seekers who have committed themselves to deepening and clarifying their understanding of the spiritual love that has stirred their souls by studying the words of others in whom that love has also arisen.

The third point that draws my attention is that the latter part of the sūtra refers to the awakening of devotional love. The word here is *udbodha*. The prefix *ud-* means "up, upward, rising forth, pressing outward" and so on. The word *bodha* refers to the process of awakening; it also connotes wisdom that dissolves ignorance, like the light of a lamp dispels the surrounding darkness. In using the word *udbodha*, our sūtra implies that Love already exists within the student, although it may be slumbering, as it were. This Love is an aspect of one's true nature that can be retrieved. Nārada implies in this sūtra that there are acts that can awaken and bring forth this otherwise hidden or unknown inherent Love.

Let us turn now to the sūtra itself. It begins with the reference to the contemplative study of devotional texts.

"Teachings on bhakti should be reflected on"

The phrase "teachings on bhakti" translates *bhakti śāstra*. The word *śāstra* means "instruction, guidance, precept, lesson" as well as "an instrument of instruction, a manual of teachings, a treatise, a composition of sacred authority." In the context of spiritual, philosophical and moral life, a śāstra is a well-organized and effective set of lessons regarding the best way to reach the goal of one's seeking, to find fulfillment of one's yearning, and to act in an ethical manner in the world. Although they were originally composed and transmitted orally, the various collections of śāstras can be regarded as what we might call "texts." Over the centuries various and numerous sāstras were written down and now can be read in book form.

Why is textual study in the context of a yogic life of devotion helpful? People will have their own experiences of Love and of the emergence of devotion in their hearts, but sometimes those experiences can be so subtle, new or powerful that they do not recognize them for what they are. Failing to understand them, people can let these experiences and intuitions slip away from them. The understanding and wisdom that is theirs can be like beautiful jewels slipping through their fingers. The study of sacred works can thus give students insight into their own experiences of Love — and, importantly, to hold onto them. So, too, it can give them guidance into ways in which they can deepen, refine and strengthen it and thereby enter more fully into the divine Presence. Indeed, according to Indian thought, students can enter into awareness of Divinity through *śāstra kṛpā*, that is to say, by grace given through the words of sacred texts.

Texts on devotion can therefore be revelatory in nature, for in studying them we can see in them expressions similar to our own love already present within us, although we may not yet recognize it, just as they can reveal to us a path that leads to experiences we may not yet have had. They can do this because, in part, they are the words of teachers, philosophers, storytellers, poets and spiritual masters who have themselves experienced divine Love in their lives and who are able and willing to share their insights and wisdom with us. These teachers know the way, as it were. They know what to look for, what to avoid, and how best to move ever further along the spiritual path. Without their guidance, seekers can stand still or become lost. Reading, rereading and studying their words, we can refresh our own understanding of Love in its various manifestations and get new perspectives on our experiences of it. In this way, we can become more established in our love and thereby remain more steadfastly in Love.

Textual study helps students avoid being superficial or even perhaps misguided in their spiritual lives. It gives them clarity of vision, refreshed enthusiasm, deeper understanding and more profound wisdom. It brings them into a community of fellow lovers of the divine Beloved who, throughout the many centuries, have refined the quality of their spiritual love and who can help us do the same.

As a text, the *Bhakti Sūtra* is itself regarded as such a śāstra, for it consists of teachings regarding the yogic path of spiritual love. The devotional tradition of which it is formally a part considers other specific texts to be bhakti śāstras, too — namely, the *Bhagavad Gītā* and the *Bhāgavata Purāṇa,* as well as the "Nārāyānīya" section of the twelth chapter of the *Mahābhārata*, which was composed sometime before the fourth century, and the *Śāṇḍilya Bhakti Sūtra*, a text I have previously mentioned.

As students on a yogic path of devotional love, we have access to countless other texts to study and contemplate, too, many of which would have been available to Nārada's students and many of which they would not have known. Some of the most profound treatises on loving God as well as beautiful devotional poems and songs in India have been composed by or attributed to such philosophers and theologians as Śāṅkara, Rāmānuja, Madhva, Vallabha, Jīva Gosvāmī, Rūpa Gosvāmī and Utpaladeva. The songs of the great poet-saints from India — Jñāñeśvar,

Eknāth, Nāmdev, Mīrābāī, Guru Nānak, Tulsīdās, Sūrdās, Kabīr, Rāvidās, Lalleśvarī (the list could go on and on) — have enflamed hearts and stirred souls throughout the centuries. So, too, we ourselves have access to scriptural texts and devotional works composed by great hearts in other religious traditions — the Hebrew Psalms, the *Song of Songs*, works by Teresa of Avila, Catherine of Sienna, St. John of the Cross, Meister Eckhart, Jalāl al-din al Rūmī, Muhammad Hāfez-e Shīrāzī: again, there are many, almost beyond counting.

You could build a whole library of these insightful, poignant, moving, sometimes quite humorous, but always inspiring contemplations, prayers, songs and poems. It is well worth keeping company with these great texts, for they help show us the contours of the path of love and devotion.

What does it mean, though, to study such texts? What are some of the characteristics of such a mode of study? I will organize my following comments around two related and important components of yogic study.

Yogic Study as Assimilation and Application

Yogic study is not simply or only a process of searching for information and acquiring objective knowledge. In the context of the yogic life, true knowledge comes through the actual and transforming experience of the content of what one studies. Study is a process of internalizing the wisdom presented by the texts one studies and then applying that wisdom in one's life. Study is active, not passive. We can think of this process through the analogy of eating food. One receives food and chews it thoroughly. Then, one swallows that food so that its nourishment can be used by the body. Similarly, yogic study is a process of assimilating the knowledge presented in the texts one studies. Then, just as the nourishment of good food is used to support the body, so too the knowledge one has assimilated through yogic study can actively be brought forward to nourish, support, enhance and refine one's larger life as a yogī or yoginī.

Given the importance and value of the yogic mode of study, I would like to take a moment to reflect further upon this process of assimilation and application.

Study as a Process of Assimilation

In a number of classical Indian spiritual traditions, the yogic practice of study includes a three-part process represented by the words *śravana*, *manana* and *nididhyāsana*. Here, the process begins and is grounded in *śravana*, which literally means "listening." We might remember, again, that spiritual lessons in traditional India were given orally by the master to the student. Here, in the discipline of śravana, a student listens closely to what is being said. It is a mindful, focused listening. We in the twenty-first century can also think of attentive reading as a form of listening.

The yogic discipline of śravana is more than simply hearing or reading words and phrases. When practicing śravana, we as yogīs and yoginīs put aside as much as possible our expectations, habitual ways of thinking and projections as we listen closely to the words presented. We earnestly open ourselves to them. We let the texts speak for themselves, rather than as we want them to speak. We listen attentively and closely so that we hear not only the surface narratives but also the subtle, less obvious, often symbolic and often more profound knowledge they express. The more a yogī or yoginī can break out of preconceived, limited ways of thinking by listening to what the words themselves are truly saying, then the more he or she can be guided by the wisdom within those words.

A next step in the process of assimilation is *manana*, which means "thinking about" or "reflecting on" what we have heard. (What I have translated as "should be reflected on" in sūtra 76, *mananan̄īya*, is closely related to this word.) This is a process of thoughtful and careful study based on a sense of appreciation for the lessons and the guidance the text presents. To undertake manana is to engage with the material at hand at a deep rather than superficial level and in a sustained rather than cursory manner. It is to ponder the teachings, to mull over them, to ruminate on them. It is to be open to the subtleties of the teachings and to the way in which they reveal their meaning to us at ever-deeper levels of understanding.

In the practice of manana we receive what we have been given and place it contemplatively into our minds and hearts. We explore the depth and breadth of what we have heard or read and relate its significance to our yogic lives. We can do this together with others who are similarly engaged in the same process, and we can do it by ourselves on a continual basis as we go through our days.

While undertaking the practice of manana it is again important that we not project our expectations or preconceptions onto the text. Rather, we let the text speak to us, tell us something, and show us a new way of seeing things. Then, as we continue to let the text speak for itself, we may then come to feel or to see that its words express our own inner experience, too. When this happens, the lessons and insights they present can seem to come from deep within our own souls.

Contemplating the meaning of devotional texts, we can thus experience an inner recognition of sorts, for in a mysterious way in them we can we can see who we truly are, or truly could be. We then can turn to the texts again and again, moving ever deeper into the process of revelation, illumination and discovery.

A third step in the process of yogic study is *nididhyāsana*. The word means "repeated entering into meditation." Following the guidance we have been given by listening and informed by our understanding gained through contemplation, we now plant that wisdom in our hearts and enter into the Consciousness that has given rise to it. Practicing nididhyāsana, we enter into meditation, and we do so on a regular and repeated basis. We can return continually to our awareness of this Consciousness, like a thirsty person repeatedly returns to a well of sweet water.

Study as the Application of what has been Assimilated

The process of assimilation is an inward process. In order for the wisdom we study to be manifest in our lives, we must outwardly activate that wisdom. In traditional terms, this is a process in which we move from what is known as *niṣkriya* to *sakriya* ways of being.

The word *niṣkriya* means "inactive" or "without doing." In its original sense, it refers to the neglect or nonperformance of one's responsibilities even though one knows what those responsibilities are. In this way, niṣkriya describes a state of mind in which one knows what to do but does not actually do it. Said differently, it characterizes knowledge and understanding that is not put into practice. When one's contemplation and study is niṣkriya in nature, it can become abstract, purely intellectual, and even, in a sense, ineffective.

Accordingly, Indian spiritual traditions stress the importance of *sakriya* ways of studying sacred texts. The word means "with action" and thus "active." Here, you draw the wisdom, understanding, insight and strength you have received and cultivated through yogic study and make them active both in your life in general and in any particular situation. The sakriya mode of being is therefore that in which you actively apply the knowledge and understanding you have gained to whatever it is you are doing. In this way, your wisdom becomes not only inwardly nourishing but also outwardly effective.

When undertaken in the context of the study of bhakti śāstra, the process of assimilating and applying knowledge is itself an act of devotion. I say this because, by undertaking this process, we inwardly open ourselves to divine guidance. We also actively show our love for the Source of that guidance itself by acting in a way that is consistent with that love.

"Practices that awaken it should be undertaken"

Nārada does not mention what these practices are; he seems to assume that his students already know what he is talking about. They may have been familiar with other texts or sets of teachings. To pick just one example of such a text with which they would have been familiar, the *Bhāgavata Purāṇa* mentions a number of such practices and attitudes. In a number of places that work gives various lists of the components of devotional yoga.

Some of those lists are short, some are quite long. In one of his discourses, the sage Śuka, the narrator of the *Bhāgavata Purāṇa*, mentions three.[48] In another place in that text, he mentions four.[49] Elsewhere in that same work, the sages Nala and Kubera mention six.[50] The teacher Kapila mentions seven.[51] Perhaps the most well-known grouping recognizes nine forms of devotional expression.[52] Still other lists from the Bhāgavata Purāṇa give us ten, eleven, twelve, thirteen, fifteen, eighteen, nineteen, twenty, twenty-four, twenty-five, twenty-six, thirty, and thirty-six modes of devotional practice.[53] Perhaps we need not be concerned with the particular number of devotional disciplines, for, as we can see, that number varies from list to list. Rather, the point here is that devotional love is nourished and expressed in many ways.

Some Devotional Practices

As a way to present some of those practices and stances presented by various lists in a more general manner, I have taken the liberty to configure them in the following way and have included a few practices described in my own words that do not explicitly appear in the *Bhāgavata Purāṇa's* various lists, although I feel they are consistent with the practices that are mentioned.

Two points should be noted. First, you will see that, grammatically, I have described these practices with present participles, that is to say, as ending in *-ing*: "remembering, worshipping, honoring" and so on. In part, this is to represent the Sanskrit suffix *-ana* added to many of the relevant words, which performs the same function in Sanskrit. I note this because the grammar suggests what I see to be an important point, namely, that these practices are to be undertaken on a continuing basis. They are not to be performed and then put into the past. Each moment, each present instant, can be infused to some degree by the attitudes and perspectives of these practices.

Second, while they are indeed important to the yogic life, it should be noted that these practices need not be cumbersome demands on your life coming seemingly from outside of yourself. As your heart opens to the divine Beloved, the sensibilities that lead to such spiritual practices can and sometimes will arise spontaneously, seemingly out of nowhere, and you can find yourself performing them freely, joyfully, reverentially and with sweet longing for the Beloved.

Remembering

Assimilating and applying what they have received through spiritual guidance and contemplation, bhaktas benefit from remembering what they have heard and studied. The act of "remembering," *smaraṇa*, is an important element of the yoga of devotion. In the context of bhakti yoga, the spiritual discipline of smaraṇa could also be translated as the "remembrance" of God. Such a practice allows seekers to embrace and hold onto what they have learned and experienced. It is to remember the Heart at all times and in all they do. Through the practice of spiritual remembrance, they maintain, solidify and continually refresh their spiritual love.

The discipline of smaraṇa also stands as the basis of the contemplative technique of spiritual "recollection." Here, you prayerfully direct your heart and mind to God; listen inwardly to God's affirming yet often silent words of guidance and support; and bring the understanding gained through such recollection outward into your life. To remember God is to continually return your heart to the divine Beloved.

Bhaktas who continually practice spiritual recollection will find that they come to hold great value in this act of remembering, for it gives them access to an ever-expansive reservoir of inspiration. Indeed, Nārada himself says in a sūtra we are not studying here, sūtra 82, that *smaraṇa āsakti* — the attitude of cherishing (*āsakti*) the performance of spiritual recollection itself — is one of the key expressions of the devotional life.

Worshipping

Once awakened, the heart longs to express its love, to share itself with God, to offer reverence to God. It does so, in part, through acts of worship and offerings of praise expressed with true, humble and warm reverence.

There are many ways in which one can offer reverential worship. As a general classification, such acts constitute what is known in Indian devotional tradition as *bhajana*, a term that rather literally refers to the act of "offering devotion" through external acts of ceremonial worship. The word *bhajana* is actually related to the word *bhakti*. Both signify the sharing of love and participating in it.

One form of bhajana is known in Indian texts as *arcana*. The term refers to the honoring of the divine Beloved by placing flowers and lighting candles in front of a sacred image that reminds the bhakta of God. This is a gentle and respectful act of homage during which one may also offer prayers or sing verses of praise.

The performance of arcana is similar to what is known perhaps more commonly in the Indian devotional context as *pūjā*. This latter term refers in classical Indian texts to acts of worship similar to those of welcome and hospitality a host performs to honor a guest — the "guest" here being God, who is understood to respond to the devotee's invitation and to visit during the time of worship. More commonly, the word *pūjā* also refers to similar acts of respect, appreciation and loving kindness offered to a sacred image. These can include not only waving candles in front of the image, but also placing flowers nearby, lighting incense, bowing one's head or body in front of the image in a gesture of humility and respect known in Sanskrit as *pranāma* and in modern Indian languages as *pranām*.

In a related practice from India, known as *vandana*, one expresses reverence for God by gently and respectfully touching the ground in front of an image of divinity, or by placing a gift of love near that image. In India, this has long been a gesture of homage, humility, gratitude and praise. (Children will sometimes touch the feet of their grandparents or parents, students will sometimes touch the feet of their teacher, and disciples will sometimes touch the feet of their spiritual master.) The practice of vandana can take place inwardly just as purely as outwardly. Here, the bhakta envisions the Beloved's presence within his or her own heart, for example, and then inwardly bows to that presence in gentle, selfless love. So, too, one can honor God's presence in others' hearts by inwardly bowing to the divine Heart within them. One way people do this is to put the palms of their hands together at the level of their hearts, with fingers pointed upward and slightly toward the person they honor in a position known as the *añjali mudrā*.

When divine love is awakened, acts of worship can spontaneously arise out of the lover's deep and reverential sense of God's grandeur and majesty as well as God's beauty and benevolence. Indeed, texts in the Indian devotional tradition speak not only of *prīti* (loving delight) expressed in worship but also of *sammāna* (reverential respect) and *bahumāna* (the holding of esteem) as characteristics of spiritual devotion.[54] This need not always be in a formal situation. Indeed, you yourself might enter into such states of worship when viewing a sunrise, or entering into a special forest glen, or standing in front of a majestic mountain. People feel a sense of worship at the birth of a child or at the death of a loved one. There are as many possibilities as there are hearts that are open to Love.

Serving

Those whose spiritual love has been enflamed often feel not only the desire to honor God through worship, but also a powerful and sometimes even undeniable longing to serve the one who has kindled that love.

Indeed, according to Nārada, one of the characteristics of genuine devotion is what in sūtra 82 he calls *dāsya āsakti*, that is to say, cherishing the attitude of service.[55] This reverential act of serving is known by several terms, the most encompassing being the present participle *sevana*. The word for service itself is *seva*.

In the history of bhakti as a religious tradition, the word *seva* was originally used many centuries ago to refer to the service that specially trained priests performed by singing devotional songs to God in temples. Then, over the years the word came also to refer to other people's act of serving the saints and spiritual masters who are immersed in love for God. In this way, we speak of *guru seva*, which is service to one's spiritual teacher. In more recent times, use of the word *seva* has expressed the understanding that service can be directed toward the world as a whole in a variety of ways.

Contemplative, religious and ethical traditions of all sorts from around the world have long valued service as an important and valuable component of the spiritual life. The awakening into Love impels the bhakta to respond by offering love in return. To serve God through seva is to express one's gratitude and to align oneself with a vision of the world embraced by divine love. In its purest form, this service is *niḥsvārtha seva*, "selfless service" (*niḥsvārtha* literally meaning "without a selfish purpose"), that is to say, service offered without any ulterior, self-centered motivations. Such an attitude of service is grounded in genuine and affirming love: for God, for others, for the world. Outwardly such service may at times be similar to what might otherwise normally be regarded as social service; the difference here is that serving God by serving others involves a spiritual understanding of the purpose of such activity. It is based in part on the understanding that God loves and lives within all people, so to serve people is to serve God.

Such selfless offering of love in service of divine Love can of course take manifold forms. It involves an active offering of one's love by offering one's capabilities, energy, time, resources and commitments to support a world loved by the Beloved. Inspired by the Love that transforms our hearts, moved by the swelling of compassion, committed to justice and to beauty, guided by hope and grounded in the recognition of the inherent value and goodness of life itself, we turn our love in the direction of a world in need of care. As we do so, we give ourselves to the divine Source of that very care. In serving Love, we serve God.

So, too, we serve God when we direct our own inner lives in the direction of the true, graceful Heart that pulsates within the movements of our own loving hearts. As we refine, strengthen and elevate our experience and expression of love, we thereby also serve the ultimate Source and ultimate Object of that love.

Honoring the Divine Presence in Others

To love God is to serve God, and one way to do this is to honor the divine Self's inner presence in other people. Continually expanding the scope of our vision, we can come to see that God dwells within all things and all beings in the universe as a whole. Our sense of reverence deepens as we enter more fully into what the *Śāṇḍilya Bhakti Sūtra* refers to as *sarvatad-bhāva*[56] — that is to say, to the attitude, mood, or perspective that allows one to see God in all things. As that text says, having seen God in others, bhaktas hold and cherish a steady love for all beings.

Swami Chidvilasananda has quoted the Russian author Fyodor Dostoyevski in encouraging people similarly to:

> Love all God's creation, both the whole and every grain of sand. Love every leaf, every ray of light. Love the animals, love the plants, love each separate thing. If you love each thing, you will perceive the mystery of God in all. And when once you perceive this, you will thenceforward grow every day to a fuller understanding of it, until you come at last to love the whole world, with a love that is all-embracing and universal.[57]

This recognition of God' presence in everything around us can bring us delight, joy and appreciation for life. It also can strengthen our resolve to do what we can to alleviate suffering in the world. In each direction we turn, we turn toward God. To each place we bow, we bow to God. In each person's face we see the face of God in the world.

For those who seek to deepen their spiritual love and refine their service, to honor others is also at times to join with one another to help each other while moving further along the path of love. Fellowship with others on the same spiritual path brings joy and a sense of friendship and community. Members of a spiritual community also lend strength to each other, encourage each other, and support each other as they experience, confront, and engage various outward and inward situations and processes associated with spiritual growth.

Such fellowship strengthens people's yogic lives, and this process thereby honors and serves the graceful work of Love in the world. Accordingly, one of the important elements of the devotional life in Indian spiritual tradition is that of *satsaṅga* — or, in modern terms, *satsaṅg* — a term that refers to an association (*saṅga*) of those who seek the truth (*sat*). In the context of devotion, the truth here is the authenticating, empowering, fulfilling, redeeming, liberating truth that is Love.

The practice of satsang — the coming together in spiritual community — is therefore another of the components of bhakti yoga. Bhaktas can share their experiences on the yogic path and help others understand their own experience. They may tell each other stories that teach yogic lessons. They may chant divine names together, study sacred texts together and meditate together. Satsang is a time in which many of the devotional practices as a whole can be performed in fellowship with others.

Honoring Yourself

Just as the divine Heart inwardly supports all beings, so too the divine Beloved dwells within you. Accordingly, just as you can honor the Soul in others, so too you can honor the Self in yourself.

To honor the Self in yourself is not vanity. It is to honor the true Self. This is the opposite of egotism, for egotism seeks to maintain a sense of self that is either superior or inferior to others. This separates you from the Heart's presence in others, and therefore leads to a sense of alienation from God. To worship the ego degrades one's relationship with God. On the other hand, to honor God's presence within you is to strengthen that bond of love.

Love for God therefore includes what in Sanskrit is known as *ātma-sammāna*: "honoring the Self." To honor and respect the true Self is to honor God's love for the soul. In this sense, bhaktas respect themselves. They are inwardly strong people. They are unmoved by other people's attempts to push them around or take unfair advantage of them. They are courageous. They are resolute. They stand firmly in Love. This is because courage, strength and firm resolution are the Self's own qualities, and bhaktas honor the Self within themselves as much as in others.

Those who honor the Self within them will strive to take good care of themselves physically, emotionally and spiritually. They will try to lead healthy lives at all levels. They will eat nourishing food, if it is available. They will get enough rest so that their bodies stay energetic and vibrant. They will be attentive to their feelings and emotions without being overpowered by them and will work diligently at transforming unhealthy states of mind to healthy ones.

It helps to get physical exercise, if possible, so that the body can stay strong, flexible, and more able to resist disease, and so that it can more readily and comfortably support the devotee during periods of meditation, study and prayer. The stretches and postures associated with the yogic practice of *āsana*, in particular, have long been appreciated by Indian sages not only for their ability to strengthen, purify, and tone the physical body but also for the harmonizing and centering effects they have on the mind and emotions. Perhaps most importantly, though, the practice of *āsana* is a form of devotion to the Beloved within, for it honors the body as the abode of the indwelling Self. Undertaken with love, the practice of *āsana* is a physical form of prayer and spiritual recollection.

Singing Divine Names

Elsewhere, in a sūtra we are not actually studying here, sūtra 37, our text says that devotional love is developed "by hearing and singing forth God's qualities." The word for "singing" in that sūtra is *kīrtana*, which also means "calling, repeating, declaring, commemorating, praising." In the practice of kīrtana one uses the voice in song as a way of expressing love in a respectful and reverential way. To sing a divine name with love helps bring Love into your heart, and from there it infuses the entirety of your being.

In practice, kīrtana usually takes the form of chanting God's names and attributes in a melodic manner. Sometimes this is done quietly and reverentially, sometimes it may become energetic. The performance of kīrtana is usually undertaken with a group of fellow seekers and lovers of God. The practice therefore is also often known as *saṅkīrtana*, the prefix *san-* meaning "with" or "together." Since the Sanskrit word for "name" is *nāman*, the practice of singing God's names together with others is known more particularly as *nāma-saṅkīrtana*.

In Indian devotional settings, this way of singing to God is done in a call-and-response manner. Here, a leader or small group of leaders will sing a phrase, and a larger group will repeat that same phrase in response. Usually, the leader will repeat the same phrase, and the group will repeat it again. Then, a second phrase will be sung and repeated, and so on. There are only a few phrases in a typical saṅkīrtana, the rhythmic and melodic repetition of which brings the singers to ever-increasing levels of delight and immersion into the various devotional sentiments.

In your own daily life you can enter into this practice in other ways, too. There are many recordings of contemporary singers and musicians singing kīrtanas, often known in modern Indian languages as kīrtans. You can listen to these recorded kīrtans as you are doing āsana practice, or taking a walk, or riding on a subway train. They can lighten your heart as you do so.

I recently was talking with a man after we had joined many others in singing a nāma-saṅkīrtana. He said that he has long enjoyed singing with others in this way. That morning though, he understood something he had never really understood before. He realized that in singing God's name over and over again he was quite literally calling out to God. He said that when he realized this his whole experience of the song changed. It was no longer just a melody he sang with others; for him, the singing of the nāma-saṅkīrtana was truly a prayer. His whole being — his heart, his mind, his body, his soul — was infused with longing.

In its form of call-and-response the song is an exchange, a sharing of sentiments, in which singers of each phrase express their own yearning to be with God. In a way, this exchange is similar to the relationship shared between God and lovers of God. Seekers reach out to God, and God reaches out to them. Each loves and yearns to be with the other. Then, within the entirety of the saṅkīrtana as a whole, in which both call and response are saying the same thing, the duality that is call and response in a sense disappears into the unity of the song itself.

This is similar to the relationship between lover and Beloved. Just as the participants in a call-and-response chant sing back-and-forth to each other, so too they call longingly to God; and, in the mystery and depths of the Heart, God lovingly calls to them. In nāma-saṅkīrtana God and worshipper remain functionally separate so that they can experience and express their love for each other. Nevertheless, at the level of the Self, lover and divine Beloved are at one with each other.

Immersing in Sublimity through the Yoga of Music

Devotional sentiments find expression not only through song; they can be drawn forth and enriched through the transforming power of music in general. In this regard, it is worth remembering that Bhagavān as Kṛṣṇa is often depicted as playing a flute, the alluring sound of which beckons the soul to come join him in his delightful play.

Sometimes people say that when they listen to beautiful music they hear the sound of God. As we know, it is not unusual to see tears rise in the eyes of people listening closely to music. At times people sit very still in their attentiveness, almost like meditating yogis. Sometimes they gently close their eyes as the music surrounds them and enters them. They may smile gently. Their hands may move gracefully, aligned with the movement and flow of the sound. Shimmers may run up and down their spines. They may nod their heads and allow their bodies to sway rhythmically. Sometimes, of course, they dance in ecstasy.

Music is rather paradoxical in a way, for although music is in a sense quite etherial, the effect of its tones, rhythms, melodies and textures on us is nevertheless quite real. Music quickens the senses and awakens the slumbering awareness. When we allow ourselves to be touched by music we can experience emotions, sentiments, moods that come from deep within us. At the same time, it stills the restive fluctuations of the mind known in yoga as *vṛttis* and softens the hard edges of the *vāsanas* and *saṁskāras*, which are the effects of unconscious memories and other mental impressions that condition our experience of the world.

The spiritual use and effect of music has been known in India as *saṅgīta yoga*, which tradition regards as one of the disciplined spiritual paths to immersion into divine sublimity. Indian texts on the nature of music speak of Nāda Brahman, the term *brahman* meaning "the ultimate power and foundation of existence," and *nāda* meaning "sound." The idea here is that the foundational source of all existence is a single, cosmic vibration or pulse. Nāda Brahman is not a physical sound as much as it is the plethoric and energetic silence out of which all physical sounds emerge. This resonant silent energy in a sense crystallizes as it variously reverberates in different physical tones, rhythms and melodies.

According to the philosophy and practice of saṅgīta yoga, the more purely we produce and attentively hear sounds ourselves, the more closely we return to and are immersed in this sublime, divine sound. Indeed, Indian musical theory and performance includes the understanding that this universal Pulsation within all things is the presence of Divinity itself. The philosopher of music and theologian, Śārṅgadeva, to whom is attributed the *Saṅgīta Ratnākāra*, a thirteenth century text, notes that,

> We worship Nāda Brahman:
> that incomparable bliss, Consciousness,
> without a second, immanent in all creatures,
> the Self through whom the world of phenomena is manifest.
> Indeed, through the worship of Nāda
> are worshipped the gods such as Brahmā, Viṣṇu and Śiva,
> for in essence they are one with it.[58]

Sometimes the music that brings forth bliss can be seemingly very simple, and yet it can still be quite effective in this regard. It seems that every time I hear the soft tones of a tambura I enter into a state that is inwardly and quietly contemplative and, at the same time, expansively joyful. As you may know, this is an unfretted lute made of a large hollow gourd and two layers of strings stretched along a long neck. The musician plays the tambura by softly and repeatedly strumming the outer strings. The resonance of the outer layer of strings then sets in motion sympathetic vibrations of the inner layer of strings, leading to the establishment of a variety of subtle, pulsating overtones and undertones.

Listening to the sound of a tambura, I often feel a deep yet dynamic peacefulness as my mind settles and my heart softens. In a sense, it is difficult to locate the source of the tones, which seems to surround me outwardly like gentle, clear light but also to rise into my awareness from the depths of my being. The multileveled, harmonious sound of the tambura calms the surface waves of any temporary and mixed emotions I may be feeling and draws me deeper into a calm yet energetic, pure state that seems to have lain underneath my awareness all along. In a sense, to listen to the tambura is like listening to the sound of the Self, waiting for me deep in my own heart.

Repeating a Mantra

The Indian mystical tradition holds that the purest and most powerful of all manifest sounds is *mantra*. A mantra is understood to be Divinity in sound form. To repeat a mantra, especially one given by an awakened master, is to participate in the divine Power by means of that sound. Among other spiritual effects, chanting a sacred mantra in reverential tones helps one open the heart and awaken awareness of the Love that pulsates with the soul. Repeating a mantra protects the feelings of devotion that arise from this awakening. It helps focus one's awareness on Divinity and thus intensifies one's experience of Love. It elevates one's yearning and refines one's emotions.

Repeating a mantra is therefore an effective component of the sādhanā of devotion. The mantra can be sung out loud, or it can be repeated quietly to oneself, often in alignment with the rhythms of the breath. This inward repetition of the mantra is known as *japa*. As you perform japa, it may help to move your fingers across a string of beads known as a *japa mālā* while you repeat the phrase or word. Soon you may find the divine name quietly repeating itself in the background of your awareness and thereby infusing and texturing all of your thoughts. Your remembrance of God becomes steadier and more constant. If performed with quiet discipline, the recollective power of japa allows you to remain always in the awareness of God's immediate presence. Sometimes the practice of japa can become so deeply pervasive of the bhakta's consciousness that the actual sound of the mantra fades into the stillness that is the foundation of all things. Entering into this silence, one performs what is known as *japājapa* (*japa-ajapa*): the constant, wordless repetition of the Word in each and every moment. The deepest prayer, then, takes place in the reverential listening to the Silence that is the source and fulfillment of all things.

Listening to Silence

The truest and finest essence of this sublimity is the quiet stillness of the Self that dwells within the heart. The Self holds and stands behind all sounds, all words, all thoughts. The Self speaks to us most fully in the heart's deepest silence.

Although we may not always be aware of it, every sound has its origin in silence. The pulse of Nāda Brahman itself moves across the enfolding fabric of this divine stillness. You might think for a moment of a painting. There can be many colors, many shapes, many textures, many patterns of visual movement in the painting. Yet, all of those things rest on an empty canvas, without which there can be no painting whatsoever. That formless emptiness holds the possibility to become any form imaginable. The same is true for sound. Anything that we hear is grounded in silence, which gives rise to and stands within all sounds.

Anything at all that comes into existence does so out of the Great Emptiness, *mahaśūnya*, which is absolute Silence. Just as the Great Emptiness has become all things and thus dwells within all things, so, too, silence lies within all sound. Therefore, the more we become attentive to silence, the more we thereby immerse ourselves in the infinite and formless Mahaśūnya, the formless home of the Beloved beyond all form.

As a yogī or yoginī, be attentive to the way in which all sounds not only arise from but also dissolve into infinite spaciousness. Dwell in that spaciousness. Listen constantly to the Silence that supports all things. There, you will hear the sound of the Self's own voice.

Meditating

The reality and nature of the Self thus can be revealed to us in the rich and dynamic silence of our inner selves. It is significant therefore that chanting sessions of all kinds end with a period of meditation. Indeed, all the many spiritual practices in the yoga of devotion could properly begin and end in meditation.

Though we may not always be conscious of it, the sustaining power and beauty of God's love flows within us all the time. To know and honor this Love and to offer our own love to God in return it is most helpful, therefore, to turn our awareness to that inner presence. Meditation is a good way to do this. In meditation we discover and open ourselves to the Love that dwells within us and that seeks to express itself through us.

Thoughts and feelings may arise in us as we meditate. Rather than getting caught up in them, however, we can shift our awareness away from the content of those changing thoughts and feelings and more toward the infinite depths of Consciousness from which they emerge. Meditation is the undistracted, calm, one-pointed attention on and immersion into the underlying, energetic, infinite, creative Source of all our thoughts.

Meditation is the graceful mindfulness of the mind itself. In meditation we shift our awareness away from the content of our thoughts and toward the capacious light of our awareness itself. We thereby open that awareness to the presence within us of the universal Consciousness that is the Self. It dwells within all things at a level that is deeper than thought, and it is of the nature of Love.

The practice of meditation opens a space within us into which foundational Love can swell of its own spontaneous, expansive nature. The more we cultivate a meditative awareness, the more we see the world through the revelatory light of Love; and the more we do this, the more we see the divine Self everywhere we look. Then, there is no beginning and no end of meditation, for each moment is illumined with the light of this awareness.

Meditation thus brings us more fully into the depths of our being and thus into our true hearts. This is where God constantly dwells. We may not experience God all the time. Yet, the more we return to our hearts, the more we enter into the Light that illumines our very existence. Meditation is therefore an important and effective component of devotional yoga. Swami Chidvilasananda has made this point in a statement that is as clear as it is succinct. "The goal of meditation," she has said, "is nothing but living constantly in the supreme love for God."[59]

Having entered into the fullness of silence in meditation, we long to return to it repeatedly and to do so in a sustained and steady manner. Directing all of our awareness and feeling toward the Source alone, we feel the subtle yet also increasingly powerful current of true devotional love. The 11th-12th century theologian, Rāmānuja, regarded meditation as an act of recollection, and said that this recollection itself "is called bhakti."[60] For Rāmānuja, then, meditation is an act of devotion.

So, too, we can meditate as a way to enter into Love. Through meditation we commune inwardly with the benevolent power that creates, sustains and fulfills all things in the entire universe. Meditation is thus a form of prayer. Becoming absorbed in meditation, we become absorbed in that ground of our being that is of the nature of unconditional Love. Drawing on that awareness, we then experience this Love as the ground of *all* being. The barriers that separate us from this Love dissolve. At the highest or deepest level of meditation, there is only Love. Bathed in it, our minds and hearts are infused with devotion.

Offering the Totality of Your Being to God

Our desire to perform spiritual practices arises, often spontaneously, as a result of the heart's grace-filled opening into Love. Sometimes we can feel completely infused or even almost overtaken with the sense of gratitude, appreciation and devotion.

Devotional disciplines strengthen, clarify, expand and deepen our spiritual love once it has been awakened. Our yearning to know, honor and serve God becomes all-encompassing and extends, finally, to the entirety of our lives. Awakened to it, we wish to offer all that we do in service of Love.

This attitude and commitment allows us to see the Self revealed in all things and to offer oneself to it in return. Elsewhere in our text, in sūtra 82, Nārada speaks of *ātmanivedana āsakti*. This refers to the devotional bond (*āsakti*) to Divinity through seeing the Self revealed in all things. With this perspective, one recognizes the Self as being introduced to us (*nivedana*) in each moment and in every situation. Introduced anew to the Self in all things, the lover of God responds with love in every context. Since the word *nivedana* can also be translated as "offering oneself," the bond to Divinity takes place through giving oneself to God in each moment. When one undertakes all things with love and sees God within all things, then one's life becomes aligned with God as love.

The *Śāṇḍilya Bhakti Sūtra*, which you will recall is an eleventh century text that is similar in ways to the *Nārada Bhakti Sūtra*, speaks of a devotional state it calls *tadarthaprāṇasthāna*.[61] This is a practice and attitude in which one offers praise, reverence and gratitude with every breath one takes, that is to say, in which one dedicates all of one's life to the expression of devotional love.

In the highest state of spiritual love, everything one does is done as an offering to God. As Kṛṣṇa says to Arjuna in the *Bhagavad Gītā*:

> Whatever you do, whatever you eat
> whatever you offer, whatever you give away,
> whatever spiritual practices you perform:
> do that as an offering to me.[62]

The teaching here is as simple as it is all-encompassing: all that you do, do so in service of God's love. When you wake in the morning, offer yourself to Love. When you close your eyes at night, offer yourself to Love. When you prepare a meal, do so as an offering to Love. If you build houses, make clothing, prune trees or defend the innocent, do so as an offering to Love. If you care for the sick, injured and dying; if you write books, make music or create art; if you protect others from harm; if you teach others: whatever you do at whatever moment in life, do that in service of God's own purpose, and God's purpose is to express Love.

Terms appearing in Chapter 5

añjali mudrā	A gesture of reverence in which the palms are placed together with the fingers pointing upward. In increasing degrees of respect, the hands are held in front of the heart, at the forehead, or above the head.
āsakti	Loving attachment, the act of cherishing, mode of devotedness.
āsana	Literally, "sitting." In the yogic context, the word often refers to a body posture or position associated with the practice of *haṭha yoga*.
ātmanivedana āsakti	Devotional dedication (*nivedana*) of all of one's life, all of one's self (*ātma-*) to God; the affectionate bond (*āsakti*) with Divinity that comes from cherishing the universal Self.
ātma-sammāna	Respecting the divine Self, honoring the true Self.
bahumāna	Holding great respect (for Divinity).
bhajana	Devotional act or set of acts of worship; worshipping. In modern Indian languages, a *bhajan* is more specifically a genre of devotional song.
bhakti śāstra	A text or set of teachings (*śāstra*) on devotional love.
Brahman	Literally, "possessed of the nature of expansiveness, powerful, sublime"; the single divine Presence within all things; the universal Ground of being.
dāsya āsakti	The affectionate bond (*āsakti*) with Divinity that comes from cherishing Divinity like a servant to a just master.
guru seva	Service (*seva*) to the teacher. When capitalized as *Guruseva* the phrase can refer to service to the divine Teacher.
japa	Practice of quietly repeating a mantra or other sacred phrase. See also *japājapa*, below.

japājapa	The practice of internalizing the repetition of a sacred phrase or divine Name. The word consists of *japa* (whisper, repetition, see above) + *ajapa* ("not *japa*, that is to say, "silent japa").
japa mālā	A string of beads (*mālā*) or other usually spherical items used as a rosary of sorts as one repeats a mantra, the divine Names, and so on.
mahāśunya	Literally, "the great emptiness." The formless Absolute, the Void, the foundational Nothingness that holds the possibility of all things.
mālā	Garland, wreath, string of prayer beads. (Not to be confused with *mala*; the latter, in some contexts, signifying a thickened, congealed clod of impurity that covers the inner splendor of the true Self.
manana	Spiritual practice of contemplative reflection on the meaning of sacred texts and teachings; also, the disciplined reflection on the inner meaning of one's experiences.
mantra	Sacred phrase, word or syllable, the repetition of which, in the devotional context, aligns one's heart with the pulsations of the divine Word.
nāda	Literally, "sound, tone." See also *Nāda Brahman*, below.
Nāda Brahman	In the mystical context, the Ultimate foundation and power (see *Brahman*, above) as the universal, divine Sound within all manifest sounds.
nāman	Literally, "name." In the devotional context, a divine Name, a name of God.
nāma-saṅkīrtana	Praising Divinity through the repetition of divine Names.
nididhyāsana	Literally, the "repeated meditation" on what one has heard and contemplated (see also *śravana* and *manana*); the disciplined practice of contemplative meditation.

niḥsvārtha seva Selfless service to one's Beloved (*niḥsvārtha*, "without selfish purpose" + *seva*, "service").

niṣkriya Literally, "without action, inactive," refers more figuratively to one who does not perform one's responsibilities; one who does not put into action what one has learned.

nivedana Literally, "making known, pronouncing;" in the devotional context, this refers to the "dedicating" of one's actions, thoughts, intentions, and so on to the Divine.

pranāma Literally, "bowing;" in the devotional context, expressing respect, gratitude and love to that which reveres. In modern Indian languages the Sanskrit *pranāma* has become *pranām*.

prīti Kind affection, affectionate grace.

pūjā Originally the singing of devotional songs in temples, the word has come over the centuries to refer to acts of reverence and worship of Divinity in general. Pūjā usually includes the presentation of flower petals, fruit, and other related items in front of an image of Divinity, often accompanied by the waving of lamps or candles and the singing of sacred songs. See also *vandana*, below.

sakriya With action, active; one who performs one's responsibilities; thus, one who puts into effect what one has learned.

sammāna Honoring, respecting, paying homage.

saṅgīta yoga The performance and application of song (*saṅgīta*) and thus other forms of music as a spiritual practice.

saṅkīrtana Literally, "singing together;" the devotion practice of people singing as a group, usually in a call-and-response manner.

sarvatadbhāva The attitude or state (*bhāva*) in which one sees Divinity in all things.

śāstra kṛpā	Grace of the sacred teachings; the illuminating and transforming power of a sacred text or texts.
satsaṅga	Literally, an association (*saṅga*) of those who seek the truth (*sat*); the coming together as fellow seekers in mutual support, encouragement and joy in a spirit of contemplation and celebration.
seva/sevana	Selfless service as a spiritual and devotional practice.
smaraṇa āsakti	An affectionate bond (*āsakti*) that arises from one's cherishing the remembrance (*smaraṇa*) of Divinity.
vṛtti	Literally, "rolling, turning;" in yogic contexts, the turning movement of the mind, often translated as "fluctuations" of the mind.
tadarthaprasthāna	Practice and attitude in which one offers praise, reverence and gratitude with every breath one takes.

PART III

Inner Transformations brought through Bhakti as a Spiritual Practice

Chapter 6

Ecstasy, Enstasy and Delight

A yogic life oriented toward bhakti involves living in ways that express and bring forth one's love for the divine Beloved. Many of the practices mentioned in Part II include outward activity of some sort. In the five chapters in Part III we will turn our attention to a number of inner experiences and transformations that can take place through the disciplines associated with spiritual love, enlivened and supported, as always, by grace. The topics of discussion in the chapters of Part III therefore generally move from relatively outward experiences of spiritual love to more inward states of being.

Like other spiritual disciplines, bhakti yoga tends to place more emphasis on the quality of one's inner state than on the circumstances or appearances of one's outer life. It is within the heart where one most fully meets God, and it is from the heart that one draws divine Love outward in recognition of God's presence within all things. The more open to that sacred presence one is, the more expansive, intense and liberating that meeting in the heart becomes, and the more lovingly responsive one becomes to others.

People will experience the effect of spiritual love in different ways. For some people it may be quiet and seemingly unobtrusive. For some, it may at times swell forth suddenly, even unexpectedly, in ways that may be noticeably different from what might be their otherwise everyday states of being. We begin Part III with some reflections on a sūtra that turns our attention to what might in some ways be rather extraordinary manifestations of spiritual love while at the same time locates the source and object of that love. Our text says:

यज्ज्ञात्वा मत्तो भवति स्तब्धो भवत्यात्मारमो भवति ॥६॥

yaj-jñātvā matto bhavati stabdho bhavati ātmārāmo bhavati

Having known which, one becomes ecstatic; one becomes stunned; one comes to delight in the Self.

— Sūtra 6

Reading these words, I am reminded of a passage from the *Bhāgavata Purāṇa* where Kṛṣṇa is speaking with his devotee Uddhava about the effect the experience of divine Love can have on people:

Where is bhakti without the melting of the heart
marked by the rise of goose bumps and
the flow of tears of joy from the eyes?
Yet, without the intensity of this love
how can one's being become purified?
The one whose words stumble because of this joy,
whose heart melts from the tenderness of love,
who weeps when feeling separated from me,
who every now and then spontaneously laughs in wonder,
at the thought of my mysterious marvels,
who sings and dances in joy, without inhibition:
the one who is joined to me through love
purifies the whole world.[63]

I suspect that you recognize at least some of these descriptions in your own experience. Sometimes, when your "heart melts with the tenderness of love," warm tears may form in your eyes or a soft shimmer of goose bumps may play along your skin. You may find that your words do indeed stumble as you try to express this ineffable joy. You may smile or even laugh out loud when you think of the marvelous mystery that is your Beloved, or your may find yourself singing and dancing freely in the expansiveness of this Love. The power of your own love elevates those around you; indeed, "the whole world" benefits from the joyful yogī or yoginī who is immersed in Love.

The joyful presence that is the Beloved is always with you, for it is within you as the divine Self. Its joy dwells within you even when you feel weary. In the *Bhāgavata Purāṇa*, the character of Nārada himself says that once, tired and thirsty from his travels across the world, he paused near a stream in a forest. He sat under a tree and meditated on the presence of the Self within, as taught by his teachers. Slowly, an image of Kṛṣṇa appeared in his heart. His mind was rendered quiet by this vision. His eyes filled with tears and a rush of goosebumps moved across his skin. He was free of sorrow and filled with joy, for he saw that there was no difference between Kṛṣṇa and his own deepest Heart.[64]

When one becomes immersed in Love one may feel oneself drawn to it again and again, a sentiment we see expressed in these words of a song from the seventeenth century by Bihāri:

> Ever since I saw Kṛṣṇa
> my eyes are drenched
> in the waters of his love;
> they keep filling with tears
> shedding them
> swimming and drowning in them,
> like the pots of a water wheel
> moving in and out of the well.[65]

These type of experiences — the rise of goosebumps, the eyes filling with tears — is known in Indian thought to be a *sāttvikabhāva*. This is a spontaneous manifestation or indicator of a pure inner state that has been elicited or drawn forth by an experience of powerful beauty and love. Nārada's sūtras make similar reference to such experiences in sūtra 68: "Their voices choking when talking with each other, with physical exhilaration, and with tears flowing from their eyes, they purify their *kulas* and the earth." The word *kula* here can mean "family" or "community;" at the mystical level, it can also refer to the "heart" in which the family or community is held.

I will say more about the *sāttvikabhāvas* toward the end of this chapter. In our current sūtra from the *Bhakti Sūtra* our text mentions two experiences that are similar to them. Nārada speaks in a single phrase of the seemingly paradoxical experience of ecstatic exhilaration and of a deep inner quieting of the mind and senses.

Before turning to these types of experience and what it might mean to include them together in one phrase, however, I would like to turn first to the sūtra's last phrase. I do this because I feel this discussion might help put the other two phrases in a perspective that might not be as apparent if we started with them.

"One comes to delight in the Self"

The association between devotional love and delight in the Self is an important one. The relevant phrase here is *ātmārāma*. The word for "Self" here is *ātman* (the "n" is dropped for grammatical reasons). The term for "delight" is *ārāma*. You will recall that, according to a number of schools of philosophical thought in India, the Self as Ātman is the universal ground of all existence, the highest or deepest level of Being in which all things have their own particular being. The devotional tradition with which the *Bhakti Sūtra* is most generally aligned, the Bhāgavata tradition, regards the divine Self as Bhagavān: the Lord, the Beloved, God.

Understood in this way, to say that one who experiences Love thereby delights in the Self is therefore also to say that one delights in God's presence in the world and within one's being. To "delight in the Self" is to share love in the totality that is God, both inwardly and outwardly. This sharing with God is the basis of bhakti itself.

When one enters into Love one enters into the bliss that is God's own nature. To help make this point, I would like to refer briefly to some ways of thinking presented by a number of theologians who lived in Bengal in the sixteenth and seventeenth centuries and who regarded God as Kṛṣṇa. They held that Kṛṣṇa possesses within himself an infinite number of divine powers, or *śaktis*. One of the most important of these they identified as *svarūpa śakti*, a term we may literally translate as "God's power to be God's own form" or "God's power to be God's own nature." Said differently, it is God's power to exist, to be real: to be God. It is this divine power to *be* that allows all other forms of existence to exist. From this perspective, the fact that the world exists, that there is being rather than nonbeing, demonstrates the Beingness of God. Accordingly, existence itself reveals the Beingness of God.

Taking this idea further, these theologians saw that Kṛṣṇa's svarūpa śakti has three components or aspects known as *sandhinī śakti*, *saṁvit śakti* and *hlādinī śakti*. These three powers are associated with God's nature as *sat-cit-ānanda*, this is to say, as being-consciousness-bliss, respectively.

According to these thinkers, it is through the power specifically of sandhinī śakti, the power to exist, that God supports his own existence and thus affirms the existence of all things in the universe, including our own. Similarly, God's power of awareness, saṁvit śakti, is the source and ground of any level of our own awareness: of ourselves, of the world, of God. And through hlādinī śakti, the divine power of joy, God takes delight in existence and, in so doing, is the source of our own experiences of joy at any level.[66]

We might think for a moment from this perspective about these three aspects of the Supreme's power to be its own form. Through the mysterious force of his power of existence, God has become all things and therefore dwells within each of us. If this is so, then we ourselves as embodied beings possess these śaktis within us, too, although of course in an infinitely reduced manner.

Similarly, from this perspective, the fact that we can know anything at all would demonstrate the presence of God's power of awareness within us. This is true even of our knowledge of God. We can seek to know God because we ourselves are to some degree an expression of God's power to know God's own self.

Finally, we would be able to experience what Nārada has called ātmārāma, "delight in the Self," first, because joy is one of the key qualities of the true Self within us and, second, because of the Self's inherent power of delight through which it delights in its own nature as unconditional joy.

Understood in this way, when we feel joy we are giving expression to God's own delight-filled power of self-recognition. God is pure Love, and through his power of joy, he comes to delight in his own nature as Love.

How does God do this? Devotional tradition in India holds that he enjoys his own nature as Love by taking form as our own experience of delight in him! In this way, then, lover and Beloved are one, united through the Self-revealing power of Love itself.

"One becomes ecstatic"

Our sūtra suggests here that the experience of this Self-revelatory Love can be one of overflowing joy. The relevant term here is *matta*, a word that suggests an exhilarating, bubbling forth of happiness and is sometimes used to describe heavenly delight. We can think of matta in this context as spiritual intoxication, as long as we are careful to remember that this is a spiritual rather than literal drunkenness. I have translated it in this sūtra as *ecstatic*, a word based on *ex-stasis*, which rather literally describes an experience beyond the ordinary, even beyond the confines of the physical body. Here, there is exuberant gladness that seems to flow outward from one's core, freeing the soul to roam through wondrous and beautiful realms.

When one becomes aware of the divine Beloved's inward presence, one *can* indeed become filled with ecstatic happiness. As just one example,

I remember one time I was meditating at a spiritual retreat center in the mountains. I became immersed in the clear and quiet inner stillness that I sensed lay beneath all the movements of my mind. Then I experienced this silence to be enlivened by a pulsation of sorts, a movement of subtle energy deep within it. I realized that this subtle energy was the same energy that supported and fueled my existence itself: my thoughts, my emotions, my body. I felt that this energetic presence knew me completely and fully, for in a sense it was me. And yet, although it pulsated deep in the stillness of my being, it was also much greater than what I normally might experience or define as myself, and I felt it to be unfathomably compassionate. Dynamic and exuberant, it was also patient and wanted only the best for me. I experienced it as pure love. Waves of this love then flowed through my body like honey. I continued to meditate for some time, moving deeper into the illuminating warmth of this love's inner presence in the form of my own awareness.

Then it was time to come out of meditation. As I slowly stood up, left the meditation hall, and stepped outdoors, everything around me seemed to be glowing with a warm and softly brilliant inner light. The otherwise rather dull brown leaves on the ground seemed to sparkle, the stones in the pavement shined in their own unique colors. The sound of the wind dancing with the long grass was a quiet but beautiful symphony. In gentle, fluid movements that seemed to reflect silent music playing within my heart, I began to sway back and forth as I walked along a path, and then to turn around slowly. Soon I was twirling in circles, my arms and hands and fingers reaching out toward the expansive horizon.

There I was, spinning around and around, with a slight smile crossing my face and my eyes softly closed in joy. It was as if I myself were not dancing, but rather as if God were dancing through me. In a moment of self-consciousness, I wondered if perhaps I looked a bit silly and hoped that nobody saw me. (Actually somebody did see me, and he gave me a big smile.) And then I heard an inner voice say, "Go ahead! Dance your heart out. God dances, too!" I felt free, for the Beloved's joyful inner presence helped me realize that sometimes our dancing expresses God's own love of life and that God wants us to share in that love.

By recounting this story, I am not encouraging people to get up and dance in the middle of a meditation hall, disturbing others around them as they do so. My point is that the experience of God's love for the human spirit frees us to experience the inner joy that is our birthright and opens us to the beauty of God's world.

The image of joyful dancing becomes a metaphor for the celebration of love for God's presence in all things, including our own hearts. I am reminded of these words by Utpaladeva, a tenth century Śaiva theologian from Kashmir, who sings to God as Śiva, whom Utpaladeva sees to be the source of all that is beautiful in the world:

That which bestows on all objects of beauty
That property of giving wonder at the mere touch —
By that very principle do those endowed with
Unwavering devotion
Worship your form.
Being self-luminous
You cause everything to shine;
Delighting in your form
You fill the whole universe with delight;
Rocking with your own bliss
You make the whole world dance with joy.[67]

Utpaladeva's words express the joyful experience of inwardly knowing and honoring this divine Presence that pervades all things:

With my eyes closed,
Relishing the wonder of inner devotion,
May I worship even the blades of grass thus:
"Homage to Śiva, my own consciousness!" . . .
May I attain that state
Where one laughs, one dances,
One does away with passion and hatred

And other such things,
And where one drinks
Of the sweet nectar of devotion.[68]

We see similar sentiments expressed in a song sung by Kabīr, a poet-saint from India who lived in the fifteenth and sixteenth centuries:

Dance, my heart! dance today with joy.
The strains of love fill the days and the nights with music,
and the world is listening to its melodies.
Mad with joy, life and death dance to the rhythm of this music.
The hills and sea and earth dance.
The world of man dances in laughter and tears....
Behold! My heart dances in the delight of a hundred arts;
and the Creator is well pleased.[69]

"One becomes stunned"

Our sūtra implies that sometimes the experience of Love swelling in the heart may be less an ecstatic experience and more a profoundly quieting one. Not only can Love draw one's spirit outward, it can also pull one deeper into the stillness of one's soul.

The phrasing here suggests that a person who has experienced Love can be in a sense overtaken by that experience. Nārada uses the word *stabdha*, "stunned" or "immovable" or even "benumbed," to describe a person who experiences it. In this case, this is not a negative state to be in. In fact it is just the opposite. It may happen quite naturally when one senses the beauty, mystery and benevolent power of the divine presence. In a way, this is the opposite of ecstasy; it is enstasy, a state in which one turns to find that presence within.[70]

I recall one time I was singing sacred chants with others in the early morning in an ashram in India. We had begun to sing together the beautiful *Śrī Kṛṣṇa Govinda Hare Murare*. The chant tells of God's nature as both a universal Lord of all people and as a gentle friend, who remains with us at all times, like a cowherd watches over his cattle. God is praised here as the Divine One who captures the heart and fills it with his loveliness as he plays the alluring sounds of his flute.

The morning air was heavy with the thick, nourishing rains of the Indian monsoon as the harmonium player who accompanied us played the first few measures of the melody. As we began to sing, she shifted one of the notes from a major into a minor key. It was a very simple change, but when I heard that note I felt an undeniable sense of poignancy rise within me. It was as if all of the human condition had found its voice in that one note. In it I heard the dignity of the human soul, the innate integrity of the human spirit, the fragile beauty of the human heart; and I heard in it the loving voice of the divine Heart's unfathomable compassion. (It is amazing what one note of music can do!)

My mind went completely still. I couldn't sing anymore. The people around me continued to offer their voices to the chant with quiet reverence, but I sat motionless. Chills ran up and down my spine for a moment. My head turned gently to one side, and then rolled gracefully to the other, then I returned to a perfect inner and outer stillness.

You might say I was stunned. I closed my eyes to hold the experience within me, for I was infused by a sense of the deep mystery of the moment. I heard the others as they continued to sing, but I sat in silence. It seemed to me that all the world's joy and all the world's sorrow was held in that timeless instant.

When I opened my eyes, I was alone. The music had stopped, the chant had ended, and everybody had left. I am not sure just how long I had been there, rendered motionless by the experience. Then, I stood up to the rhythm of the rain falling on the courtyard nearby and moved into the rest of my day.

A 15th-16th century poet-saint from India, Mīrābāī, felt such powerful love for her lord, Kṛṣṇa, that she would enter into complete stillness upon hearing the sound of Kṛṣṇa's flute. She composed songs telling of such experiences. In the following lines from one of them, we hear of her being moved to quiet by her experience of the divine presence. Mīrābāī speaks of the banks of the Yamunā, a river that flows near the town of Vṛndāvana, where Kṛṣṇa dwells, and of the deep sense of stillness she feels when hearing the flute:

> On the banks of the Yamuna
> The flute was heard.
> The Flute-Player has captured my heart,
> My soul has not strength to withstand.
> Dark Himself,
> Kṛṣṇa is seated on a dark blanket
> By the waters of the Yamuna.
> On hearing the sounds of the flute
> I lose body-consciousness,
> My body remaining like a stone.[71]

Mīrā's words here suggest that she was so moved by the sound of Kṛṣṇa's flute that she entered into the yogic state of *pratyāhāra* in which the outward pull of the senses was reversed and she became immersed in her Beloved's presence at a subtle rather than physical level. For his part, Kṛṣṇa, too, was like a yogī, sitting on a dark blanket near the river. Inwardly sharing their love, both Mīrābāī and Kṛṣṇa enter into inner communion in the full, powerful stillness of Love itself.

"Having known which"

The word *jñātvā*, "having known," presents a linguistic resonance of sorts with the classical Indian notion of *jñāna*, "knowledge." In classical Indian thought, knowledge is not simply intellectual familiarity with a topic. Genuine knowledge is the full and direct experience of that which is known. Indian sages have used an effective simile to make this point: we can hear *about* mangos over and over again until we become quite expert in recounting what others have said about their shape, size, color, and so on. Yet, we cannot really know what a mango *is* in its essence until we ourselves have tasted one. The same is true for Love. Here, knowledge of Love comes from direct experience of Love.

When one in some way experiences God's love, then there can be spontaneous expressions of that experience. One's feelings and responses to love as it emerges from the depths of the soul can be similar to those we experience when touched by beauty.

To help make my point, I would now like to return our attention for a moment to the Indian notion of sāttvikabhāva mentioned earlier in this chapter. This is a pure (*sāttvika*) expression of an inner state (*bhāva*), so described because it arises from a pure heart without being fabricated or manipulated.

Indian aesthetic philosophy and psychology have identified a number of such sāttvikabhāvas, each of which is manifest in a physical manner. A typical list includes some of the manifestations of internal states we have already mentioned: the stumbling over words when trying to express oneself verbally, having warm tears form and flow from the eyes, the feeling of goose bumps playing across the skin and a sense of deep inner stillness. Other sāttvikabhāvas include an unexpected rise in perspiration, a trembling in the body, a shift in skin tone, and a sense of the benevolent dissolution of one's being, as if the boundaries of the individual self and larger universe fade as one enters into the expansiveness of the Self.[72]

Philosophers in India have noted not only these different states of emotion but also have taught that they may be experienced at various degrees of intensity. These levels of intensity are sometimes described in terms of heat and fire. A person's experience may be said to be "smoking" (*dhūmāyita*) when an emotion or set of emotions is gently felt but can be suppressed. It is "kindled" (*jvalita*) when at least two or three of the sāttvikabhāvas reveal themselves and are difficult to hold back. When four or five of these inner states are distinctly felt and are too strong to contain, then one's experience may be said to be "inflamed" (*dīpita*). One experiences the "blazing" degree of intensity (*uddīpita*) when six, seven, or even all eight of the sāttvikabhāvas are clearly manifest and impossible to ignore. Each of these is a spontaneous response that can be similar to the emotions we may feel when we open ourselves to the presence of Love, and our hearts begin to burn with devotion.

As you enter into Love you may experience similar feelings. It is also fine if you do not. Your own entry into spiritual love need not necessarily be marked by the rise of these particular sāttvikabhāvas, nor do you need to think of this list of responses ranging from "smoking" to "blazing" as definitive and exhaustive. In other words, do not worry if you have not experienced one or more, or even any, of these sāttvikabhāvas or cannot locate the intensity of your experience within these levels of intensity. This would in no way mean that you have not known the rise of Love. I list them here more as information and to support you if you have indeed experienced these and wondered what was happening. Furthermore, as we will see in a later chapter, higher experiences of spiritual love become increasingly finer, such that Nārada at one point describes such experiences as "extremely subtle."[73]

In any case, sūtra 6 suggests that sometimes people know God's presence in dynamic ecstasy and sometimes in quiet enstasy. The fact that they can inwardly experience Love to begin with is because the Self that is the abode of Love is of the nature of both expansive joy and deep stillness.

That Nārada notes these two experiences together in one sūtra suggests to me that they are actually expressions of the same Love. Indeed, even in the highest levels of ecstasy there remains a quiet stillness in the heart. So, too, when one enters deeply into that stillness, one experiences a sense of dynamic expansiveness. The pulsations of ecstasy and enstasy merge in the fullness of Love.

Terms appearing in Chapter 6

ārāma	Delight, especially delight in the beauty of something.
ātman	A term for the single, universal, divine Self within all things.
ātmārāma	Delight (*ārāma*) in the divine Self (*ātman*).
jñāna	Knowledge; in the contemplative and devotional contexts the experiential as well as intellectual knowledge of the divine nature and presence.
pratyāhāra	The yogic withdrawal of the sense organs from the objects of sense; thus, a quieting of the senses in a move toward inward stillness.
śakti	Literally, "effective ability, power;" in the devotional tradition, this is God's inherent divine Potency. In the Tantric tradition, śakti is pure, divine energy, often associated with the divine Feminine.
sat-cit-ānanda	In Vedāntic thought, the divine Nature as consisting of Being (*sat*), Consciousness (*cit*) and Bliss (*ānanda*).
sāttvikabhāva	Literally a pure (*sattvika*) expression of an inner state (*bhāva*). In the aesthetic and devotional contexts, this is a spontaneous, unfabricated expression of an emotion (*bhāva*) that has been drawn forth by an experience of powerful beauty and love. Such outward manifestations of powerful inner experiences include tears forming in the eyes, goosebumps running across the skin, a stumbling with words, and so on.

—○ *Table III* ○—

A Classification of the Divine Power to be Its Own Nature

(See *Caitanya Caritāmṛta* 2.8.118-119)

svarūpa śakti		
Divinity's inherent power (*śakti*) to be its own divine nature (*svarūpa*).		
hlāldinī śakti	*saṁvit śakti*	*sandhinī śakti*
God's inherent power of Delight, the ultimate source of all human experiences of joy in the world. Associated with the quality the Vedānta recognizes as *ānanda* (Bliss).	God's inherent power of Awareness and thus the ultimate source of the human ability to be aware of anything; associated with the quality the Vedānta recognizes as *cit* (Consciousness).	God's inherent power of Beingness and thus the ultimate support all of existence; associated with the quality the Vedānta recognizes as *sat* (Being).

Chapter 7

Brighter Splendor in One's Love

From the yogic perspective, bhakti is a spiritual discipline, a *sādhana*, a word we remember literally means "leading to the goal." The goal of bhakti is immersion in what the *Nārada Bhakti Sūtra* describes as *paramapreman*, "supreme love." This definition of bhakti as the highest spiritual love implies that in some sense there are also lower levels of love. As a sādhana, a yogic life of devotional love can take us upward through these various levels.

That they are in some sense lower does not necessarily mean that these forms of love are not valuable (although, as we will note in this chapter, there are some forms of devotion that can actually be harmful, and we should be careful to avoid them). Rather, they are preparatory in nature. When developed in the context of a yogic life, they can lead to higher forms of spiritual love.

In this chapter we will consider some of the differences between various preparatory forms of bhakti and the highest state of devotional love, as our sūtras present that state, and I will offer some thoughts regarding how one might move through these levels through various yogic spiritual practices. I will focus that discussion by referring to sūtras 56 and 57. We will look at these two sūtras as a unit rather than separately.

गौणी त्रिधा गुणभेदादर्तादिभेदाद्वा ॥५६॥

gauṇī tridhā guṇabhedād-artādi-bhedād-vā

Preparatory [bhakti] is of three kinds according to the difference in one's nature or to difference in distress and so on.

— Sūtra 56

ऊत्तरस्मादुत्तरस्मात् पूर्वापूर्वा श्रेयाय भवति ॥५७॥

uttarasmād-uttarasmāt pūrvapūrvā śreyāya bhavati

Each succeeding one becomes
more splendid than the preceding one.

— Sūtra 57

"Preparatory" and *"more splendid"*

The term translated as "preparatory" in sūtra 56 is *gauṇī*. It would be more literally translated as "associated with specific qualities or properties." It is related to the word *guṇa*, a point to which I will return shortly.

The term for "more splendid" in sūtra 57 is *śreyas*, which is the comparative form of the word *śrī*, meaning "splendor, light, beauty, goodness." This is why I have translated *śreyas* as "more splendid." It could also be translated as "more beautiful" or "more excellent."

I will turn to the phrases "each succeeding one" and "the preceding one" later in this chapter. For the moment, though, we should note that, taken together, sūtras 56 and 57 imply that there are various types of devotion with different characteristics that can prepare the bhakta for higher forms of spiritual love.

Philosophers and teachers in the devotional tradition in India present a number of ways we could identify various levels of devotional love. For our current purposes, I will base my comments only on the phrasing in these two particular sūtras. According to sūtra 56, there are three kinds of such preparatory devotion, and that these three can be distinguished according to differences in one's temperament or according to one's motivations in offering devotion. We turn our attention initially to the latter description.

"According to . . . difference in distress and so on"

The term *artādibheda* can be broken down into three components. *Bheda* means "difference." *Ādi* means "beginning" and here can be understood to refer to the first word in a list of characteristics. And *arta*, means "distress." So, *artādi* would refer to a list of words beginning with "distress." That there are other entries on the list is implied by the reference to the beginning of it. We can assume that students at the time of these sūtras would already have been familiar with that list. Nārada here is reminding them of it by saying simply "artādi," which accordingly I have translated as "distress and so on."

For those who cannot infer the reference here, this phrase might understandably cause some initial puzzlement. What could it be referring to? It seems likely that Nārada has in mind a passage in the *Bhagavad Gītā*. Here, God as Kṛṣṇa tells his disciple Arjuna that there are different types of lovers of God. All four consist of good people. Yet, the text notes that there is a type that in some manner is closer to Kṛṣṇa than the others. That passage reads:

> There are four types of good people
> who worship me, O Arjuna:
> one who is in distress, one who seeks knowledge,
> one who desires wealth, and one who is wise.
> Of these, the wise one is the best,
> the one who is in constant union with me,
> whose devotion is one-pointed;
> for I am supremely dear to him,
> and he is supremely dear to me.
> All of these are worthy of respect,

but the wise one I truly regard to be myself —
the one who, with a disciplined soul,
abides in me, the supreme goal.[74]

The first kind of worshipper mentioned here is one who turns to God because he or she has fallen into misfortune of some sort. Such a person is distressed at a turn of events and worships God in hopes of relief from this unhappiness. The second type of devotee is one who worships God because he or she is intrigued by the idea of God and wants to gather more and more knowledge about God. The third type worships God because he or she hopes to gain materially from this devotion. We ourselves can imagine various such desires in our own world. Perhaps such a person wants to pass an examination, or to get paid more money, or to hold more social status, or perhaps to be given entry into heaven at the time of death. There are of course countless such possibilities.

Kṛṣṇa distinguishes these three types of devotee from a fourth, the latter of whom he says "abides in me, the supreme goal." The phrasing here suggests that the other three types of devotee are not yet immersed in the highest state.

If we take this list as an example of different levels of devotion, what distinguishes the first three forms of bhakti mentioned here from the highest form? Looking closely at these verses, we see that each of those first three types of devotion is offered with an ulterior purpose of some sort: one type of seeker wants relief from unhappiness, another looks for intellectual excitement, and a third hopes to gain something from the relationship with God.

Again, there is nothing wrong with any of these three types of devotion. As the *Bhagavad Gītā* says, all such devotees are "good people" who are "worthy of respect." As we know, many people turn to God when confronted with sorrow, illness or painful confusion in their lives. This is as appropriate as it is good, for God is compassionate and strong, and is the source of solace. Similarly, it is commendable that bhaktas come to an increasing understanding of God's nature so that they can align their lives in harmony with divine Wisdom. It is important to make good use of the intellect and all of its capabilities. So, too, the worship of God does indeed open people to the experience of wealth of a sort, for God is a benevolent and generative force that continually showers the human spirit with a graceful intention of wellbeing. I am referring here less to outer wealth than to inner wealth. As bhaktas mature spiritually they come to experience increasing gratitude for the immense inner richness that is God's munificent love for them. No number of outward material possessions can match this inner wealth.

So, there is value in each of these three types of devotion. The problem arises when people's ulterior purposes are actually of more concern to them than is their love for God. One danger is that the person who turns to God in order to gain something — relief, intellectual stimulation, material wealth — can tend to forget about God once that purpose has been met. God becomes a tool, as it were, that may be placed aside when that tool seems no longer needed. Devotion with an ulterior motive is a utilitarian form of devotion that does not last. It comes and it goes, and it is always susceptible to disappointment and discouragement if things do not turn out the way one hoped they would.

Each of these three types of devotion is an example of what is known in Indian thought as *haitukī bhakti*. The term means "devotion with a purpose" and characterizes devotion that is offered as a means to attain an end of some sort. It is also known as *sopādhi bhakti*, which is devotion that is a mixture of desires, motivations and inclinations.

On the other hand, there is a possibility of devotion without an ulterior motivation, this is to say, of *ahaitukī bhakti*. So, too, there is *nirupādhi bhakti*, devotional love that is not mixed with lower motivations. Such higher devotion is given without any purpose other than to express love for the divine Beloved. Accordingly, the highest love is also described in a number of other related ways. It is *eka bhakti*, one-pointed devotion; *kevala bhakti*, devotion solely to the divine Beloved; and *ananya bhakti*, devotion to none other than God, and thus to the true Source of all love.

Love offered with an ulterior purpose is a form of conditional love, and conditional sentiments of love can arise from what might otherwise be self-centered concerns. In a passage expanding our lines from the *Bhagavad Gītā*, the *Jñāneśvarī* describes the power of self-concern as like a rushing river and says that "In the stream of egoism, spouts of infatuation with learning, wealth, and power gush out."[75] On the other hand, love offered without other motivations is unconditional in nature and therefore is a higher form of devotion, for the highest form of love itself is unconditional love. Returning to the image of the river, the *Jñāneśvarī* has Kṛṣṇa say: "Only those who have served Me with devotion have succeeded in crossing it."[76]

These passages from the *Bhagavad Gītā* and the *Jñāneśvarī* imply that we can find increased freedom from the swirling currents of egoistic concern, and that this freedom comes through unconditional love for God. We are free from limitations in our devotion to the extent that we approach the divine Beloved with no intentions other than to express our love.

"According to the difference in one's nature"

Another way sūtra 56 classifies preparatory kinds of devotion is according to the various characteristics or qualities of one's inner state. The relevant term here is *guṇa*.

In using this term, our text draws on vocabulary from a classical philosophical tradition in India known as Sāṁkhya. According to Sāṁkhya thought, all things that exist in the universe consist of various combinations of three basic and preexistent qualities. Each of these three is known as a *guṇa*, a word that literally means "thread" and that also otherwise means "quality, characteristic, property, attribute." These guṇas are known as *tamas, rajas* and *sattva*. Tamas is a quality of darkness and heaviness and thus of thickness, dullness and solidity. Rajas is the quality of energy, excitement, heat, and of thus of movement, passion and generative urgency. Sattva is a quality of clarity, purity, light and calm effulgence, and therefore of quiet, goodness, beauty and wisdom.

Tamas is the densest of the three qualities and tends toward keeping things the way they are. Rajas is capable of bringing change and transformation. Sattva is the clearest, most serene and most splendid relative to the others. The adjectival forms of these nouns are *tāmasa*, *rājasa* and *sāttvika*: thick, energetic and pure, respectively.

There are also gradations within each of these three guṇas, each relative level being characterized in the same manner. So, tamas guṇa as a whole includes a continuum that encompasses dark thickness (tāmasa-tamas), energetic thickness (rājasa-tamas), and pure thickness (sāttvika-tamas). Similarly, rajas guṇa as a whole includes coagulated energy (tāmasa-rajas), active energy (rājasa-rajas) and pure energy (sāttvika-rajas). And, sattva guṇa as a whole encompasses thick purity (tāmasa-sattva), energetic purity (rājasa-sattva) and pure purity (sāttvika-sattva).

So, in this sense, our experience of life is woven on nine variations of the three foundational gunas. Then, each of these nine is said to include a similar continuum within itself, and we have 81 subtypes. The possibilities grow mathematically.

Understood from this perspective, it is the various configurations of these threads that form the fabric of our various and particular physical, emotional, mental and spiritual lives. States of being that have tamas in them tend toward heaviness, inertia and thickness; those that have more rajas in them are more energetic and transforming; and those that have more sattva in them are closer to a state of clarity and light. These configurations keep changing according to which of the guṇas — heaviness, energy, purity — predominates at the moment.

Yogic philosophy informed by Sāṁkhya thought holds, however, that deep within each person is an original, harmonious state of being that is not conditioned by the changing interactions of the gunas. This ground-state of inner equanimity is free of all discoloring influences. It is luminous in its inherent splendor. Here, all the guṇas stand in balance and harmony with each other. Then, pushed, pulled, and stretched by various forces of cause and effect, this is to say, through *karma*, and through the force of one's own intentions, these three preexisting and originally balanced threads weave themselves into the various patterns that determine the nature and quality of our experience of ourselves and of our world at any given time.

These patterns are understood first to form the subtle inner fabric of our thoughts and concepts as well as of our emotions, feelings and passions. The possible permutations are endless, depending on the amount of each of the guṇas present relative to the others and the manner in which the guṇas are combined with each other.

The process then continues as we project the inward mental and emotional patterns woven by the gunas outward, conditioning the way we see and experience the external world itself, and thereby the way we act in that world. People whose inner life is woven primarily on tamas will tend to experience the world as dark and heavy. People whose inner life is woven on rajas will see the world through the color of their passions. Those whose inner state is threaded by sattva will experience a world textured to that extent with qualities of beauty and light. The actual nature of our inner state may change from moment to moment as the web of the guṇas fluctuates. At times we may feel dense. Other times we are energetic. And at times our inward state is illumined by the light of wisdom.

When understood from a yogic perspective, the variously interweaving relationship of these three primary guṇas thus forms the fabric on which our inner lives in all our complexity as well as our particular experiences of the world are woven. Each one of us has a different temperament, if you will, fashioned by the particular influence of these preexistent threads. This includes our devotional sensibilities, which also can be said to be textured by the guṇas. Some people are more tāmasa in their devotion than others, some more rājasa, and some more sāttvika. The *Bhagavad Gītā* makes this point in the following passage:

> The faith of embodied beings is of three kinds:
> depending on their own nature:
> sāttvika, rājasa, and tāmasa.

Now, hear about this —
every person's faith is in
accordance with his or her temperament.
A person is made of faith.
Whatever faith that person has, thus that person is.[77]

What might tāmasa, rājasa and sāttvika types of devotion be like, respectively? You may want to contemplate this question for yourself, informed by your own experience in your life. But, in general, we can say that there are some helpful as well as less than helpful aspects of all three kinds of devotion.

Using this Indian notion of the gunas as an interpretive tool, we could say that bhakti in which the guṇa of tamas predominates could be, for example, rather dry, dull, unimaginative, or lethargic. Here, you may not really feel much emotion, but go through the outward acts of devotion almost out of rote habit or from a rather constricted sense of obligation. Such devotion is not really bad or improper. It's just that it can be rather sterile. It can have little vitality and, as such, can be rather unproductive.

At its worst, tāmasa devotion can be harmful, even sinister. Blind and unthinking devotion to God that is based on closed-mindedness is a form of tāmasa sensibilities, for it tends to be based on a limited and stagnant understanding of God and to re-enforce feelings of arrogance and superiority. I shudder at the thought of how much injury, suffering and degradation has been inflicted on others throughout history by people who selfishly feel that they either have the only true understanding of God when others do not, or that God loves them more than God loves others. Religious sensibilities based on any form of bigotry, racism, condescension or any other degrading attitudes toward others express "dark" or "thick" forms of understanding and, as such, are dangerous forms of devotion.

Yet, there are also positive components and possibilities within tāmasa bhakti. Devotional actions performed dutifully and humbly kindle our love, even if they are undertaken without much initial or obvious sense of movement upward. Musicians may not feel much when practicing the scales over and over on their instruments. Yet, this practice allows them to reach levels in their art in which deeper and more powerful feelings can find expression. Devotion, too, involves practice (*abhyāsa*) — and practice makes perfect in spiritual love as much as it does in other endeavors. So, if and when you are feeling dull and of the nature of tamas in your devotion, keep doing those sorts of things we noted in Chapter 5 that stoke the fire of your spiritual love. This is part of what makes bhakti yoga a true sādhana.

An energetic devotion woven primarily on rajas can similarly be both detrimental and beneficial to the cultivation of higher spiritual love. On the one hand, it can be impatient, incautious, and judgmental. So, too, rājasa displays of devotion can be showy, flamboyant, and self-serving. They can, on occasion, be an expression not so much of emotions of pure love but rather of a coarse emotionalism in which a number of self-centered desires, demands, fears and expectations get jumbled up together and presented outwardly as if they were feelings of devotional love.

On the other hand, of course, rājasa devotion can be quite helpful to yogīs and yoginīs, for it brings transforming energy to their sādhana and to their expression of love in the world. It is rājasa-bhakti that fuels the fire that burns in the lover's heart. It enlivens bhaktas' thoughts, commitments and intentions. Throughout history people's passionate loving energy has directed their longing to serve God in countless ways: by taking care of their bodies, minds and hearts; constructing and maintaining beautiful sacred spaces; offering benevolent concern for others by supporting worthy and beneficial social causes; expressing love by working in hospitals and clinics; cultivating and distributing nourishing food; insuring that people have proper housing; protecting people from harm and danger; sharing in the wonder of life by teaching in schools. The offering of love in active and energetic ways is an expression of rājasa bhakti.

Similarly, devotion woven on sattva can have both lower and higher forms. Regarding the former, there is the possibility of pretense. You can imagine, for example, a person who rather showily wears a plastic or goofy devotional smile, or who speaks in artificial and self-conscious tones that fairly drip with "spirituality." Or, we might imagine a person who almost compulsively performs acts of worship that actually seem more neurotic than loving.

Higher forms of sāttvika bhakti express an increasing clarity of mind, an expanding purity of heart and a deepening calmness of spirit. Sāttvika bhaktas tend to cultivate refined emotions rather then get caught up in coarse emotionalism (more on this in the next chapter). They turn their mindfulness toward the subtle inner forces working within themselves and within others. They are receptive to knowledge gained through study and reflection. They tend toward contemplation and meditation.

Just as there are various combinations of the guṇas, so too there are combinations of these different types of bhakti. Bhaktas will experience and express different forms of devotional love at various times, and perhaps various types at the same time. Even the most rājasa of bhaktas will experience longing to meditate, for example, and sāttvika bhaktas can often wish to express love actively in the world. Tāmasa bhaktas can bring their solidity and steadfastness to their other devotional yearnings. All of these various forms of devotion based on the guṇas can serve lovers of the divine Beloved as they move upward on the path of yoga.

"Each succeeding one becomes
more splendid than the preceding one"

We recall that the word for "more splendid" in sūtra 57 is *śreyas*, literally, "of more *śrī*" and thus "more lustrous, more radiant." In this phrase our text is saying that spiritual love can become increasingly resplendent as it moves from one type of devotion to another. Our sūtra is referring to various levels of devotion based on one's motivations that are conditioned by the guṇas. One way we could understand this phrase would therefore be to say that love offered unconditionally is more splendid than love offered with an ulterior motive. Another way would be to say that devotion grounded in rajas could be, for example, more splendid than devotion based in tamas, and devotion based in sattva could be more splendid than devotion based on rajas.

There is still another way to understand this phrase, too. The reference to preceding types of love for God could also refer to each of these forms conditioned by one's motivations or by the gunas *before* each is illumined by the full light of unconditional Love. From this perspective, any and all of the levels of devotion can be infused by that light at any time. When this happens, that particular level — whatever it is — is more splendid than it was previously, and this is true from moment to moment as we move further along the path of spiritual love. When there is love, each step on the path of yoga can seem to be even more splendid than it was previously. The process continues throughout the yogic life. I am reminded here of a particular sūtra in the *Śiva Sūtras* from about the ninth century noting that all the "stages of yoga [bring] wonder!"[78]

In either case, we might pause to note three points here. The first is that we can think of all the forms of spiritual love to which sūtras 56 and 57 allude as being potentially helpful and productive in their own ways. Some are more filled with light, as it were, than others. Second, there is the possibility of our elevating our love toward higher levels no matter what our seemingly natural tendencies and proclivities may be. Third, by using the verb *bhavati*, "becomes," our text assures us that the movement toward these higher forms of love is indeed possible.

Moving toward Increasingly Splendid Love through Yogic Discipline

One might wonder: what can I do to be less conditional in my love and increasingly free of my predilections in the way I offer expressions it? In such instances, we can use techniques of yogic discipline to help us. There are many such techniques. For our current purposes, I will mention four that come to us from traditions of Indian spiritual practice. They are the cultivated spiritual disciplines of: diligent self-inquiry, illuminating discernment, beneficial dispassion and renunciation. All four are supported and enlivened by the power of grace. These components of the spiritual life are important elements of yogic sādhana in general and thus merit some discussion.

Openness to Grace

In some ways the process of inner purification and the turn toward freedom can be difficult. Our hidden motivations can be so hidden that they are virtually invisible to us. This is one reason why bhaktas cultivate and deepen their trust in Love. Unconditional in nature, Love is not bound by preconditions. The strength and power of God's compassion dissolves the knots that tie up a mind and heart preconditioned by the guṇas and leads ultimately to the freedom to experience the expansive reality that is Love. It is an act of grace when supreme Love reveals itself to you, when it takes form for you. The more you put your deepest trust in Love, the more you become open to it and at one with it. We remember what Kṛṣṇa has taught Arjuna, quoted earlier: "Whatever faith a person has, thus that person becomes."

Another way to say this is that our faith opens us to God's grace. As the *Bhāgavata Purāṇa* says, Bhagavān is pure Consciousness.[79] Therefore, God is not influenced by any preconscious forces. In this sense, God is *nirguṇa* — without guṇa — and thus not bound by any predetermined qualities. God is of the nature of pure freedom and pure spontaneity. God as ultimate Love has no selfish motivations. God's intention is to reveal Love. This pure and selfless intention is the source of God's grace, and it is this grace, in part, that frees us from our own entrapping predilections. When we remember and align ourselves with God's affirming love, then we are open to grace.

Self-Inquiry

In order to move forward mindfully in our sādhana of devotion, it will be helpful to be as aware as possible of just what our motivations in offering devotion are. Without this mindfulness we can continue to get stuck at lower levels without our knowing it. This means we need to be honest with ourselves. We need to ask: Who am I? What is the true Self? Is what I am thinking and doing consistent with the nature of that true Self?

In the context of the yogic life, diligent self-inquiry is known as *ātmavicāra*, which literally means "movement into the self." It is also known as *ātmaniveśana*, or "entering into the self." The practice involves a process of attentively discerning the quality and direction of one's thoughts, actions, desires and so on. There can be, and often are, layers of our inner lives that veil or distort our experience of the true Self, Ātman. As we lose sight of the true Self, we feel separate from it, often without even knowing that we feel this separation. Then, we allow those desires, motivations, insecurities and habitual ways of thinking that arise from the feeling of separation to determine our actions in the world; we think and behave in a manner that is not aligned with the Self and its affirming nature as Love. Our lives become driven by falsehood grounded in misunderstanding of who we really are as embodied beings loved by Love. This is to say that we feed our ignorance, *avidyā*. The remedy for this is to return one's attention to the true nature of the Self through meditation, contemplation and study.

In yogic sādhana this practice of ātmavicāra includes not only the contemplation on the nature of Ātman, but also the active, candid and courageous honesty with oneself in noting just what one's motivations and desires are in any given situation relative to nature of that Self. So, again, the seeker asks: What am I doing? What are my intentions here? What am I experiencing? What am I projecting? What am I hoping for, expecting, demanding? What is my real purpose in acting or thinking in this way?

Honest answers to such questions help dissolve pretense and self-deception. The process may be difficult at times since it can uncover aspects of ourselves we may not particularly like. But it can also be liberating. As we go further and deeper into our self-inquiry we can discern the effects of various forces working within us: past experiences, fears, disappointments, impulses, desires, wishes, the contours of our relationships with others and so on. When they are discerned, there is more possibility of release from them, just as the light of the sun burns off thick layers of fog covering the land. Then, we can move forward, illumined by a wisdom that reflects the light of the Beloved's compassionate presence within us.

Illuminating Discernment

One step we can take toward elevating our love for God is therefore to practice continual self-inquiry, through which we can become more aware of our motivations in offering that love. As we do so, we may come to see what parts of our devotion are less pure than others. Once we recognize this, we can then begin to refine the essence of pure love from within those less pure forms.

To do this, we can practice illuminating discernment or discrimination, *viveka*. This, then, is a second step in this four-step process. In the context of bhakti as a sādhanā, this is a disciplined attentiveness by which we distinguish between what is truly loving and that which seems pleasant but merely reinforces our own narrow desires.

The *Kaṭha Upaniṣad*, from roughly the third century BCE and thus a much earlier text than the *Bhakti Sūtra*, offers a helpful set of teachings that support such a yogic practice. It distinguishes between *śreyas* — a term you will recall I have translated in Nārada's sūtra as "more splendid" — and what it calls *preyas*, which in this context could be translated as "more pleasant."

> The more splendid [*śreyas*] is one thing, the
> more pleasant [*preyas*] is another.

> Their purpose is different. Both bind a person.
> Of these two, it is better to take hold of the more splendid.
> Those who choose the more pleasant will miss their goal.
> Both the more splendid and the more pleasant present themselves.
> A wise person discerns them,
> and chooses the more splendid over the more pleasant.[80]

Such discernment takes practice, for it can be easily distracted. As a spiritual practice, viveka is an important element of yogic sādhana. We see the work in the title of an important philosophical-devotional text from ninth century India, the *Vivekacuḍāmaṇi* (the "Crest-Jewel of Discernment"), which notes that such discipline finds support in what are sometimes known as the six virtues: inner tranquility, self control, equanimity, trust, and contemplative composure.[81]

Beneficial Dispassion

Having discerned the difference between what is loving and what is not, we can try to loosen the grip of narrow self-centeredness that otherwise discolors our unconditional love. This spiritual practice is known as *vairāgya*, often translated simply as "dispassion."

In the bhakti context, this practice does not mean that we abandon our passions, if by this we mean our joys, commitments and experiences of wonder. For our purposes, I would prefer to translate *vairāgya* as "beneficial dispassion." The word suggests the loosening of our addictive desires for the pleasant rather than the liberating yearning for the splendid. By doing so, we can more fully feel genuine Love rather than the transient emotionalism that sometimes gets confused with it.

You can think of vairāgya as a process in which, while continuing to practice self-inquiry and illuminating discernment, you then separate various inner impulses from each other, and thereby assume control over the pull of harmful desires and their seeming need for gratification. This leads to the experience of an inner calm that allows you to see more clearly your true heart and its relationship to your Beloved.

Renunciation of Narrow Self-Centeredness

With the equanimity that comes with vairāgya at its various levels, you can turn away from the allure of self-centered desires in favor of truly selfless spiritual love. This is the yogic practice of *saṁnyāsa*, renunciation. The word implies a "throwing off" or "putting aside" of one's attachment to the more pleasant over the more splendid. In some yogic contexts, the act of renunciation is one in which one turns away from attachment to and participation in the world and enters into a life of asceticism. It is a turning away from the desires of the self (lower case "s") and into the depths of the Self. This is the renunciation exemplified by traditional *saṁnyāsīs* in India who undertake a yogic life untethered to any home, having thrown off bonds to the world of family, marketplace and social life in service of a liberating experience of the Self within themselves.

In traditional India, such saṁnyāsa is reserved for people in the fourth and final stage of their lives, having given themselves to the responsibilities incumbent on them first as students, then as householders, and then as elders living contemplative lives in forest retreats. So, too, saṁnyāsa describes the renunciation of worldly motivations and attachments undertaken by people who in other religious contexts might be called monks and nuns.

However, this throwing off of one's bonds to the world need not be part of a yogic life illumined by bhakti. Here, saṁnyāsa can be understood to be the renunciation of selfish motivations, in general, in one's devotion to God. As this kind of saṁnyāsī, you most certainly do not need to turn away from your family, your work or the larger human community. Such renunciation does not go against your benevolent attachments and responsibilities. Indeed, it is not so much a rejection of the self (lower case "s") and its world as much as it is a gentle affirmation of the universal Self that dwells within those attachments and which you honor, in essence, by attending to your responsibilities.

Therefore, in the context of bhakti, while the practice of renunciation at first may seem negative, it actually is a positive one. Here, we let go of all those selfish, unloving forces and misplaced values that distract us from experiencing and expressing the Love that is the Beloved's nature as the true Self.

These four yogic disciplines — self-inquiry, illuminating discernment, beneficial dispassion and letting go of narrow self-centeredness — support and nourish each other. Through the practice of self-inquiry we become aware of our true motivations in doing what we do or believing what we believe. Through illuminating discernment we can more clearly distinguish true spiritual love from devotional attitudes and experiences that feel pleasant but may actually be more self-centered than others. Then, through beneficial dispassion, we quiet the motivations based on any selfish intentions we have discovered and brought to awareness. Finally, through renunciation we let go of even the most subtle, yet nevertheless constricting, forms of selfishness and give ourselves to the expansive Love that is the nature of the true Self.

This yogic letting go of self-centered motivations then allows us to deepen our practice of self-inquiry even more, which gives rise to the possibility of even clearer illuminating discernment, more thorough dispassion and more liberating renunciation of self-centeredness — and the whole process of yogic refinement itself becomes increasingly effective as we move toward states of love that reveal themselves to be more splendid than previous ones.

An Implication: The Highest Devotion is Love for God beyond Characteristics

The unconditioned and unconditional source of all our experiences of Love, God is not defined and limited by the web of the gunas. In this sense, God is *nirguṇa* in nature, "without guṇa." As such, God is not an object among objects or a thing among things. God is the ultimate divine Field without which there can be no existence whatsoever, the boundless potential by which anything becomes actual. Accordingly, the nirguṇa Foundation of existence is sometimes described with such terms as Mahāśunya, the "Great Emptiness."

From the nirguṇa perspective, God as the Great Emptiness has no characteristics, no qualities, no size, no texture, no shape. And yet, God remains the source and basis of our existence and the ultimate object of all our yearning. One implication of this would be that, at the highest level, devotion is offered to the divine Beloved beyond all form. Such devotion is *nirguṇa bhakti*. It is also known as *śuddha bhakti*, "pure devotion," for its splendor is not defined by the color of any particular guṇa.

Nirguna bhakti or śuddha bhakti is in some ways a difficult kind of spiritual love, for we as human beings tend to a longing to direct our love to something or somebody that has some sort of characteristics we can see, touch, hear or imagine. The problem is that, as we do so, we can also tend to remain in a devotional world defined and conditioned by the guṇas and thus limit our ability to enter and serve the infinite and unconditional expansiveness that is God's nature. Although devotion to Divinity without form can be difficult, it is also in some ways the highest level of devotion; for here there is no false idolatry, no insistent emotional clinging to a particular physical form or image of God, no limiting of the Beloved's boundless nature.

In the Mystery of Pure Devotion
The Formless Beloved can be Adored within Form

While, in some ways, nirguṇa bhakti may be difficult to attain, there is also a delightful mystery here, too. Just as the universal and unconditioned Self stands within the conditioned particularity of all things, so too the formless Beloved can be honored, loved and worshipped in a particular form.

In this latter case — devotion to the Beloved within form — we can speak of *saguṇa bhakti*, the word *saguṇa* literally meaning "with *guṇas*" and thus "with qualities." While it is true that the Great Emptiness embraces and frames all of existence, it is also true that all things emerge from and thus give form to this plethoric void, just as all sounds arise ultimately out of pure silence.

This means that, while a continually refined and purified saguṇa bhakti can lead ultimately to nirguṇa bhakti, so too the unbounded nature of nirguṇa bhakti can nourish, deepen and elevate saguṇa bhakti. Accordingly, just as there is no need to cling to a physical form of the Beloved, there is also no need to turn away from that form, either.

In the end, saguṇa bhakti and nirguṇa bhakti can and do support each other, for the formless Beloved and the Beloved with form are, from the devotional perspective, one and the same. I suspect that this is one reason why bhaktas continue to express profound respect and reverence to physical reminders of this fact of embodiment: images, saints, awakened teachers, our own physical bodies and those of all others in the world. And this is why even those devotees who are least attached to physical forms of God nevertheless find joy in offering their reverence to particular forms and delight in being in their presence. They experience formless Love pulsating in the movements of their own loving hearts, and they see the face of the formless God in the faces of their fellow human beings.

No matter what level one may be in one's devotion, those who cultivate spiritual love will always have help in their sādhana through the grace of the divine Beloved. Indian devotional thought holds that the formless power of the divine Presence is expressed through various saguṇa forms for the devotee's sake, no matter what stage of spiritual development that devotee may have attained. That graceful Love is "like the wind, which assumes the fragrance of whatever it blows across."[82] Love's splendor brings light to each level of our devotion. Turning our hearts toward the Source of love, we turn toward the Splendor that is Love.

Terms appearing in Chapter 7

abhyāsa Continuing, disciplined spiritual practice.

Ātman The single divine, universal Self that is the foundation of all relative selves. The true Self within all selves; the divine Presence within all things.

ātmaniveśana "Entering into the self," the discipline of diligent self-inquiry. See also *ātmavicāra*, below.

ātmavicāra "Moving into the Self," the spiritual practice of diligent self-inquiry by asking such questions as "What is the real Self? Who am I? What keeps me from knowing the Self? What motivations lead me to act in certain ways?" and so on.

avidyā Not-knowing, ignorance; specifically, ignorance of the true Self.

gauṇī Of the nature of a *guṇa* (see below).

guṇa A characteristic or quality; a constituent property of one's physical, psychological, and spiritual nature, understood to be three in number: *sattva* (lightness, purity, goodness), *rajas* (energy, passion), and *tamas* (thickness, darkness, ignorance).

karma Literally, "action." The universal law of cause and effect that holds that any situation is the result or effect of a cause that precedes it. Said differently, *karma* is the power that binds cause to effect and effect to cause. In Indian thought, all of one's thoughts, deeds and intentions have an effect on the world and thus on oneself.

mahāśunya The Great Emptiness.

nirguṇa Without (*nir*) characteristics or qualities (*guṇa*).

paramapreman Supreme love.

preyas That which is pleasing to the senses and desires.

rajas The characteristic or quality (*guṇa*) of energy or passion.

sādhana	Spiritual discipline, a set of spiritual practices, the yogic life.
saṁnyāsa	Yogic renunciation.
sattva	Conditioning or preconditioned quality (guna) of purity, lightness, goodness.
śreyas	More splendid, more beautiful, more auspicious, better, more excellent. (The comparative form of *śrī*, see below).
śrī	Splendor, beauty, auspiciousness.
tamas	Conditioning or preconditioned quality of darkness, heaviness, or ignorance.
vairāgya	Yogic beneficial dispassion.
viveka	Yogic discrimination between what is real from what is not real, valuable from what is not valuable, loving from what is not loving.

Table IV

Some More Types of Bhakti

(See also Tables I and X)

haitukī bhakti	Devotion that has an ulterior purpose or motivation.
ahaitukī bhakti	Devotion that is offered without any ulterior purpose or motivation; thus, selfless devotion.
saguṇa bhakti	Bhakti that is conditioned by the *guṇas*; thus, light-filled devotion (*sāttvika bhakti*), energetic devotion (*rājasa bhakti*), and heavy or dark devotion (*tāmasa bhakti*). Saguṇa bhakti also refers to devotion to the Beloved with characteristics, that it to say, devotion to Divinity with form.
nirguṇa bhakti	Devotion that is not conditioned by one's personal predilections or psychological predispositions. Nirguna bhakti also refers to devotion to the Beloved without characteristics or form.
sopādhi bhakti	Devotion that is mixed with extraneous desires, motivations and inclinations.
nirupādhi bhakti	Pure, unmixed devotion that is free of extraneous desires, motivations and inclinations.
aśuddha bhakti	Bhakti that is impure (*aśuddha*), that is to say, devotion that is discolored by selfish intentions and tendencies.
śuddha bhakti	Pure (*śuddha*) devotion that is not discolored by selfish intentions and tendencies.

Some Synonymous Phrases

ananya bhakti	Devotion that is given to the Beloved alone rather than toward that which distracts from genuine love.
eka bhakti	One-pointed devotion. Devotion that is directed to the Beloved only.
kevala bhakti	Devotional love that is offered to the Beloved alone and to no other.

Chapter 8

Refinement of the Emotions and Deepening of Devotional States

We turn now to a consideration of the place of one's emotions, moods and attitudes in a yogic life illumined by bhakti. Our textual reference will be to sūtra 79. The relevant term in that sūtra is the Sanskrit *bhāva.* It is a word with many levels of meaning. It can be translated as "way of being, state of mind, mood, temperament, attitude, disposition, personal manner." At another level, it can mean "one's true nature, the essence of one's being" and thus "soul" and "heart."

The word *bhāva* itself comes from a Sanskrit verbal root meaning both to "be" and to "become." So, bhāva literally means both "existing, being" and "coming into existence, occurring." The word thus suggests both a state and a process. That which *is* undergoes a process of *becoming*, and thus of manifesting, disclosing, revealing. Similarly, that which is *becoming* eventuates as that which *is*. Accordingly, from the yogic perspective, it is important to understand how one's emotions and attitudes, as bhāvas, both express and affect one's inner state and how one's inner state affects one's outward experience. Bhāvas both draw us toward our hearts and allow us to express our hearts' sentiments. At the deepest, most refined levels, emotions — especially those associated with love — can open a way to the soul's communion with the divine Beloved in the depths and expanse of the divine Heart.

Before we turn to our sūtra, it will be important to note that yogic traditions in India have regarded the emotions in two general ways. One point of view — one that I will *not* take in these comments — sees the emotions as forces that can hinder a seeker's movement forward along the spiritual path. From this perspective, emotions are temporary fluctuations of the mind that arise out of latent memory traces, unconscious motivations and sensual desires that are conditioned by people's projections, expectations and habitual tendencies. The emotions are understood here to distract, confuse, and mislead the spiritual seeker and thus to get in the way of liberating knowledge free of such distortions. Some yogic traditions therefore urge people to free themselves from the effect of their emotions as much as possible.

In general, the philosophy of bhakti as a sādhana does not take this position. If it were to do so, then how would bhaktas understand and work with their yearning for the divine Beloved — an emotional longing that can be as undeniable as it is powerful? Are bhaktas to abandon that longing? The answer is, no, they should not. Neither should they turn from feelings of joy, sadness, courage and so on. Bhakti-oriented philosophy holds that the emotions, rather than being an obstacle to communion with Divinity, can open the way to that experience.

However, bhakti yogīs and yoginīs should not confuse beneficial emotions with the dynamics of self-centered desire. Accordingly, before we turn to the sūtra at hand, it might be helpful to reflect for a moment with a yogic perspective on the difference between emotion and desire.

Emotion Arising out of Fullness vs Desire Based on a Sense of Lack

From a yogic point of view, people desire something when they feel that they themselves are lacking in it. They seek to obtain the object of their desire as a way to fill that absence. Therefore, understood from a yogic point of view, desire is based in a self-centered motivation.

An emotion, on the other hand, arises from an inner state of mind or heart that in some way already exists. In this sense, an emotion does not arise from a sense of lack. Rather, it expresses an overflowing of sorts. (In this regard it might be helpful to remember that the English word *emotion* derives from a Latin word meaning "move outward.") Sometimes, as we know, this movement from within can feel like agitation that seems to explode. Other times, of course, it can feel like golden honey rising from the depths of our hearts. In any case, as bhaktas, we can affirm the presence of our emotions as expressions of the fullness of our embodied existence as human beings.

As bhaktas we can and should honor our yearning. We are to be careful, though, to make sure that this longing is less insistent on gratification of desire than on service to Love itself. This is to say that, as yogīs and yoginīs, we are to distinguish emotions of love — affection, fondness, endearment, tenderness, adoration, delight, longing, joy, gratitude, caring concern, compassion and so on — from the pull of desire based on a feeling of not having something. Doing so, we turn toward the Love that already moves in its fullness within us.

Emotions do tend to get caught up in desires. Therefore, in order to distill the Love that moves within their hearts, bhaktas, as yogīs and yoginīs, can work to refine their various emotions by reducing and freeing themselves as much as possible from narrow self-centered desires otherwise associated with them. This process of refining of the emotions takes yogic discipline, a point to which I will return shortly.

Even when independent of desire, our expressions of love-based emotions can also be quite jumbled and mixed up with each other. Accordingly, the yogic life involves the distillation of these manifold emotions from each other so that we can experience the single, embracing, sublime Source of all of them. From the bhakti perspective, this Source of all forms of human love is Love itself. Of course, sometimes that Source can be buried under the web of coarser forms of attitudes, feelings and sentiments we often associate with our human love. Thus, our yoga of devotion involves the refining of our emotions and strengthening of loving states of mind so that we may be immersed in the fullness of their true Source, which is divine Love.

Before considering the yogic process of refining the emotions and the importance of deepening beneficial attitudes, let's turn now to sūtra 79. It reads:

सर्वदा सर्वभावेन निश्चिन्तैर्भगवानेव भजनीयः ॥७९॥

sarvadā sarvabhāvena niścintair bhagavān-eva bhajanīyaḥ

God alone is to be worshipped by those without worry all the time with all the heart.

— Sūtra 79

*"God alone is to be worshipped by those with-
out worry all of the time with all of the heart."*

The word for God here is *bhagavān*: the one who shares, the one who distributes beneficence and care, the one who gives love bountifully. Our sūtra thus says that one is to offer reverence to God as Bhagavān. The relevant verb here is *bhajanīya*: "to be worshipped." It is related to the noun *bhajana*, "worship," the reverential, sanctifying and transforming process of participating in and sharing the Love that is Bhagavān's nature. The words *bhagavān* and *bhajana* are related to the word *bhakti*, all having something to do with the sharing of love in the fullness of Love.

It is important to note the word "alone" (*eva*) in this sūtra. In Sanskrit, *eva* is used to stress the word or phrase with which it appears. In our current sūtra, *eva* adds emphasis to the word Bhagavān.

We can interpret the effect of this emphasis in two ways. The first is that, when there is highest bhakti, then God is the sole object of one's devotion. Sometimes we may say we love God, but actually our love for money, material possessions, social prestige and so on determines the focus of our lives. In this case, our devotion is not for God *alone*. However, as our sūtra holds, bhakti is love that is directed to God.

In this regard we might think of the *gopīs* as examples of this focused adoration of the Beloved. According to texts such as the *Bhāgavata Purāṇa* and other devotional literatures, the gopīs are young village women who feel deep, joyful, sometimes poignant, but always unwavering loving devotion for their beloved Kṛṣṇa and for nothing else. One well-known story says that the gopīs' yearning for Kṛṣṇa was so strong that, hearing the tones of his flute as he played it beyond the edge of the village, they dropped all they were doing to follow that beautiful, compelling sound into the dark and unknown depths of the forest beyond the village, where they met him and danced in pure bliss with their Lord through the night.[83]

A second way we could interpret the word for "alone" in our sūtra is that we can look for God in whatever we experience, for God is the Source of all that comes to us. In whatever our lives may bring us we have an invitation to recognize God's presence in our lives. The world is filled with beauty and with beautiful things. The bhakta appreciates them fully and deeply. However, guided by teachings such as this sūtra, the bhakta does not worship those things by themselves, for they have no existence without God. In their beauty the bhakta sees expression or revelation of the divine Presence within all of existence. When our hearts are open to Divinity within all things, then when we look with adoring wonder into the eyes of a child, we are, in essence, adoring God. When we gaze with awe into the brilliant sunrise or deep into the midnight sky, we worship God. When we listen attentively to the sounds of voices, or of musical instruments, or of the wind blowing across a field, we worship God. Whenever we eat food or drink water, we worship God. Whenever we bow in reverence in front of a sacred image in a temple, we worship God. Whenever we wipe tears of sadness or of gratitude from our eyes, we worship God. As our sūtra is telling us, it is Bhagavān and Bhagavān *alone* who is the object of our worship.

"By those without worry"

The word *niścinta* quite literally means "without thought" yet also means "without concern" and thus "without worry." I understand the use of the term here in two ways.

One way is to recall that the affirming Source of all existence, the divine Heart, is of the nature of exuberant joy, *ānanda*. God can therefore be worshipped in our own expansive joy. Worry constricts joy. Sometimes people think of God as an oppressive, domineering, negatively judgmental figure. It is important to remember that, from a bhakti perspective, God loves you, has always loved you, and will continue to love you. When there is genuine response in one's heart to divine Love, then one's life is directed by that response and one offers one's own love in return without worry.

A second, related way to understand *niścinta* would be that worship is to be undertaken with confidence in the reality of Love. Trust dissolves worry. When one trusts Love, then one is less torn by uncertainty and doubt, and more infused with gratitude.

Of course, there may be times in life when you experience doubt in the reality of God. This can be a healthy doubt, for it leads one to greater maturity and sophistication in one's faith. It is good to question religion and religious beliefs, for to question is literally to be on a quest for meaning. The religious quest that accepts doubt thereby both challenges and is the antidote to superficial, immature belief. Religious sensibilities that do not accept questions are liable to the dangers of monolithic absolutism and fanaticism.

Ultimately, God is beyond the reach and capabilities of the human mind to describe, imagine and understand. The more we engage the mystery that is God, though, the more we are able to experience that Mystery. Love requires trust, and trust is a form of faith. But openhearted faith is not the same as blind dogmatic belief.

Faith in divine Love is based in the experience of human love in all of its delightful, poignant, touching, transforming ways, even in a world that does not always seem to express such love. When there is faith, there is the possibility of movement forward in life within its uncertainties. The world will always present us with complexities, contradictions and vicissitudes. Yet, when there is love for God, that love will remain steady and trusting and, in this sense, without worry.

"All of the time"

At the highest levels of bhakti, the sharing of God's love encompasses and directs all of the bhakta's life. Participating in Love need not take place just once a week, or a few times a day, but rather *sarvadā*, "always," or "all of the time."

God's love supports, enwraps, and nourishes us from instant to instant. Without that Love, we have no being, no existence, for Love is the foundation and basis of our existence. We cannot be separate from God and still exist. When we inhale, we inhale in God's love, and when we exhale, we also exhale in God's love. When we wake, and when we sleep, we do so in God's love. When we eat, walk, take care of our families, work at our jobs and give attention to our communities, we do so in God's love. When we sing God's name, when we study sacred texts, when we offer ourselves in service, when we honor our bodies and when we meditate, we do so in God's love.

The more we truly know God as Love, then the more we can live in awareness of that Love in each moment of our lives, and the more we can respond by offering our own love, from moment to moment, in grateful return.

"With all of the heart"

The word for "all" here is *sarva*. It is joined here to the word *bhāva*. As I have said previously, the word *bhāva* itself carries several related meanings. To review briefly, in part it means "existing, continuing to exist, particular essence" and thus also means "soul, heart." I understand the term to be used here in this latter sense. When these two particular words, *sarva* and *bhāva*, are put together, the resulting combination *sarvabhāva* means "all of one's being" or "the whole of one's existence" and thus also "with all the heart," as I have translated it here.

What would this mean? Well, think of what you mean when you tell a person you love that you do so "with all your heart." Your love is unbounded, undiminished, true, unconditional, strong, deep, genuine, unfeigned. When you love another with all your heart, you love from the entirety of your being, from the depths of your soul. So, too, you can love Bhagavān with all your heart. When you share these qualities of love with the Highest, the Source of all love, then the fullness of your love emerges from and flows toward God as Bhagavān.

Our sūtra is saying here that, just as Bhagavān is to be worshipped all the time, *sarvadā*, so too the divine Beloved is to be adored with the intensity and fullness that is all of one's being, *sarvabhāva*. This implies that there is more than one way to worship God, for your heart holds and expresses many delights, hopes, concerns, longings and satisfactions. The heart is the hub of the many bhāvas, if we now understand this term also to refer to inner states, ways of being, temperaments, attitudes, dispositions, feelings, sentiments and emotions. Accordingly, if I may use a play on words here, we could say that God is to be worshipped both "always" and "in all ways."

This notion that God can be worshipped in all the heart's states distinguishes the bhakti perspective from other yogic views that see the emotions and similar sentiments as distracting forces that interfere with the yogī's or yoginī's advancing on the spiritual path.

At the same time, bhakti as a yoga involves the recognition that some emotions are in a sense coarser than others. This does not mean they are bad. It means that they are not as pure as others. They are mixed with other emotions. I will say more about what this means shortly. For now, it is important to note that a yogic life informed and directed by bhakti sensibilities turns in part on the purification — this is to say, the refinement — of the emotions. As they are refined, they become both more subtle and more powerful at the same time. Refining the emotions, the bhakta distills an increasingly pure essence within them — an essence that is of the nature of pure Love. The yogic life as sādhana allows the bhakta to immerse more and more deeply into this fine Sublimity, the ultimate Source of which is divine Love itself.

Nārada's use of the word *sarvabhāva* in our current sūtra thus not only encourages us to cultivate and express love for the divine Beloved with all our hearts, it also gives us an opportunity to consider and reflect further and more particularly both on the nature of the various levels and types of bhāvas and on ways in which we can make use of the emotions, feelings, attitudes and so on as we move forward along the spiritual path. This is what I will do in the following sections.

Levels of Bhāva

Indian thought holds that some emotions and similar sentiments are more superficial than others. Said differently, some are deeper than others. More superficial bhāvas tend to come and go and to move on the surface of one's experience. Such a surface emotion is described as a *vyabhicārabhāva*, a transient emotion, that is to say, an emotion a person feels in the moment at hand yet goes away as time passes. A deeper emotion is known as a *sthāyibhāva*, an "abiding emotion," for it remains within a person's deeper experience even if it is not outwardly experienced at any particular moment. Some schools of thought intuit a third level of bhāva underneath these two. They refer to it as *mahābhāva*, the "great state." I will return our discussion to the nature of this mahābhāva shortly.

A transient bhāva often mixes with other bhāvas as it comes and goes. Because it is mixed up with others it is not as purely itself as it would be if it were unmixed. You might think of waves on the surface of an ocean. They rise and fall due to various causes and move across the water, meeting with other waves and temporarily changing shape. Similarly, we experience different emotions that come and go. Like the waves on the ocean, a transient emotion moves across the surface of our experience as it combines with others before it fades away, usually to be replaced by another set of similarly temporary feelings.

Perhaps an example would be helpful. Think for a moment of the nature of infatuation. An infatuation can be delightful in some ways: stirring, exciting and invigorating. But it may also be somewhat frightening, for you may sense that the object of your infatuation may not feel the same way about you, or that you may make a fool of yourself, or that your feelings may change, or that the feelings themselves are inappropriate. Maybe the person who draws your emotions unconsciously reminds you of somebody you once knew, or admired, or envied, or wished in some way you could be like. An infatuation is usually a combination of several emotions. Most infatuations are also temporary, too.

Now think of the deeper energy that drives infatuation. An infatuation reflects a longing of some sort. What is that yearning? Some of it may be hormonal, in which case the energy will dissipate when the object of desire is gained. At this level, infatuation expresses desire. At a deeper level, though, we may feel infatuation because we actually long to express love in our lives. The object of our desire is a momentary glow of an ember in the darkness. What we really want is the fire itself. The temporary surprise, happiness, fear, disappointment, anger, and other transitory emotions we feel on the surface are expressions of a deeper and abiding longing. Therefore, if we purify the surface feeling of infatuation by distinguishing and separating it from other feelings such as intrigue, excitement, frustration and so on, then we can more fully immerse ourselves in its truer, deeper essence, which in this case is the yearning to express our love.

Due to the dynamics of time and the limitations of space, the outward object of our infatuation will eventually change in some way or move out of our lives and probably become less compelling to us. And yet, the yearning will still remain, for what we really long for does not change in time and is available no matter where we are. This is because, at the deepest or highest level, the true object of all of our love is God, a point I have made previously and to which I will return again.

So, an infatuation may be a form of a transient emotion, *vyabhicāra-bhāva*, that is mixed in nature and expresses itself on the surface of our experience. On the other hand, an abiding bhāva, *sthāyibhāva*, moves more in the depths of our experience. So, too, it remains longer. We may not feel it on the surface of our experience at a particular moment, yet it is nevertheless still there. It is powerful and dynamic yet also quiet and, accordingly, subtle. It is also pure, in the sense that it is not a mixture or combination of other bhāvas. It is like a deep ocean current that is not really affected by the movements of various temporary surface waves.

You might think of a time in which you burst into laughter in a humorous situation. At that moment you may have experienced a combination of emotions, depending on the setting: perhaps delight, or surprise, and so on. Indian thought holds that this momentary experience of mirth would not be possible if there were not already present within you the possibility of happiness. You may not feel happy all the time, yet the potential to do so nevertheless remains within you. It is a more permanent aspect of your emotional being than is the more temporary moment of laughter. Similarly, the delight you may feel in that moment, or the surprise, are themselves made possible by your deeper, more permanent capability to experience those transient emotions to begin with.

Just as a person swimming in the ocean will experience the movement of surface waves but may not feel the presence of the deep current, so too a person will experience a temporary emotion but may not always feel an abiding emotion, at least on the surface of his or her awareness. Similarly, Indian thought holds that, while perhaps it is less readily or obviously experienced, an abiding emotion or state is deeper, more lasting and purer than a temporary surface emotion.

Because it is more permanent, purer and more powerful, an abiding emotion is in a sense more real than a surface emotion. Indeed, according to this line of thought, a transient emotion would not even exist if there were no abiding emotion underneath it, just as there could be no surface to an ocean if the ocean had no depth. On the other hand, the repeated or sustained experience of a surface emotion can deepen it into an abiding emotion. As we will note later in this chapter, there are important ramifications in the yogic life of this possibility of deepening a bhāva.

Rasa as the Pure Essence of an Emotion

Indian thought holds that each and any deep and abiding mood or emotion itself has its own pure essence or *rasa*, a word that connotes a delectable, subtle juice or flavor. The rasa of an emotion is like the essence of a perfume: it is that emotion's purest, finest quality that exists within all manifest expressions of that emotion.

So, to return to the example above, when purified of other sentiments, experiences leading to moments of laughter, *hāsa*, express a deeper, more abiding potential for joviality, *hāsa sthāyibhāva*; and the pure essence of this joviality itself is the even deeper essence of buoyant happiness known as *hāsya rasa*. The same would hold true for the experience of other emotions. So, for another example, the temporary experience of fortitude, *utsāha*, expresses a deeper and more abiding potential to experience courage, *vīra*, and the essence of this deeper *vīra sthāyibhāva* is an even deeper state of emotional strength and commitment known as *vīra rasa*, the powerful pure essence of courage itself.

Each of the various rasas is itself and in its own way a manifestation of an encompassing, single rasa sometimes known as *ekarasa*: the "one essence" of all rasas. Accordingly, at their most refined and deepest level, all emotions in their own way give expression to a single essence. Tradition regards this ultimate, deepest rasa as *mahābhāva*: the "great state," the "sublime emotion." This mahābhāva is the state of Love itself. To relish this Love in its purity is described as *mahānubhāva*, the "great experience."

According to devotional theologians and philosophers in India, this ultimate essence of all rasas, this great state, is none other than *bhakti rasa*, the essence of spiritual love. Love is the source of our happiness, our courage, our steadfastness, our sense of wonder, just as it is of all other emotions that emerge from and express a deep affirmation of existence.

This way of viewing the emotions is based on the understanding that at the very core of our being moves a divine force that gives rise to and supports the inherent goodness and value of existence. This is the power of God's own Love. The emotions variously express that affirmation. Sometimes Love reveals itself more directly than at other times. Sometimes it may lie concealed in emotions that may not seem to express it. Experiencing and refining the emotions grounded in their love, the bhakta remains attentive always to the divine Love that is their source and purest essence.

The Yogic Refinement of the Emotions

As a simple exercise in developing the openness to more abiding levels of emotion, you might notice your feelings when, for example, you find a beautiful flower whose stem has been broken. You may experience a momentary sense of sorrow, *śoka*. As you do so, allow your spirit to dwell in that feeling.

Then, distinguish the sentiment of sadness from the immediate sensual experience of the flower itself. This is to say, experience pure sadness without identifying it with the flower as the object of that sadness. When you distinguish your feeling of sorrow from the object of that sadness, you can come to see that you already have the emotion of sorrow itself within you and that the flower has drawn that emotion into your awareness.

Then, distinguish this abiding emotion of sorrow from other feelings you might experience in view of the flower, such as a sense of wonder in front of its beauty or some other sentiment. Separate the sadness from the different emotions that express themselves in the mixture of your outward experience. In other words, distill the sadness from within the other emotions. Refine your experience of sadness. Experience it as itself, independent of other emotions. As you do so, you will enter into the abiding emotion of sorrow itself, *śoka-sthāyibhāva*. You can also do this with any of the other bhāvas you may be feeling in the emotional mixture of your experience.

Continuing in this exercise in refinement, you can enter even more deeply into this abiding sentiment of sadness. As you do so, you may then taste the deep essence of that emotion itself, which in this case is the essence of compassion, *karuṇā rasa*. You would not feel sadness in your experience of the flower if you did not already possess the capability of compassion.

Refining and entering even deeper into that state of compassion, and distinguishing it from the essence of other rasas, you then can experience the ekarasa, the single essence within all rasas. This is the mahābhāva. This great bhāva is none other than love.

In other words, the source of your sadness at seeing the broken flower was your inherent capability to love. Your sense of wonder at the flower's beauty also emerges out of love. Immersing your awareness into the refined essence of this love, you can taste the nectar of divine Love itself, which is the Source of your own love. Entering more fully into that Love, you can bring its light more fully into your life as a whole. That Love remains with you, even when you are no longer in the garden and the sadness you felt for the broken flower has passed.

Even anger, *krodha*, can be based in love — if it is anger that arises from the sense that a person's inner dignity, either someone else's or our own, has been mistreated. This is in part the source of our sense of justice and of our respect for others. Of course, it is important to repeat, our feelings in this regard may be driven and distorted by narrow self-concern. Again, it is necessary to distinguish emotion from desire, as they are understood from a yogic perspective. If there is no selfish desire involved, then the foundational source of righteous anger still rests in a deep affirmation of the inherent value of existence. It therefore has its origins in love.

The difference between a yogic use of anger and a non-yogic use of anger is that, whereas a non-yogī clings to the transient emotion and gets caught in a web of other transient emotions temporarily associated with it, a yogī distinguishes anger based in love from other less-loving temporary emotions; gives appropriate response to that loving anger; and then allows the temporary emotions themselves to pass. At the same time, the yogī refines the energy of the loving anger so that he or she experiences its pure essence — here, *raudra rasa*, fierce courage in the face of unloving sentiments — and then refines the essence of that courage even further until he or she tastes the purer essence even within it. This essence is the mahābhāva, and this mahābhāva is love. Understood in this way, the source of one's courageous commitment to righteousness and justice is therefore one's love for God. The same holds true for all emotions in their most refined form.

Beneficial Dispassion in the Yogic Refinement of the Emotions

A key to the yogic use of emotions is therefore to experience the changing waves of the surface emotions yet not to be caught in them. Here is another way to say this: We can enjoy the dance of life without getting caught in our various dramas. This process of becoming free from drama so that we can enjoy the dance takes place within the larger sādhana of spiritual love as a whole and thus includes, once again, the yogic practices of continual and diligent self-inquiry and illuminating discernment between what is truly loving and what is not. (See Chapter 7 for a brief discussion of these yogic practices.) Each of these spiritual disciplines is important and necessary. Without scrupulous self-inquiry we can remain distracted by our selfish desires and will not progress spiritually as quickly as we might otherwise. Clear discrimination allows us to recognize and distinguish different emotions we may be experiencing and therefore be more able to isolate them from each other. Then, we can see them more for what they are, unalloyed with others.

The process of refinement continues, as before, with the discipline of beneficial dispassion. The yogic discipline of vairāgya is itself said by some Indian philosophers and theologians to consist of different levels or stages, namely: the striving stage, the separation stage, the one-sense stage, the controlled stage and the highest stage.

At the "striving" level of dispassion, *yatamāna vairāgya*, we recognize that there is benefit in moving toward inner equanimity and we undertake effort to become less entangled in the outward pull of the surface emotions. By continuing practice in this regard, we can gain more awareness of inner states. Then, at the "separation" stage of dispassion, *vyatireka vairāgya*, we distinguish the various components of our inner experience. We may notice the presence of, say, happiness, or sadness, or loneliness, or contentment, or any other of the countless feelings and emotions that play in the mind. At the separation stage of dispassion we observe the way in which these inner states express themselves in the flow of our thoughts and moods. Rather than letting these sentiments carry our attention in their own direction, we merely watch them come and go, differentiating them as they rise and fall in the movements of the mind. We observe them, acknowledge them, and — not clinging to them — let them dissolve into the spaciousness of the mind and heart.

Having separated the various states of mind and noted the flow of thoughts, we can then mindfully focus our awareness on a single object. This is the "one-sense" stage of dispassion, or *ekendriya vairāgya*. In Indian psychology, the mind is regarded as one of the sense organs and, as such, can be either distracted or focused, in a manner similar to the way the other five senses can be distracted or focused. At this "one-sense" stage, we direct our attention away from the five outward senses and hold it instead on the subtle, inner essence of the object of awareness. In a yogic life of devotion, this object would be the divine Beloved, as we experience that sublime Presence within the object of our love.

Continued practice then can take us to the "controlled" stage of dispassion, *vaśīkara vairāgya*. Having become aware of the wandering nature of self-centered desires, we tame them by not entertaining them.

We thereby calm the otherwise seemingly uncontrolled jumpiness of those harmful desires based on a sense of lack by holding our awareness in the reality that is the Beloved's steady and abiding presence in our hearts.

This yogic movement through levels of beneficial dispassion leads toward the highest stage of beneficial dispassion *parāvairāgya*. Here, we can become free from habits and thoughts that distract or interfere with our movement into Love. This letting go of attachment to surface emotions brings an increased ability to experience all of them in their deeper purity, richness and vitality, for we are no longer ensnarled by our feelings. This leads to a certain freedom from the bonds of desire while at the same time experiencing the fullness of the emotions.

The Importance of Attitude

As I hope these comments in this chapter so far have indicated, any emotion, feeling or other state of mind or heart can reveal and give us access to a deeper Love, if it is refined and used productively. At the same time, it should be said again, as yogīs and yoginīs we can work to refine our understanding and expression of our emotions and other sentiments so that they are less confused and muddied by the force of harmful desires. Our moods and feelings can take us in different directions, depending on their nature and what we do with them. At the extremes, we can establish and get caught in harmful emotional patterns that distract or degrade our love, or we can use our emotions to come closer to Love itself.

This is one reason why our intentions and attitudes are so important in the yogic life. (Remember, "attitude" is one way to translate *bhāva*.) To explain this, I would ask you to think once more of the relationship between transient surface feelings and deeper, more abiding emotions. If a surface emotion is entertained repeatedly, it can take on a more permanent and deeper nature. Once it has become more permanent, it can then affect the rise and fall of other surface emotions. If we allow negative thoughts and desires repeatedly to hold sway over us, then their effect on us will become deeper, more permanent and, in this way, more harmful. On the other hand, if we set out repeatedly and more often to express love in our lives, then the love we do feel in passing moments will become increasingly deeper and more lasting.

Accordingly, it is important that, as yogīs and yoginīs, we hold an intention to strengthen our healthy, loving emotions. If we do not hold this intention, this attitude, then the love we feel in any given moment may soon dissipate. If we keep an attitude that is open to and supports love, then the love we do feel becomes ever stronger.

The Use of Devotional Settings

Transient sentiments arise in some context or another. Indian thought calls such a setting for an emotion a *vibhāva*. For example, a glimpse of the rising moon may lead you to a sense of wonder. Similarly, entering a sacred space may evoke from you a mood of reverence. Sitting in a quiet, calm and clean place for regular meditation can give rise to the contemplative mood. This is one reason why it is important to honor such settings for yogic practices. They help you strengthen beneficial devotional attitudes, and this can help you experience deeper levels of an abiding devotional emotion.

There are two types of such settings. There is a setting that awakens or ignites a devotional mood. This is known as an *uddīpana vibhāva*. There is also a setting that supports or takes hold of a mood once awakened. This is an *ālambhana vibhāva*.

You can probably recall examples of awakening settings in your life. You may have found that you felt the inner presence of the divine Beloved as you sat quietly in meditation. Perhaps you experienced a powerful moment of insight as you read a great one's words or studied a sacred text. Or, you may have felt a surge of love when you heard the first notes being played by musicians at the beginning of a sacred or beautiful song. You may have felt at such times that the setting — the meditation room, the words, the music, and so on — has somehow brought forth from within you a feeling of love that you sense has been there all along but perhaps has been dormant. The setting has awakened it in you.

There can be innumerable such awakenings throughout our lives. For some people, they might happen every few years, or perhaps once in their lifetimes. On the other hand, they can also take place several times a day, even several times an hour. Some people experience them almost continually.

In any case, once an awakening to Love has opened your heart, then you can strengthen the positive emotion it releases by returning to a setting that nourishes this mood.

This is to say that you can then establish a supportive setting for your devotional sentiments. For example, if you have found that you feel the presence of God when you sit in a particular place, then go back to that place whenever you can. Enter it with deep respect and reverence. Immerse yourself in the atmosphere, steep your spirit in the quiet yet vibrant energy of the sacred place. In this case, that setting serves both as an awakening setting and a supportive setting at the same time.

Similarly, it helps to establish a particular place in your home where you can meditate. Return to it knowing that it is a special place. Feel the expectancy associated with waiting to rejoin the Beloved within you, and then feel delight when the presence of love enters your heart.

The undertaking of yogic practices themselves serves as both an awakening and supportive setting for a life of spiritual love. Such settings are established when you listen to and contemplate the words of a spiritual master. You can repeat a mantra through japa-repetition. Study the sacred texts. Carry an image of your Beloved in your mind and heart. Meet with others of like heart to share your experiences and insights in the spirit of satsang. Perform selfless service in the name of the Beloved for the welfare of the larger world.

These practices of bhakti yoga, and others like them, can serve as ways to awaken, nourish and strengthen devotional sentiments. When you experience emotions of love that arise in these settings, then relish those feelings. Immerse yourself in them. Don't just let the warmth of love pass through you and then dissipate. Experience that love. Feel it. Honor it. Go deeper into it.

As you do so, you will strengthen the supportive devotional mood even more. Then, the supporting attitude itself will become an awakening cause, which can then be strengthened still more by an even deeper and more focused devotional practice. It is an ever-refreshing cycle. This is one reason why the further you move along the path of spiritual love the more you may delight in the disciplines and practices of bhakti yoga, for they allow you to adore the divine Beloved all the time, with all the heart.

Terms appearing in Chapter 8

(See also the vocabulary in Tables V-VIII, below)

ālambhana vibhāva A particular setting or context that supports an emotion, mood or state of mind once it has arisen.

bhajana Literally, "sharing" one's adoration for the divine object of one's devotion through acts of worship and song. It thus comes to mean both "devotional worship" and "singing sacred songs of devotion." This Sanskrit word is the source of the vernacular word *bhajan*, meaning "devotional song."

bhāva Initially, *bhāva* means "coming into existence" and thus "existing, being;" thus, "a way of being" and thereby a "state of mind, temperament, attitude, personal manner" and also "mood, feeling, sentiment, emotion." In some contexts it also means "inner essence" and "soul" and thus "spiritual heart." The term also characterizes various modes of relationship with Divinity. Indian thought recognizes different levels and types of *bhāva* (see Tables V and VI, below).

eka rasa The single (*eka*) sublime "juice" or "flavor" (*rasa*) that stands as the purest essence of all of the heart's emotions.

hāsa Laughter, mirth.

krodha Passionate anger.

mahābhāva The "great state, sublime state" that is Love; similarly, the devotional love that supports, stands within, and yet also transcends all other states.

mahānubhāva The great (*mahā*) experience (*anubhāva*); this is to say, the experience of *mahābhāva* (see above).

rasa Literally "sap, juice," thus "delectable flavor;" from this it comes to refer to the "sublime essence" of an emotion or inner state.

śoka Sorrow, grief, sadness.

sthāyibhāva	An abiding (*sthāyi*), deeper emotion that remains within the heart even though it may not be experienced on the surface of one's feelings.
uddīpana vibhāva	A setting or context (*vibhāva*, see below) that awakens or ignites a particular emotion or mood.
utsāha	Fortitude.
vaśīkara vairāgya	The "controlled" (*vaśikara*) stage of beneficial dispassion (*vairāgya*).
vibhāva	An external setting or context that gives rise to or supports an emotion or mood.
vyabhicārabhāva	A transient (*vyabhicāra*) mood, feeling, sentiment and so on (*bhāva*) that moves at the surface level of the emotions.

Table V

Levels of Bhāva as "Feeling, Sentiment, Mood, Emotion"

vyabhicārabhāva	*sthāyibhāva*	*rasa*	*mahābhāva*
Transient (*vyabhicāra*), superficial.	Abiding (*sthāyi*: literally "standing"), deeper.	The pure essence of an emotion.	The "great bhava;" the state grounded in, supported by and infused with pure, sublime Love.

Table VI

Some Sectarian Classifications of Bhāva

A Conventional Devotional Vedāntic Classification	A Conventional Vaiṣṇava Classification	A Conventional Śaiva and Śākta Classification
pūjā bhāva A worshipful state, which finds expression and direction in instances of external worship. It can also refer to the inner state in which one can approach the moment at hand as if one were approaching the sacred.	***dāsya bhāva*** In which one offers service to God as a servant would to a loving and kind master.	***paśu bhāva*** The animal-state of devotion. Draws on qualities we might associate with those of a tethered, domestic animal. Like a cow on a rope follows a farmer who leads it, so too one whose devotion of this nature trusts God and looks to God for guidance.
stava bhāva An attitude of praise in which one brings an appreciative response to the Love revealed in God's divine names and qualities.	***sākhya bhāva*** In which one feels a deep and loving friendship with God.	***vīra bhāva*** The hero-state of devotion; has an active, energetic quality. This is a form of devotion involving a courageous engagement in the yogic life in service of the divine Beloved.
dhyāna bhāva The attitude of meditation, in which one holds the attitude of entering attentively into the contours of the spiritual heart, the home within one's own being of the divine Heart that pulsates within all beings.	***vātsalya bhāva*** In which one feels love for God that is likened to the unconditional, fearless, gentle love a mother feels for her child.	***divya bhāva*** The illumined-state of devotion; can also be translated as the "bright" or "heavenly" state. It is associated with the intellect and thus with study, contemplation and meditation.
brahma bhāva Absorption in the divine Presence. In the devotional context, here one would allow the light of Love to shine within one's own awareness so completely that this Love would envelop and illumine all one's other sensibilities.	***śānta bhāva*** Characterized with a sense of peace and of easeful trust in God.	
	mādhurya bhāva A devotional state that expresses a powerful, compelling love that is like paramours meeting secretly. It can also be like the sweet committed love that is reminiscent of the mature affection one can feel for a spouse or life-partner, in which case this devotional attitude is also known as *kānta bhāva*.	

Table VII

Levels of Beneficial Dispassion (*Vairāgya*)

parāvairāgya
The highest beneficial dispassion in which one is free from narrowly self-centered habits and thoughts that limit one's unconditional love.

aparāvairāgya
The "non-highest" level of beneficial dispassion.
It is said to consist of four stages:

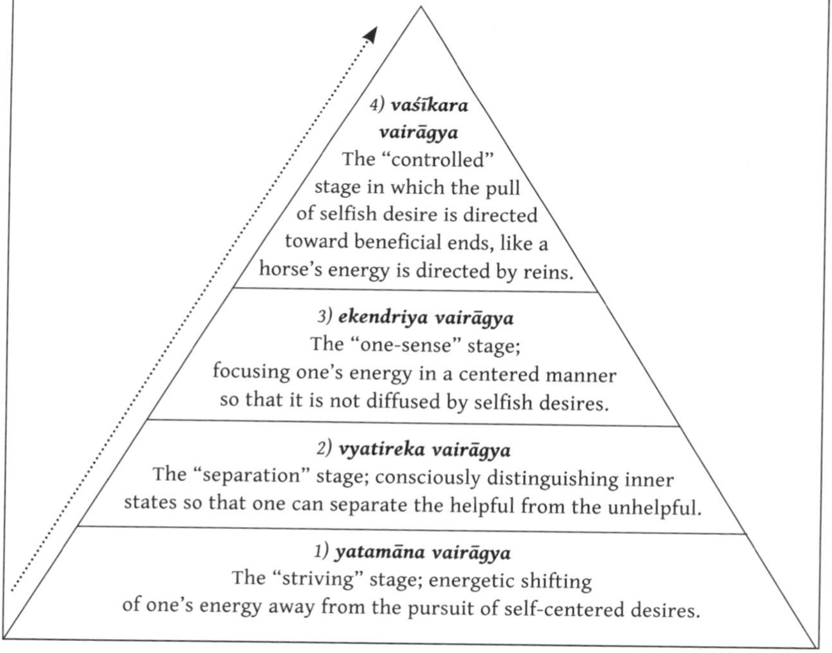
*4) **vaśīkara vairāgya***
The "controlled" stage in which the pull of selfish desire is directed toward beneficial ends, like a horse's energy is directed by reins.
*3) **ekendriya vairāgya***
The "one-sense" stage; focusing one's energy in a centered manner so that it is not diffused by selfish desires.
*2) **vyatireka vairāgya***
The "separation" stage; consciously distinguishing inner states so that one can separate the helpful from the unhelpful.
*1) **yatamāna vairāgya***
The "striving" stage; energetic shifting of one's energy away from the pursuit of self-centered desires.

Table VIII

Types of Rasa

Classical schools of Indian aesthetic thought recognize at least eight *rasas* as the pure, refined essence of an emotion:

śṛngāra rasa	The sublime emotional essence of mature, beautiful affectionate love.
hāsya rasa	The emotional essence of mirthful, exuberant happiness.
karuṇā rasa	The essence of deep compassion.
raudra rasa	The essence of fierce, righteous anger.
vīra rasa	The essence of heroic courage.
bhāyanaka rasa	The essence of fear.
bībhatsa rasa	The essence of disgust.
adbhūta rasa	The essence of wondrous surprise.

Some schools also recognize a ninth rasa:

śānta rasa	The sublime essence of Peace.

And some devotion schools recognize a tenth, namely:

bhakti rasa	The sublime emotional essence of devotional love.

Chapter 9

Equanimity, Mindfulness and the Calming of Harmful Desire

The refinement of the emotions and other sentiments brings a bhakta deeper into the sublimity that is the Heart. Those who taste the essence of spiritual love, bhakti rasa, can find that its delicate flavor gives definition, direction and meaning to their lives as yogīs and yoginīs. They can more fully experience the richness of their emotions and yet are not pushed and pulled about by them. Within the movements of their emotions themselves bhaktas can stand in a deep and pervasive equanimity of being.

This is not to say that they no longer have any yearning. Bhaktas remain filled with longing to honor, adore and serve the divine Beloved dwelling in the true Heart. As their yearning deepens and matures, though, they come to an increasing understanding that their love is distorted when their devotion is driven by hidden motivations or otherwise self-centered desires. As yogīs and yoginīs they become more able to distinguish the yogic difference between unconditional yogic yearning and conditional desire and to affirm the power and direction of their longing while dissipating their selfish desires.

In a sūtra we will not have time to discuss here, sūtra 21, Nārada points to the *gopīs* as examples of this higher form of bhakti. You will remember here that, according to tradition, these are simple, unlettered village women whose love for Kṛṣṇa is pure, total and encompassing. In the wisdom of their hearts, they understand the difference between selfless love for the Beloved and devotion that is given for selfish motivations. The *Bhāgavata Purāṇa* tells of their understanding that this lower type of devotion, "is a pretense that is maintained until the object has been obtained." The gopīs liken such attraction to that of birds for trees from which they have eaten all the fruit. Such birds fly away from the trees; their desire fades when the object that fulfills that desire is no longer needed.[84]

In this image of those who love the Adorable one, the gopīs do not seek selfish satisfaction of their expectations or insistent desires. Their love is not based on a sense of lack. Rather, their longing is directed to Kṛṣṇa, who draws from them a Love that already exists in their hearts. This God-centered yearning releases that Love in the gopīs, who then experience it in their emotions. Kṛṣṇa describes them in this way: "Their minds are always on me. I am their life-breath. Their purpose is me. . . . Their hearts are given to me, their most Beloved, their life, their soul."[85] Unlike desire that fades and dissipates when it is fulfilled, the gopīs' emotional love for Kṛṣṇa is constant, abiding and given to him at all times. The many things they do throughout the day give them a setting to remember Kṛṣṇa: "while milking the cows, threshing, churning, cleansing the floor, rocking cradles of crying babies, watering the garden, cleaning and so on, the gopīs sing of Kṛṣṇa, their hearts filled with love for him."[86]

In two other sūtras we do not have space to discuss here, sūtras 22 and 23, Nārada notes that, even in this higher devotion, bhaktas are continually to direct their love to the supreme Beloved so that they do not distort the purity of their love with otherwise selfish desires or motivations. As embodied beings, bhaktas' feelings and emotions are very human in nature. Yet, they direct their emotions less toward accommodating their egoistic desires and more toward communion with the true, Highest object of their love. In sūtra 22 we read that, "Even in the case of the gopīs, there can be no objection regarding their forgetfulness of knowledge of God's magnificence." This is to say that the gopīs' sentiments were always informed by their remembrance of God. As sūtra 23 says, "For without that [knowledge, the gopīs' passionate sentiments] would be like that of decadent lovers." As we have noted in Chapter 7, the bhakti tradition recognizes the difference between devotion with an ulterior motivation and devotion without such motivation, and regards the latter as the higher form of spiritual love. Desire associated with what Nārada describes as "decadent lovers" is different from the gopīs' longing because, whereas the former is based on self-centered use of another as the object of desire, the gopīs' love is centered on God, the true Object of their yearning itself.

Continual mindfulness of the Beloved reduces one's tendency to seek gratification of one's narrowly self-centered desires. This mindfulness thus establishes and nourishes an inward state of contentment and equanimity. When there is less attachment to the gratification of these desires, then there is more possibility for mindfulness of God's unconditional freedom, beauty and love. This mindfulness sharpens one's awareness of God's constant presence, enriches one's reverence and deepens one's gratitude.

In this chapter we will reflect on the contours of these reciprocal and mutually supportive states of equanimity, mindfulness and the calming of narrowly self-centered desire. We will begin with the latter characteristic. As a way to focus my comments, I will refer to sūtra 7:

सा न कामयमाना निरोधरूपत्वात् ॥७॥

sā na kāmayamānā nirodharūpatvāt

It does not arise from desire because it is of the nature of calming control.

— Sūtra 7

At first, the point of the sūtra may seem to contradict to some degree what we have seen in the previous chapter, namely, that God can be worshipped with all the emotions, moods, attitudes and so on. A key to resolving possible confusion in this regard is, again, to remember the difference between a desire and an emotion. As you recall from Chapter 8, a desire is based on a sense of lacking something while an emotion is grounded in an inner state that already exists. With this in mind, let's turn to the sūtra at hand.

"It does not arise from selfish desire"

The operative term in this phrase is the word *kāma*, a word which, like so many words dealing with love, has various levels and shades of meaning.

Across the literatures of India throughout history, the word *kāma* generally refers to a longing of some sort, a wish that seeks to be realized, and thus a desire that reaches for fulfillment. This is often understood in quite positive ways. You might recall that in the Introduction I quoted and discussed verses from the *Ṛg Veda* regarding the divine force of Love-yearning that draws Being itself out of Nonbeing. According to that perspective, without this procreative, divine longing-to-be there would be no creation, and thus no transformation, no completion, no fulfillment. The word that early sacred song uses to refer to this power is *kāma*.

Over time, the word came also to refer to this universal impulse toward creation as it moves within the human psyche. Kāma in this sense is sexual longing. The sexual impulse is one of the most personal expressions of the universe's own pull toward existence. It drives the divine yearning-to-be and the divine yearning-to-share one's self. As such, sexual longing and acts of sexual love are two of the most important, valued and beautiful components of human existence.

On the other hand, the generative and loving force of kāma at the sexual level can also be constricted by self-centered motivations. In this case, procreative longing finds expression in the pursuit of self-centered pleasure at the expense of another, who is used as an object of this desire. In this sense, kāma is lust rather than love. Lust is a distortion of Love. Its source lies in the power of creative longing, yet it is a delimiting expression of that longing. Kāma in this sense is not a yearning to express an inner fullness but rather is directed toward satisfying a perceived sense of lack. In this latter use of the term, kāma is therefore a form of desire, as I characterized it toward the beginning of this chapter.

By extension, by the time of the *Bhakti Sūtra*, kāma came to be understood by some philosophers to be characteristic of lust of any sort. One can lust for power, or for riches, or for attention from others. Understood in this way, kāma is not so much a loving, creative force but rather a manipulative impulse that seeks satisfaction by gaining control over the object of desire. This is the sense in which I interpret the use of the term in this sūtra.

Desire that is driven by kāma, when the word is used in this manner, is impermanent and exhaustible. This is because feelings driven by kāma may be satisfied for a moment, but then either the object of desire changes and no longer brings this satisfaction, or the lover, having in some way gained the object of desire, loses interest in that object. In any case, the satisfaction the lover once felt disappears or fades. Then, losing this satisfaction, the lover feels desire again, and the whole cycle repeats itself. In this way, kāma is almost like addiction. The feelings it brings may be quite pleasant, but they do not last and eventually lead to disappointment, a returning sense of lack, or, worse, of futility and meaninglessness.

Desire characterized as kāma, thus understood, may feel like love in some ways, for love is certainly also a satisfying and pleasing state to be in. But such desire is not the highest kind of love, nor does it therefore characterize supreme devotion. Therefore, when sūtra 7 says that supreme love "does not arise from kāma" it thereby urges bhaktas to be mindful of their motivations in offering their devotion.

Tradition therefore distinguishes what is at times called *sakāma bhakti* and *niṣkāma bhakti*, the former being devotion offered with self-centered desire for some sort of pleasure or gain, and the latter being devotion that is offered without desire for selfish gratification.[87] Unlike sakāma-bhaktas, who would offer bhakti to satisfy a desire of some sort, niṣkāma-bhaktas do not offer devotion to the Beloved to please themselves, but rather because their love for the Beloved rises spontaneously in their hearts. Similarly, whereas sakāma bhakti turns on attachment to or manipulation of a temporal object of desire, niṣkāma bhakti is love for the eternal Beloved, whom the devotee honors and cherishes but does not seek to control. So, too, whereas feelings associated with sakāma bhakti can become old and stale, those associated with niṣkāma bhakti remain ever fresh and ever new. In selfless love there is always the sense of discovery, spontaneity, wonder and mystery.

The opposite of kāma in this sense of lust is preman, love. Whereas kāma as lust is manipulative, seeks self-centered gratification, is temporary and exhaustible and leads ultimately to disappointment, preman as love honors that which is loved, does not seek to satisfy egoistic desires, is permanent and inexhaustible, and leads to true and lasting fulfillment.[88]

Viewed in this way, preman is niṣkāma in nature, that is to say, it is without kāma. At its purest level, preman becomes paramapreman, the highest and purest love. As we know from sūtra 2, this is the level of love — paramapreman — of which Nārada speaks in his *Bhakti Sūtra* as a whole.

When the first part of our current sūtra says that devotion "does not arise from kāma" it is therefore saying that love, in its highest form, is not influenced or driven by self-centered desire. The second half of the sūtra leads us to a fuller understanding of the state of highest spiritual love by juxtaposing it to that reference to kāma.

"It is of the nature of control"

Here, Nārada tells us that bhakti as paramapreman is characterized by an inner state he describes as *nirodha*. In the yogic context, nirodha has at times been interpreted as a stopping of something, as in the rather frequent translation of Patañjali's definition of yoga as the cessation (nirodha) of the fluctuations of the mind.[89]

I interpret the use of the term in the current sūtra somewhat differently. The word *nirodha* rather literally refers to an enclosure of some sort, as for example a corral in which horses may be kept from wandering. That they are held in a corral does not mean that the horses cease to exist; rather, it is that they do not scatter in various directions pursuing satisfaction of their particular desires. As living beings, they continue to embody the energy of life, yet this energy is controlled. The corral thus holds a living, energetic calmness of sorts. The horses' strong energy can then be harnessed and directed in beneficial, transformative ways when they are guided from the corral.

The same would be true of the energy of our yearning. We can understand the word *nirodha* here to describe a yogic state in which we fully experiences the presence of energetic Love within us, yet we also distinguish the fullness of this inherent Love from the impulse of temporary desires based on a sense of lack. When the craving that fuels our harmful desires is not fed, those desires can calm down and cease to exert their manipulative pull.

Those who practice bhakti yoga will therefore be attentive to their true motivations for offering devotion to God and will work to free themselves from the pressures of self-centered kāma. They can do this through the continuing practices of self-inquiry, illuminating discernment, beneficial dispassion and renunciation we have already discussed in Chapters 7 and 8. When there is a stilling of self-centered desire there is a calming of one's insistence for conditional gratification and thus more possibility of openness to unconditional Love.

To immerse in Love is to return to the true Heart. It is to remember God, the divine Presence, at the purest level of our own hearts. While there may be a tendency to forget this Presence, it is never absent from us. The Heart pulsates in all things. Its Love can be revealed in manifold ways. We can turn toward it in any and all moments of our lives. Forgetfulness of the Heart, on the other hand, dissipates one's sense of Love as real and as ultimately valuable. Forgetfulness also adds force to the sometimes insistent demands of our narrow self-centered desires. Perhaps this is in part why Nārada says the following in sūtra 77:

> **सुखदुःखेच्छालाभादित्यक्ते काले प्रतीक्षमाणे**
> **क्षणार्द्धमपि व्यर्थं न नेयम् ॥७७॥**
>
> ***sukha-duḥkhecchā-lābhādityakte kāle pratīkṣamāṇe***
> ***kṣaṇārddham-api vyarthaṁ na neyam***
>
> Relinquishing happiness, dissatisfaction, self-centered willfulness, worldly gain, and so on, when there is attentive awareness in every moment, not even half an instant should be passed uselessly.
>
> — Sūtra 77

"When there is mindfulness in every moment,
not even half an instant should be passed uselessly"

We turn first to the second part of the sūtra, which marks the importance of developing and clarifying one's constant attentiveness to the moment at hand. This is an awareness of the unique particularity of each instant, framed by the larger vision of God's encompassing presence within all moments.

The adjective *pratīkṣamāna* means "of the nature of *pratīkṣa*," the latter word meaning "turning the eyes upon, looking at, beholding, respecting, venerating." I have translated *pratīkṣamāna* as "mindfulness" to suggest a state of undistracted, immediate, attentive awareness of what is happening in the moment at hand.

You might recall for a moment seeing something that drew all of your attention. Perhaps it was a delicate flower, into whose petals you paused to look closely. All thoughts of other concerns disappear for the time being while your mind is held on the beauty in front of you. Here, your gaze is pratikṣamāna in nature. In the spiritual context, that attentive awareness of something can deepen into a state of respect, reverence and even veneration.

Entering into a state of mindful awareness, you are more able to see an object as it really is in this very moment. Here, your attentiveness in a sense allows the object to present itself in its own pure nature. In the clarity of such awareness, you can be more open to experience the immediacy of the object in the moment, that is to say, in a way that is not mediated by your own preconceptions and desires. This leads you to a sharper, clearer and more refined appreciation of it in its unique particularity.

You can apply this same mindful attentiveness wherever you are and in whatever you are doing. Nārada says that it is to be practiced at every moment (*kāle*, literally "in time"). Each and every instant in the flow of time gives you a setting to practice appreciative mindfulness. Mindfulness enables you to listen in an expansive, focused, attentive way to the sound of rain on the roof, the whisper of snow being blown across an open field, or the chatter of leaves quivering on their stems as the breeze crosses over them. When your fascination is held undistracted by the tiny universe that is held within the clear brilliance of a dewdrop on a blade of grass, this is mindfulness. Mindfulness allows you to feel the subtle movement of air on your upper lip as you breathe, the gentle pressure of your eyelids against your eyes, the soft weight of your tongue on the floor of your mouth. Mindfulness clears the noisy clutter of your thoughts and brings your appreciative attention right to the moment at hand, as it presents itself to you.

Here is an exercise in mindfulness you can undertake. Imagine that each new second in your life is your very first experience of the world. Turn your eyes to what is in front of you. Let's say you are holding an apple. Look at that apple as if you had never seen anything before, much less that particular apple. I suspect that you would feel a sense of wonder and of delightful mystery. Isn't that apple gorgeous?

In fact, each and every moment is brand new. It has never happened before. When you experience the newness of the moment at hand, then what you might otherwise experience as ordinary in a way becomes extraordinary. When you sweep the floor with mindfulness you feel the pressure of the broomstick in your hands; you hear the sound of the brushes as they move across the floor and see the textures, shapes and colors of the small objects you sweep into the pan; you experience the flow of time as you step from one foot to the other. Attention to the simple act of sweeping the floor becomes an invitation to celebrate the miracle of a universe in which there are such things as brooms, floors and you to sweep them. It could so easily be different. None of this could exist whatsoever.

As you read these words, realize that this moment right now is a completely new moment. And here is another one — right now — and another, and another. Time is ever-new. What a wonder existence is!

Sometimes when sweeping the floor or reading a book you might find that a desire creeps into your mind. Perhaps you wish you were doing something else. The degree to which that desire infuses your awareness is the degree to which you are no longer living in the moment at hand. When that happens, you may tend to lose your sense of appreciation, respect and reverence for the moment at hand. If this tendency becomes generalized and extends to your experience of other moments, too, then one possible result is that you can eventually lose your sense of the appreciation for life itself.

On the other hand, when we become more aware of the moment at hand we feel a sense of the mystery of life, and thus open ourselves to the experience of wonder. Each moment becomes sacred. Our gratitude deepens and widens.

This is one reason why meditation can be so helpful. When you meditate you bring your awareness precisely to the current moment. You can do so in a number of ways. Sitting quietly, you may focus your attention on the sensations in your body and on the subtle flow of energy that courses through it. You can become aware of the movement of your breath: the rise and fall of your abdomen, the expansion and contraction of your chest and back muscles, the cooling and warming flow of air across your lips, tongue and throat. You can become aware of the beats of your heart and of that pulse as it appears in the arteries in your neck, temples, legs, and arms. You thus notice that there is change and movement within your body, even as it sits very still, as one moment passes to the next. You see that each moment both flows from the previous one and yet also exists in its own completeness and uniqueness. At the physical level, there can be no stopping of this movement. The body does not cling to one moment over another. In the supportive Love that is the divine Heart, each moment is new.

Similarly, in meditation you can become aware of the movement of thoughts and images rising into and passing through your mind. In non-meditative states, we allow our thoughts a kind of free reign because we are not really aware of them as they emerge; alternatively, we cling to certain thoughts and, in so doing, inwardly resist the emergence of a new pulsation of consciousness. In meditation, though, we observe our thoughts in the same way we observe the rising and falling of our breath. We see them come into our awareness, and we see them dissolve within it. We experience less attachment to them, and thus become more a witness of them. In so doing, we both experience our thoughts and are free from bondage to them. Again, we see each moment to be new.

As you develop this witness consciousness, *sākṣī bhāva*, you can more clearly see the deeper concepts or attitudes that direct and condition our thoughts. A thought may be driven by an expansive benevolence on your part, or it may narrate a constricting self-concern. It may be driven by hope, or it may arise out of fear. It may repeat a memory, or it may express a fantasy. Most often, any given thought is framed and energized by a number of underlying emotions, desires, values and motivations. Immersed in witness consciousness, you become more aware of these forces that push your thoughts. You see them as they are. As you do so, you are freer to determine which forces you want to cultivate and which you will allow to dissipate.

In deeper levels of meditation the object of one's awareness is not only the physical and subtle experiences of one's body, the movement of one's thoughts, and the ideas that condition them; here, in deep meditation, the object of one's mindfulness is that very awareness itself. Meditation involves the gentle, disciplined freeing of the mind from its constricted patterns and the focusing of one's attention on the Source all one's thoughts and feelings. Meditation is the awareness of Awareness itself.

This is to say that meditation is a way in which you can bring your attention to the moment at hand. You become more fully aware of the mysterious, wonderful fact of awareness, and as you do this, you become more immersed in and illumined by the reality of the supreme Consciousness of which your own awareness is an inseparable reflection. This unencumbered, clear, illuminating awareness of Awareness itself is a deep state of witness consciousness.

Mindfulness in its various forms thus opens your heart and your mind not only to the wonder of existence but also to the presence of the Self, the true Heart, which you are able to know because you can see it *pratīkṣamāna*: right in front your eyes, as it were. The state of attentive mindfulness represented by the term *pratīkṣamāna* in this sūtra is therefore similar to that of witness consciousness, that is to say, of *sākṣī bhāva*.

The clear attentiveness gained and strengthened by meditation can then be brought to your life in general. When we are mindful, we can be more aware of the effect that our thoughts have on our actions and of the effect our actions have on the world. Mindfulness strengthens and enables our self-inquiry and thus makes possible our ability to see what we might need or want to change about ourselves. It gives us more clarity regarding our relationship to others, our responsibility to the community, and our place in the natural world. Mindfulness allows us to live completely, and thus to experience joy and contentment.

Mindfulness therefore increases our ability to experience the fullness of existence. This is true in times of sorrow, loss, or death of a loved one as much as in other times; for, even in these times — perhaps especially in them — we can have the sense of the fragile wonder and value of life.

Clear attentiveness leads, then, to a sense of reverence, and mindfulness can become a form of prayer and contemplation. Practicing mindfulness, we come more to experience the divine Presence in each moment. Mindfulness opens us to the presence of unconditional Love. With mindfulness we are more able to see in all things the face of the universal Self, to hear in all sounds the voice of the Self, to feel in all that moves us the touch of the Self. As Kṛṣṇa says to Arjuna in the *Bhagavad Gītā*:

> With mindfulness of me,
> with love shared with me,
> offering to me, act with reverence for me.
> Steadfast in this manner,
> you will surely come to me,
> having immersed yourself in yoga,
> with me as the supreme goal.[90]

Nārada stresses the importance and value of this sense of a sanctifying, attentive awareness by saying that the bhakta should try not to let this mindfulness slip for even the slightest moment. As our sūtra says, not even half an instant should be allowed to pass uselessly. Life is already so short! Once it has passed, that half-instant cannot be retrieved. It is not to be wasted.

"Relinquishing happiness, dissatisfaction,
self-centered willfulness, worldly gain, and so on"

How might we understand this sūtra in the context of a loving, life-affirming worldview? What might it mean to say that one is to turn away from happiness, sadness, willfulness, worldly gain, and other states of being? Are bhaktas not to have any sense of intention in their lives and in their spiritual practices?

No, this is not what this sūtra means, and I say this because the weight of the lessons in the other sūtras throughout the larger text counters this idea. Again, emotions such as happiness and sadness are to be affirmed.

One way I understand this sūtra, then, is to go back to sūtra 7 and to its assertion that supreme love for God "does not arise from desire." When there is conditional, self-centered desire, rather than loving emotion, one places one's own preferences above one's alignment with the true Heart. Seeking gratification in this way re-enforces the egoistic tendencies that seek fulfillment but which ultimately lead to disappointment or to a discouraging sense of limitation and frustration because such desires can never truly be fulfilled.

Applying this prior point to our current sūtra, we can say that the happiness Nārada says is to be renounced is a kind of happiness that arises when one's narrow self-centered desires are met. Seeking this kind of happiness can distance one from the experience of Love. Therefore, if we are to live more in the light of Love, then we live life more as yogīs and yoginīs who place increasingly less value on seeking satisfaction of those desires.

The same would hold true for what our sūtra calls unhappiness. Again, I most certainly am not saying here that one should feel no emotions at times of sadness. The sorrow one feels when tragedy takes place in the lives of others or when a loved one suffers can be the purest instance of sorrow there is. Such sorrow reveals the presence deep in one's heart of karuṇā rasa, the essence of compassion.

Rather, I understand our sūtra to be referring to that the kind of unhappiness or disappointment that arises when one's expectations and demands have not been met. When this happens, one feels a certain disease with things: "dis-ease" being a rather literal translation of *duḥkha*, the word I have translated in this sūtra as "dissatisfaction." When one is caught in duḥkha, one cannot fully celebrate and take joy in God's presence, no matter what the situation may be. Therefore, in higher forms of spiritual love, the lover does not insist that one's relationship to God be the way he or she personally wants it to be. In this way, he or she is more open to God's actual and genuinely fulfilling, graceful presence.

A similar interpretation can be applied to the renunciation of willfulness. The word here is *icchā*, which otherwise simply means "will" or "wish." The word is usually used in a positive sense. Indeed, God as Creator said to create the universe through the power of the divine wish, icchā. Similarly, yogic thought holds that we can and should offer the world our own best wishes and intentions. The power of the yogī's or yoginī's intention drives movement forward and upward along the yogic path. So, there is nothing wrong with icchā, as such. Rather, again, our sūtra seems to be saying that it is a certain kind of icchā that is to be relinquished. It is that willfulness that arises from a limited and egoistic motivation to have things the way one wants them to be rather than as the loving Heart would want them to be, or that desire that comes from a sense of lack versus a benevolent wish that comes from an overflowing sense of offering. For this reason, in this context I have translated the word as "self-centered willfulness."

We can understand the renunciation of worldly gain in a similar manner. The relevant term in this sūtra is *lābha*, a word generally associated with the act of acquiring or obtaining. Again, from a yogic perspective, there is of course nothing wrong with the process of attainment. Certainly, the entirety of the yogic life is directed to the attainment of increasing levels of spiritual completion and wholeness.

Accordingly, our sūtra does not seem to me to be speaking here of this kind of beneficial kind of lābha, but rather of self-centered motivation for artificial prestige, profit or worldly gain. Unfortunately, throughout history there have been people who have sought to use what otherwise looks like devotion to God for their own purposes. They may invoke God's name not so much out of reverence for God, but rather in the interest of gaining attention, political influence, material wealth or some other form of self-centered attainment. At higher levels of devotion, this sort of motivation is to be renounced.

The last component of the phrase under consideration is the simple word *ādi*, which means in this context "and so on." By using this short word, Nārada is saying that there are other intentions, values, and attitudes besides those he has just mentioned that bhaktas are to relinquish if they wish to move further along the path of devotion. You might reflect on the phrase here and contemplate this question: "What other perspectives and motivations beside those listed in this sūtra might I renounce because they obstruct my own progress on the path of Love?"

Terms Appearing in Chapter 9

duḥkha — Ill-at-easeness (*duḥ-kha*: literally "dis-ease"), uneasiness, dissatisfaction, unhappiness, misery, suffering.

icchā — Power of the will; thus wish, intention. The term is often used in a positive sense: creative will, effective wish. Nārada uses the word to represent self-centered intention, wish or desire.

kāla — A moment in time, instant, occasion; time in general. Thus, the locative *kāle* means "in time" or "in the moment."

kāma — Desire, especially sensual desire. In its earlier Vedic usage, the word connotes a positive, creative or procreative power of desire. Over time it came to imply sexual longing and pleasure. In the yogic context, the word came to refer to self-centered desire for gratification of any sort. Nārada uses the term in this latter more negative sense.

lābha — Literally, "obtaining, gaining" and thus "acquisition, profit, wealth." In spiritual contexts, the word is usually used in a positive sense: the "obtaining" of spiritual splendor. Nārada's use of the term, on the other hand, implies the selfish pursuit of external wealth and profit.

nirodha — Often translated in yogic contexts as "cessation," the word originally means "enclosing, confining, restraining." I have translated it in this chapter as "calming control" to suggest the process of restraining otherwise uncontrolled desires.

niṣkāma bhakti — Devotion that is offered without self-centered desire or intention. See also *sakāma bhakti*, below.

pratīkṣa — Literally, "turning the eyes upon, looking at" and thus "beholding, respecting, venerating." See also *pratīkṣamāna*, below.

pratīkṣamāna "Being of the nature of *pratīkṣa*" (see above); thus, "looking at, attentive to." I have translated the term in this Chapter as attentive, undistracted "mindfulness."

sakāma bhakti Devotion that is offered with hope for satisfaction of a specific desire of some sort. Devotional thought generally holds that this can tend toward the offering of devotion with an ulterior motivation and see this form of devotion to be less pure than *niṣkāma bhakti* (see above).

sākṣī bhāva The state in which one views the world and oneself from the perspective of the wise, discerning, independent, nonjudgmental inner "witness" (*sākṣin*: literally, "with the eyes" and thus "observing, seeing, witnessing;" the word appears here as *sākśī* for grammatical reasons).

Chapter 10

Inner Freedom, Expansiveness, Constancy, Sublimity, Serenity, Joy

The last three chapters have had a rather sustained and fairly heavy emphasis on yogic sādhana in the context of devotional love. Comments and reflections in the next two chapters will continue somewhat in this manner while at the same time point out more directly some more of the delightful inner transformations a yogic life can help bring about and support. In this chapter we will look at two sūtras to which over the years I have found my own attention returning. I find them to be compelling and inspiring. We begin with sūtra 54, which reads:

> **गुणरहितं कामनरहितं प्रतिक्षणवर्धमानम्**
> **अविच्छिन्नं सूक्ष्मतरम् अनुभवरूपम् ॥ ५४ ॥**
>
> ***guṇarahitaṁ kāmanarahitaṁ pratikṣaṇavardhamānam***
> ***avicchinnaṁ sūkṣmataram anubhavarūpam***
>
> It is free of limiting qualities, free of self-centered
> desire, ever-expanding, uninterrupted, most
> subtle, of the nature of inner experience.
>
> — Sūtra 54

"Of the nature of inner experience"

I will turn attention first to the last phrase in the sūtra. The "it" to which the sūtra refers is the larger topic of the text as a whole — namely, bhakti as paramapreman: supreme love.

Here, our sūtra describes this love as *anubhavarūpa*. You will recall that the word *rūpa*, "form," also connotes the essential nature or particular quality of something. The first part of this compound *anubhava*, sounds quite similar to *anubhāva*, the latter of which refers to a physical gesture or indication of an emotion or mood. The two words are different in meaning, though. The word *anubhava* — the one we find in this current sūtra — can be translated as "experience."

In Indian philosophical thought, anubhava refers to knowledge that comes from one's personal observation of the object of that knowledge. Accordingly, the word is also sometimes translated as "perception" in the sense that psychologists speak of perception, that is to say, as the way we understand and interpret something we have become aware of. When we perceive something — say, a green lime — we first become aware of its existence. Our awareness of the lime comes through our experience of it. We then interpret and understand the object of this experience by describing that form as "green."

Drawing on this example, we can say that it is by means of anubhava, personal experience, that we come to know the nature of the world itself. However, as we have previously noted several times, yogic thought in general holds that one's experience of the outer world is itself conditioned by the nature of one's inner state.

I will illustrate this point with another example. Imagine that you and I are walking down the same street together. I look at the street and see the garbage that has collected along it. "What an ugly street," I say. On the other hand, you look out and see all the flowers growing along its side, and you say, "What a pretty street!" We have both looked at the same outward setting yet we have seen completely different streets, as it were. This being the case, where does the actual "street" we see reside? Is it out there in front of both of us?

Well, if it were "out there," unconditioned by our perception, then we both would see the same street. Yet, we don't see the same street. Why? This is because the "streets" we do see in some sense stand within us, in our own particular inner states.

What does this have to do with the experience of God as Love? The same understanding holds true, ultimately, for your experience of God. You may experience God as external to you and then act as if that object of your love is "out there" somewhere. This is of course appropriate, when one considers the infinite nature of God and of God's presence in all existence. However, even this experience of God as "out there" — *as an experience* — actually takes place within you.

If God existed completely outside of your experience, then you simply could not experience God at all. You could not even *say* that God exists external to you, for you would not have any experience of God on which to base this assertion. So, even though you may experience God to exist in the outer world, your experience of God is necessarily an inward one.

Accordingly, the experience of God outside of you also means that God is present within you! In perceiving and responding to God's presence in the world about you, you are experiencing God within you.

Put differently, the very fact that you experience love for God means that Love already dwells within you in the form of your experience of love.

This is to say that the divine Beloved is not only the object of a bhakta's experience. The Beloved dwells in the bhakta's inner experience of love itself, as an experience.

This is another reason why contemplation and especially meditation are helpful elements in a sādhana of love and devotion, for these are ways by which bhaktas can discover and enter into the contours of their inner experience. The more deeply they do so, the more they can perceive the presence of the Love that is the inward support of all existence — even of their own inner and personal experience of existence. They then can see the "street" from the perspective of love. Their experience of the outer world, and therefore their behavior in that world, is illumined by the light of that inner experience of Love.

"Most subtle"

The word for "subtle" here is *sūkṣma*, a word that we find in a variety of spiritual texts from India. The yogic insight that a person's outward experience is fashioned by the quality of his or her inner state lies behind a similar notion, for example, that the objective, physical body (*sthūla śarīra*) is enlivened by living energy within it, in the form of what is called the subtle body (*sūkṣma śarīra*). The physical body is supported by the living power of the subtle body, which suffuses it from within. From this perspective, our experiences in the physical world as embodied beings are made possible by a deeper, subtle foundation within us. The same could be said for our thoughts and emotions.

In using the word *sūkṣma* to describe the nature of bhakti, Nārada encourages bhaktas to be aware of the actual source of any experience of love in any form or at any level. When you feel the stirrings of love as you look at a flower opening its petals, or a child learning to hold a pencil, or an elderly person combing her thinning hair, you might ask yourself: where does this love come from? Is its source the object? If it came from, say, the flower, then everybody who looked at that flower as an object would experience love for it, and I am not sure this would be the case, any more than everybody sees the same street, as it were. Yet, *you* feel this love. So, this love must come from within you, in the form of your experience of the flower, the child or the elderly person. Your experience of their loveliness, *as an experience*, takes place at a subtle level within you. Your openness to that experience then draws that love from within you, a Love that is your true nature, for it is the nature of the Self that dwells within you. Your loving feelings for others thus allow the Self to reveal Itself within you. This Self-revelatory power is none other than the power of Love itself; and this is the true Beloved.

There are different degrees to which one can experience or allow Love to reveal itself within us. A yogic perspective holds that the more subtle an experience is, the closer it is to its foundation in the Self. Some experiences of love are outwardly more physical than others. This does not mean that they are wrong or bad. It does mean, though, that they are less subtle than the others and therefore further from their Source.

Our sūtra describes spiritual love not only as *sūkṣma*, but as *sūkṣmatara*: "the most subtle, the subtlest of the subtle." Nārada is therefore saying here that supreme Love is the finest, the most refined, state of love.

As one who feels love, you may at times feel tremendous emotions associated with that love. Yet, even in those moments, the finest essence of those powerful experiences remains extremely subtle. You can of course hear love expressed outwardly, yet supreme Love itself speaks in the quietest of whispers, sings with the softest of voices, pulsates with the most delicate of movements.

Characterized as sukṣmatara, the experience of supreme Love would be truly exquisite in nature. Even in the most powerful emotions and experiences of human love stands this finest essence. It is quiet, and it is complete. It moves in the perfection of the Heart, where it always has been and will always continue to dwell.

If we could remain in that sublimity that stands within all experiences of love, then we thereby might abide in the state that our sūtra describes as sūkṣmatara. What an exquisite state that would be to live in!

"Free of limiting qualities,
free from selfish desire"

These two phrases translate the Sanskrit *guṇarahita* and *kāmanarahita*, respectively. You will recognize the word *guṇa*. We have already had opportunity in Chapter 7 to discuss the ideas it represents. As a reminder for you, in the yogic context, the weaving together of various guṇas textures our understanding and experience of ourselves and of the world. As we have seen, the effect of the guṇas can be used productively in the yogic life. The influence of the guṇas can limit bhaktas to various degrees depending on the relative presence of tamas, rajas and sattva. In our earlier discussion we noted the idea that *gauṇī* forms of bhakti — those associated with the guṇas — are preparatory relative to what tradition calls *śuddha bhakti* or pure spiritual love.

The word *kāmana* in the second phrase is related to *kāma*, a word to which I gave some attention in Chapter 8. From the perspective held by the *Bhakti Sūtra*, I defined kāma as "selfish desire" or as "desire that seeks self-centered gratification." It is to be distinguished from preman, which is unconditional love.

The word *rahita* in *guṇarahita* and *kāmanarahita* means "separated from, absent of, independent of." I have translated it here as "free of" as a way to suggest a state of spiritual freedom from a bondage of sorts.

To be *guṇarahita* is not to be bound up by the guṇas. It is therefore to be free of prepatterned, preconditioned, and therefore limiting characteristics and predilections. It is to be released into the spontaneous, unconditional state of pure Love.

Similarly, to be free of attachment to the gratification of selfish desires, *kāmanarahita*, is to be free of bondage to them. Here, one's self-centered pursuits have been transformed into a benevolent wish to give love to others and to God. One inwardly experiences the pure and benevolent Love that is the true nature of the spiritual heart.

It may take much effort on our parts to free ourselves from constricting predilections and from our pursuit of self-centered desires. This is, again, one reason why bhakti yoga constitutes a genuine sādhana. In previous chapters we have noted at some length various components of a yogic life dedicated to such spiritual discipline, so perhaps there is no need to repeat them here. Given the need for effort, we can also be reassured that those disciplines are supported, as always, by grace.

"Uninterrupted"

I suspect that in some way or another and to some intensity or another you have tasted the nectar of Love in your yogic life. Although such experiences may be fleeting or sporadic, they can reveal to you the reality of Love itself.

If even a brief glimpse into Love can be so compelling, just think what it would be like to live always in that state! Is it possible to do so? Our current sūtra says that the highest level of bhakti is, indeed, *avicchinna*: "uninterrupted."

We can understand this in two ways. The first is quite literal. In some experiences and expressions of devotion there is a break (*vicchinna*) in the flow of love. Such sentiments can come and go. On the other hand, the experience and expression of the highest state of love is unbroken (*avicchinna*). Here, there is no wavering from Love. A person in this state lives in love for God all the time and expresses devotion to God in everything he or she does. That love, like the Heart from which it emerges, is constant and ever-abiding.

A second way to understand this reference to uninterrupted love is more experiential and perhaps more applicable to those bhaktas who feel they have not yet reached this state. We remember that elsewhere our sūtra says that love is available to us in our own inner experience and that it is supremely fine. Here, our sūtra is saying that it is also avicchinna: it is always with us.

Your own experience is always your own experience. Life continues from moment to moment in an uninterrupted way. The same is true for Love. Its foundational presence remains always within us. It is there even when we do not feel it. So, too, the powerful yet subtle essence of supreme Love exists within all our experiences of relative love. Accordingly, divine Love dwells subtly if perhaps hidden within your momentary experiences of love at any level.

Love is available to you always. It stands within all of your feelings and sentiments, even though at times it may be distorted, discolored and veiled by them. It flows, silently, from the core of your being, like a wellspring of sweet water rising from the depths of the earth. You can bathe in this delightful Love wherever you are. Walk along a quiet path and you feel Love. Weave your way through a crowd on a noisy city street, and you feel Love. Listen attentively to the sound of rain on pavement and you feel Love. Hear the sound of a child singing and you feel Love. Drift into sleep at night and you feel Love. Wake into the morning and you feel Love. Ever present, ever quiet, ever fine, Love as the expression of the divine Presence, remains with you, within you. It is avichhinna: uninterrupted.

"Ever-expanding"

In the remaining description of spiritual love in sūtra 54, our text says that it is *pratikṣana-vardhamāna*. The word *pratikṣana* in a sense captures what I was just talking about. It means "continuing at every moment." It is what I represent here by the word "ever." *Vardhamāna* means "increasing, swelling, growing."

I interpret this phrase in three ways. One way is that the heart's elevation into higher forms of love is ever-expansive, for love itself is an expression of the divine Heart's own expansive Love. The highest Love toward which we are drawn does not fade when there are changes in our external situation. It remains undiminished by the fluctuations of our moods, feelings, thoughts, emotions and other sentiments conditioned by the guṇas. God's love is unbounded by limitations of finite space and time. Therefore, it stands within each instant and in all places. God's powerful and loving presence supports each and every moment of life. Accordingly, each moment presents a new setting by which one can turn toward Love.

A second way to understand this phrase would be that spiritual love is ever-increasing in its intensity. By this I do not mean that one's devotional feelings are necessarily more and more outwardly obvious. Remember that spiritual love itself is finely subtle and of the nature of inner experience. Therefore, to say love is increasing is to say that it becomes more exquisite and more clearly known within one's own inner experience. As one enters more fully into the state of spiritual love one experiences the reality of God, the ultimate Source and Object of one's love, with swelling intensity.

A third way we can think of devotional love as ever-expanding would be to remember from our discussion in Chapter 6 that a person who experiences Love thereby experiences delight in the divine Self. To delight in the highest, universal Self, Paramātman, is to delight in the expansive nature of that divine Presence within all things. This Presence is God, who is Love. To love God is to participate in a Love that is of an expansive nature. Our love for God then swells outward to embrace others: the members of our families, those in our communities, and eventually, as our love expands, the people of the larger world.

Spiritual love is therefore ever-expanding in its availability, its intensity, and its extent. Because the divine Heart is infinite, that Heart's love can never be encompassed. So, no matter how much love we ourselves experience and express, there is always, always, more love to expand into.

In sūtra 60 our text adds two more characteristics of this spiritual love:

शान्तिरूपात् परमानन्दरूपाच्च ॥६०॥

śāntirūpāt paramānandarūpāc-ca

"It is of the nature of peace,
and it is of the nature of supreme joy."

— Sūtra 60

"It is of the nature of peace"

The word for "peace" here is *śānti*. It is a beautiful word. It can also be translated as "tranquility, quiet, calmness of mind." Śānti is an easeful state of inner freedom, for in this peace there is no bondage to the cycles of disappointment driven by self-centered desires. The peace that is śānti is not a passive, unmoving, static peace. I am reminded of the saying: still waters run deep. Those places in a powerfully flowing river where the surface current churns the least are those places where there is the most depth. So, too, śanti is quiet and deep, yet also expansive, dynamic and nourishing.

The spiritual peace I am speaking of here is one that finds expression in the whole of one's being. Śānti is associated with tenderness, humility, benevolence, strength, forgiveness, patience, dignity, respect, gratitude and reverence. It characterizes the experience and expression of that which is true, valuable and holy. The divine Heart itself is filled with the strength of peace, and it moves deep within the human heart as the soul's truest nature.

To speak of peace in the devotional context is also to call to mind the relationship between surface devotion and deep devotion. On the surface, our feelings of devotion can be quite powerful yet perhaps also unsteady. One moment we may feel confidence in our connection with the Beloved, in another we may feel uncertain or unclear about that relationship. One moment we may feel acknowledged, another we may feel overlooked. We may feel encouraged, or we may feel disheartened.

These feelings express an unsettledness in our sentiments. They keep changing as they rise and move through us, like individual waves on the surface of the ocean. Deeper devotional love is not defined only by the quality of these surface feelings. It dwells deep within the heart. It finds expression in these changing outward forms, yet it remains also in the depths, even when those transient feelings subside. At the core of your being stands the abiding silence of Love, and that love is *śāntirūpa*: "of the nature of peace."

Bhaktas orient their yogic lives away from the pull of selfish desires and more toward the peace that is the divine Heart. As the *Bhagavad Gītā* says,

> One who has conquered the [narrow desires of the] self,
> one who is peaceful:
> that one is immersed in the Supreme Self.[91]

In the larger spiritual context, peace is the setting in which all beings at all levels of existence dwell in concord with each other within the embrace of the divine Heart. In traditional Indian perspectives, peace holds the universe together: all beings everywhere, in all realms — on the earth, in the skies and in the heavens above them — are joined to each other through peace. It is for this reason, in part, that the study and recitation of sacred texts in the yogic context, as with other spiritual practices, often begin and end with a threefold affirmation: *śānti, śānti, śānti.*

"And it is of the nature of supreme joy"

Here our sūtra uses the beautiful term *paramānanda-svarūpa* to describe the inner state toward which the sādhana of devotion brings bhaktas. *Svarūpa* in this context means "of the nature of" something or "of the essence of" something. *Ānanda*, as it is represented here, means "joy." It is often translated as "bliss." *Parama* means "highest, supreme." This is a state in which there is boundless, exuberant joy grounded in the experience of the universal Self's presence in the contours of the bhakta's own spiritual heart.

Devotional yogic thought in India has long held that this bliss is the divine Self's true nature and that the experience of the joy that is this true Beloved brings fulfillment of one's yearnings at all levels of one's being. To be at one with the universal Self is to be at one with the ultimate Source and Object of that yearning. The *Bṛhadāraṇyaka Upaniṣad*, dating to roughly the seventh century BCE, uses the same term as our sūtra does in reference to a single Self dwelling within all manifest beings: "This is [the heart's] highest goal. This is its highest treasure. This is its highest realm. This is its highest joy (*paramānanda*)."[92]

In this highest state of contentment, one's narrowly selfish desires fade and dissolve as one enters into the unconditional joy that is the Self. The *Bṛhadāraṇyaka Upaniṣad* also describes that state as "one's [true] nature that is free from craving" and uses an image of love to illustrate this point: "As a man in the embrace of a woman he loves knows no difference between what is without and within, so too a person in the embrace of the conscious Self knows no difference between what is without and what is within."[93] The *Chāndogya Upaniṣad*, another text from roughly the seventh century BCE, also uses language reminiscent of loving enjoyment to describe the experience of the Self, and identifies *ānanda* as the culmination of such enjoyment: "Truly, one who sees this [Self], who thinks this [way], who understands in this [way], has fondness for the Self, has playful delight in the Self, has union with the Self, has joy in the Self (*ātmānanda*)."[94]

Indian thought holds that we are able to experience this unconditional joy because the Self that is of the nature of ānanda dwells deep within us as the universal foundation of our existence itself. As the sages in roughly the fifth century BCE whose words form the *Taittirīya Upaniṣad* have taught, "Truly, beings that are born here are born from ānanda. When born, they live by ānanda, and when departing, they enter into ānanda."[95] Though we may not know or experience it, joy is therefore the very essence of our being, and as such it can infuse all dimensions of our lives.

In a relatively long passage, the *Taittirīya Upaniṣad* makes this point when it speaks of five layers of a person's embodied existence.[96] (In his short, pristine work known as *Ātmabodha*, "Enlightened Self Knowledge," the influential ninth century philosopher, Śāṅkara, referred to these as the five *kośas*, or "sheaths," of the Self. The word *kośa* has often been used since then to refer to these layers.) The coarser levels of our existence are closer to the surface, as it were. The more subtle, powerful, determinative levels of our existence lie deeper within us.

Here is a summary of that passage. At the outer level, a person is a physical body. The Upaniṣad calls this physical form a self "filled with food" or "made of food" (*anna-maya*). Both within and pervading this nourishment body, a person has what the text identifies as a self "made of life-breath" (*prāṇa-maya*) that enlivens the physical body nourished by food. Without that living breath, the physical body would not continue to have life. Within yet also pervading this body made of living energy is a self "made of mind" (*mano-maya*). This is the mental level of one's existence: one's thoughts, ideas, concepts, attitudes and so on. This is why, from this perspective, the quality and direction of our thoughts influence the way we live and act in the world. Within and pervading this body made of mind is a self "made of intelligence" (*vijñāna-maya*). This is to say that thoughts arise from a deeper foundation, which is the capability of understanding itself.

Then, the Upaniṣad continues to say, within and pervading the self made of intelligence and understanding is a self "made of joy" (*ānanda-maya*). According to this view, this is the innermost level. Said differently, at the very core of our being, at the deepest level of our existence, stands the reality that is ānanda.

What a compelling view this is! Bliss is our deepest, truest nature. All other levels of our being, in their various ways, embody this core joy.

Why is it that we do not experience this inherent bliss that is our true nature? Yogic thought holds that this foundational joy is hidden and distorted by one's thoughts, motivations, attitudes, perspectives and so on. These then take form as desires, for which we seek external satisfaction. Yet, ānanda itself is a pure and deep inner joy that is not dependent on or conditioned by external circumstances. In its fullness it lacks nothing. It is of the nature of pure, unconditional Love. There is a boundless spaciousness to ānanda. When it is not constricted by narrow self-centeredness, it expresses itself through our own expressions of love in various forms and at various levels. This, then, is one of the purposes of the yogic life: to turn toward the joy within us so that it can be expressed in the world around us.

A yogic sādhana informed by this vision of ourselves consists of honoring and giving expression to all of these levels of our existence. It begins at the level of nourishment (*anna*). We recognize that the world offers itself to us in a way symbolized here as food. The web of existence as a whole nourishes us. Knowing this, we come to see that we, too, are to offer ourselves back to the world by sharing our grateful love in a way that nourishes the world in return. As we share our love, we thereby also share the universal life-breath (*prāṇa*) that supports life in all living beings. Then, we turn our attention to the mind (*manas*) and to its potential to envision beneficial states of being. We focus the mind by honoring and returning to the qualities of intelligence (*vijñāna*) that condition the nature of the mind itself. The Upaniṣad describes such intelligence with a metaphor of a body: "Faith is its head, the right is its right side, the true is its left side, the yogic life is the main part, and the great one [that is to say, the Self], is the lower part, the foundation."[97]

These levels of existence as envisioned by the Upaniṣad — existence made of nourishment, life breath, mind and intelligence — are infused by joy, which stands at the center. As we progressively move deeper into these levels we thereby return to the self consisting of that bliss. We do so through a disciplined spiritual life that makes beneficial use of the body and mind in service of illumined awareness. The yogic life in this way leads to supreme joy, what Nārada has called *paramānanda.*

The *Bhakti Sūtra* describes the highest state of love. Sūtras 54 and 60 give us compelling descriptions of this love. When we enter into this highest state, we enter into the peaceful joy that is of the nature of inner experience, free of all limiting qualities, free of self-centered desire, continually expanding and uninterrupted. We enter into the finest Love.

Terms appearing in Chapter 10

ānanda	Unconditional joy, bliss.
anubhava	A personal experience or perception of something. The compound word *anubhavarūpa* means "of the nature of experience." The word *anubhava* is not to be confused with *anubhāva* (see below).
anubhāva	An "indication of a mood" or "sign of an emotion" such as a look or a gesture; not to be confused with *anubhava* (see above).
anubhavarūpa	See *anubhava*, above.
avicchina	Unbroken, steady, constant.
guṇarahita	Free of or released from (*rahita*) the nature of preconditioned qualities or tendencies (*guṇa*).
kāmanarahita	Free of or released from (*rahita*) selfish desire (*kāmana*).
kośa	A "sheath" or "layer" of the Self. Vedāntic texts sometime speak of five such *kośas*. See Table IX, below.
manas	The mind, the mental organ.
paramānanda-svarūpa	Literally, of the nature (*svarūpa*) of supreme bliss (*paramānanda*).
paramātman	Supreme (*parama*) self (*ātman*); in devotional contexts the reference here is to God as the supreme Self of the universe.
prāṇa	Breath, life-force, living energy.
śānti	Peace; pervasive calm.
sthūla śarīra	One of several terms for the physical body; literally, "solid" (*sthūla*) "support, frame, body" (*śarīra*). Compare *sūkṣma śarīra* (below).

śuddha bhakti — Devotional love (*bhakti*) that is pure (*śuddha*) in nature, that is to say, not mixed with other motivations or intentions.

sūkṣma — Subtle, fine, intangible.

sūkṣma śarīra — One of several yogic terms referring to the subtle dimension of one's being; often translated as "the subtle body." Literally "subtle, intangible" (*sūkṣma*) "support, frame, body" (*śarīra*). Compare *sthūla śarīra* (above).

sūkṣmatara — Most subtle; thus, finest, exquisite (see *sūkṣma*, above).

Table IX

A Vedāntic Scheme of the Concentrically Layered Nature of One's Embodiment

(See *Taittirīya Upaniṣad* 2.1-5 and Śaṅkara's *Ātmabodha* 15)

Moving from outer/most physical layers, towards inner/most subtle layers.

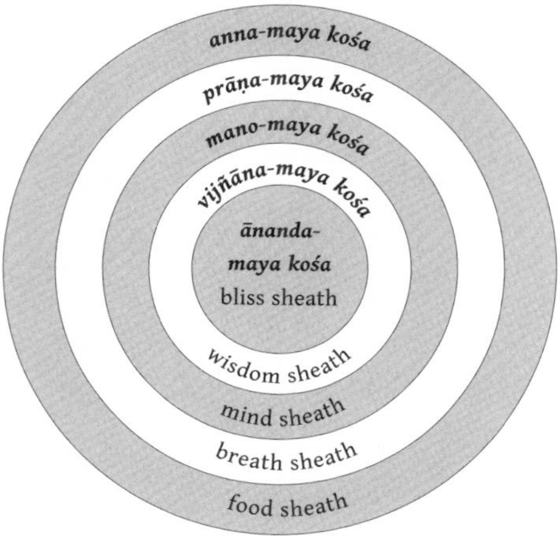

anna-maya kośa	The physical body, what tradition calls the sheath (*kośa*) that consists of (*maya*) food (*anna*).
prāṇa-maya kośa	The dimension of one's being consisting of "breath or "life force" (*prāṇa*) that stands within yet also pervades the physical body.
mano-maya kośa	The dimension of one's being consisting of the mind (*manas*: the word is spelled *mano* here for pronunciation purposes); the aspect of one's self that consists of one's thoughts. This mental layer or "body" stands within yet also pervades the physical and energetic layers.
vijñāna-maya kośa	The inner dimension of one's self that has deep wisdom (*vijñāna*) and that both stands within and pervades the mental, energetic and physical layers.
ānanda-maya kośa	The layer of the self that is made of bliss (*ānanda*); the deepest and most pervasive dimension of one's being that consists of pure, unconditional joy; the true Heart that stands at the core of one's being and that, when released, pervades the entirety of one's wisdom, knowledge, living energy and physical body.

Chapter 11

Communion with the Divine

Our text has given us the opportunity to reflect on the nature of the highest love as an ambrosial, free, expansive, steadfast, splendid, fine, peaceful, supremely joyful state. The essence of this state toward which the yoga of devotion leads is itself the essence of the divine Heart's own nature. We can share in the Heart's essence when we enter into and express love. Absolute, divine Love is reflected in our own particular and individual love. God is not separate from the loving impulses and yearnings of the human spirit.

Yet, the state of spiritual love may seem rather vague and unformed for some people, who might want to experience it in a more definite manner. One reason this may be so is because they are not sure just what the ultimate object of their love is, so they seek it in ways that may actually hinder their experience of it. For other people, the experience of devotional love may be strong, but they don't really know where to direct it and thus it may seem to them to dissipate. Still other people may find that the level of their love has reached a plateau of sorts. They continue to feel and express it, but it doesn't seem to get any higher or deeper. The possible result is that it becomes seemingly rather predictable, ordinary and mundane.

Our text gives bhaktas resources to understand such situations in the yogic life. In one breath, Sūtra 9 both implies the state of communion of the relative heart with the divine Heart and gives guidance regarding a yogic life oriented toward that communion. It reads:

> तस्मिन्ननन्यता तद्विरोधिषूदासिनता च ॥९॥
>
> ***tasminnananyatā tadvirodhiṣūdāsinatā ca***
>
> And, in this, there is non-otherness and
> disinterest in that which goes against it.
>
> — Sūtra 9

The phrase *and in this* links this sūtra with a preceding one, sūtra 7, which as we have seen in Chapter 9 says that bhakti is characterized by an inner calmness gained by becoming less and less driven by one's harmful desires. In other words, "and in this" refers to this state of spiritual love.

"There is non-otherness"

This phrase translates the Sanskrit *ananyatā*. At the most literal level, this simply means "of the nature of not-other." True to the sūtra style, Nārada's economy of words here invites contemplation that can go in more than one direction.

One way to understand the use of the word *ananyatā* here is that, in love, there is a state of togetherness shared by God and the lover of God and that, at the deepest or highest level, God is not separate from Love. Thus, in Love, there is no alienation of soul from Beloved. I like the way a contemporary commentator on this sūtra has rendered the phrase as "there is not-being-other to God." He expands this by saying that "loving God, *bhakti*, is a sharing in God's very being" and that "loving is the mutual sharing between two who are not 'other' to each other."[98] Said differently, in the encompassing state of Love, there is a non-otherness — this is to say, there is a communion shared — between subject and object, self and Self, lover and Beloved.

In this not-other devotion, the lover shares the same essence with the One who is loved. We sometimes hear of bhaktas immersed in an ocean of nectar or of becoming one with absolute Consciousness. This is to say that lovers of the Beloved become so infused with Love that their love becomes not-other to the Love that is God.

A second way I understand the phrase focuses on a yogic perspective through which this unity-in-love can be realized. The state of supreme love is that of non-otherness because, in the inner stillness of this love, there is an unwavering focus on God as the ultimate object of love without being distracted by self-centered desires that would otherwise pull our attention. In this way, the word *ananyatā* represents the realization that, in bhakti, there is a sharp clarity of vision directed toward higher states of love. When there is this love, there is nothing other than God as the object of that love.

Such an interpretation would be supported by a passage from the *Bhagavad Gītā* where Kṛṣṇa teaches Arjuna that the intensely focused love for God brings vision of and immersion into God:

> Indeed, through devotion that is not-other
> can I be known,
> be truly seen in this form,
> and be entered into, O Arjuna.[99]

This understanding is reminiscent of the yogic practice of one-pointed awareness, *ekāgrata*, in which one brings all of one's attention onto a single object. This focus gives great power to one's otherwise diffused awareness. You might think of this practice as being like a laser, which takes all the various wavelengths of light, converts them into one single wavelength, and directs that powerful beam in a single direction. As we know, the intensely focused light from a laser carries such powerful energy that it can perform functions far beyond the capability of diffused light.

Similarly, love that is focused on the Beloved gains energy and transformative power. Not dissipated and thus not weakened, such love becomes increasingly strong.

Devotion that is characterized as *anayatā* is known as *ananya bhakti*. The yogic tradition holds that the disciplined one-pointed attention on a single object can transform a person's inner state such that he or she in some way becomes the same nature as that of the object being meditated upon. For example, Patañjali's *Yoga Sūtra* refers to a state of *samyama*,[100] which we can translate as a "convergence." That text tells us, for instance, that one who meditates one-pointedly on compassion becomes compassionate.[101] Accordingly, we could also say that one who holds one's awareness on Love becomes more loving. Similarly, from the devotional perspective, undissipated love for God brings such a lover into communion with the divine Beloved. As Kṛṣṇa teaches Arjuna in the *Bhagavad Gītā* in reference to the divine Presence:

> This is the supreme Spirit, O son of Pṛtha,
> to be attained through undissipated devotion,
> within which stand all beings,
> and by which the whole universe is pervaded. . . .
> With your mind fixed on me, be devoted to me;
> Worshipping me, offer reverence to me.
> Disciplined in this way, with me as your supreme goal,
> You yourself will come to me.[102]

Expanding on this latter verse, the 11th-12th century theologian-philosopher, Rāmānuja, described *ananya bhakti* as being like oil poured from one vessel to another. It is an apt simile: such devotion is steady and unbending as it moves in a single direction toward its object. The words Rāmānuja gives Kṛṣṇa are worth quoting:

> Focus your mind uninterruptedly, like a flow of oil, on me, the supreme lord. . . who shines with the brilliance of a thousand rising suns. [Focus] on me, the ineffable ocean of beauty. . . . While focusing your mind on me, may you be filled with overwhelming love for me. When you have understood me to be the boundless and incomparable Lord, devote yourself to worshipping me. . . . [I am] your innermost Self. Establish yourself in me because without me your Self would be unsupported.[103]

A passage from the *Bhāgavata Purāṇa* gives support to our twofold understanding of the not-other nature of spiritual love both as both not-being-other to God and as undissipated and focused on God. Here, Kṛṣṇa uses a simile of the Ganges River flowing uninterruptedly to the ocean to describe the highest discipline of love that leads to the realization of God:

> When, inspired by the mere hearing of my goodness,
> the mind streams toward me
> like the uninterrupted flow of the Ganges to the sea . . .
> when love is directed to the supreme being,
> the divine presence in all hearts:
> . . . this is the glory of the highest discipline of love
> by which one . . . enters into me.[104]

That same text defines bhakti itself as this focused, loving attention on the highest, divine object of true devotion. It says:

> When all the energy of the senses,
> which are ordinarily dispersed through external contacts,
> is purified through devotional practices;
> when one becomes focused purely on the Beloved,
> without any ulterior self-centered motivation;
> when nothing else overpowers this focus:
> this state of mind is called "bhakti."[105]

In this not-otherness with the Love that is God there is dissolution of narrow self-centeredness and thus the dissolution of the sense of separation from God. Jñāneśvar makes this point when he has Kṛṣṇa teach Arjuna that,

> This devotion must be like showers of rain which have no other place to go, apart from the earth; or like the river Ganges, which with its abundant waters again and again seeks out the ocean, which is its only refuge. In such a way, a devotee lives his life in me with wholehearted and unswerving love, becoming one with me. . . . When fire is lit from fuel, the fuel becomes fire and is lost from sight. The sky remains dark as long as the

> sun hasn't risen, but when it appears, the light shines forth.
> Similarly, through direct experience of me, egoism vanishes;
> and with the disappearance of egoism, duality passes away.[106]

"Disinterest in that which goes against it"

The movement toward this "non-other" form of love is indeed a worthy devotional sādhana toward which a bhakta can aspire. It does not always come easily. With Utpaladeva, one may wonder:

> When shall my mind
> Indifferent to all else through love's intensity
> Tear open the great door latch
> With a loud bang
> And finally arrive in your presence, O Lord?[107]

Our current sūtra seems to acknowledge the power of this yearning. With the phrase "distinterest in that which goes against it" it indicates that the process of aligning with the divine Beloved involves turning from that which contradicts, interferes with or constricts love.

The word "disinterest" translates *udāsinatā*, literally, "of the nature of sitting apart from something" and thus also "unencumbered, free." The phrase "in that which goes against it" translates *tad-virodhiṣu*. The "it" here refers to the single-hearted, absorbing love for God that the first part of the sūtra has just mentioned. The word *virodha*, the basis of *virodhiṣu*, means "opposition, incompatibility, contradiction, antithesis." The phrase thus implies that there are forces, motivations, or states of being that interfere with this intense devotion. Our current sūtra does not say what these opposing forces are. (In Chapter 4 we discussed the importance of defeating the various "inner enemies" that hinder spiritual progress and maturity.) I interpret the oppositions to love meant by the phrase *tad-virodhiṣu* to be those misplaced interests that distract one from or are not consistent with one's yearning for the divine Beloved.

Those forces that obstruct one's communion with the divine Heart are those that increase one's sense of separation from It. The primary mechanism that brings about this sense is one's own narrow self-centeredness in all of its subtle as well as its grandiose forms. The sense of being separate from or alien to God is the source of basically all spiritual problems. It arises when one defines the self only in limited and small terms. Yet, the true Self within you is magnificent, expansive and great. Identifying exclusively with the small self can lead you to understand yourself and others in constricted and possibly degrading ways and then to arrange your priorities and conduct your life in ways that re-enforce this misunderstanding. You may act in ways that do not honor the inherent value and worth of a soul that is loved by God. This misunderstanding of who you really are would also be a source of a possible sense of superiority over others, just as it is a source of a feeling of inferiority. Such misunderstanding could then lead to arrogance, or to timidity. It inflates egoistic pride, just as it feeds feelings of resentment and inadequacy and fuels a sense of lack.

This narrow and limited sense of oneself is not consistent with the expansive and splendid fullness that is the Self that participates in God's nature as love. It creates a feeling of separation from God. Influenced by this misunderstanding, one thereby degrades oneself and gets in the way of one's own truly fulfilling relationship with God.

So, following our sūtra's guidance, bhaktas who seek to be one with the Beloved will turn away from seeking gratification of narrow self-centered desires. This need not be an ostentatious rejection of those desires; rather, it is the discovery of the much greater and fulfilling yearning to know and love God. As one moves deeper into the reality of Love, one becomes more infused and at-one with that Love. In this way, *ananya bhakti* is thus a state in which there is a non-otherness, *ananyatā*, between lover and Beloved.

Those who open themselves to God become infused with Love, for Love is God's own nature. Open to that Love, they become immersed in it. As sūtra 70 says,

तन्मयाः ॥७०॥

tanmayāḥ

They are absorbed in that.

— Sūtra 70

The key word in this phrase is *maya*, which I have translated as "absorbed in" yet could also correctly be translated as "filled with, full of, made of." (It is not to be confused with *māyā*, the latter of which in some Vedāntic schools of Indian philosophical thought means "projected mental illusion" and in some Tantric schools refers to the "differentiating power of supreme Consciousness.") The "that" in the sūtra refers to bhaktas' unconditional love that is not constrained or limited by their personal predispositions and predilections. Accordingly, it is not driven by selfish desires or ulterior motives of any sort; it is one-pointed love directed toward God alone. So, by the phrase *tanmaya*, our sūtra is speaking of bhaktas who are so filled with love that they are absorbed in it.

At one point in the *Bhāgavata Purāṇa* Kṛṣṇa teaches his disciple Uddhava about the way in which the devotee whose love is pure becomes immersed in God's nature. Kṛṣṇa draws on an important yogic idea that the mind becomes attached to the objects on which it focuses. He says, that

> The mind that continually thinks of objects
> becomes attached to those objects,
> while the mind that is in continual remem-
> brance of me becomes dissolved in me.
> Therefore, become collected in me,
> your mind purified in my state.[108]

Elsewhere, the *Bhāgavata Purāṇa* tells of some gopīs whose life situations made it such that they could not leave their homes to follow the sound of Kṛṣṇa's flute and dance with him in the forest. Describing these gopīs who could not physically be with the outward form of their beloved Kṛṣṇa, the *Bhāgavata Purāṇa* says that these lovers became inwardly absorbed in the quality of his state by entering into meditation. This is to say, they entered into their hearts. Doing so, they became immersed in the essence of Love, and thereby in Kṛṣṇa's own essence as Love. Immersed in this Love, they communed inwardly with Kṛṣṇa as Paramātman, the Supreme Self.[109]

If we think of our yearning to be with the divine Beloved as similar to that of these gopīs, then we can honor and fulfill that yearning by entering into our hearts. We can do so in any and all of our life's situations. We can draw on our love at any time and in any setting. In the language of sūtra 70, we can be "absorbed in that." Absorbed in love, we can share love with those around us and with the world. Doing so, we share Love with God.

Terms appearing in Chapter 11

ananya bhakti Devotion (*bhakti*) that is given to none other (*ananya*) than the Beloved; the phrase can also be understood to refer to devotion to the divine Presence that is not-other to one's deepest self, that is to say, to devotion in which there is communion with the Divine.

ekāgrata In the yogic context, this is the disciplined focusing of one's awareness on a single object. In the bhakti setting, this would be the disciplined and heartfelt focusing of all one's devotion on the divine Beloved.

maya "Consisting of, made of, filled by, immersed in." Thus, for example, the Vedāntic notion of the *ātmā-ānanda-maya*: the "Self that consists of bliss." The word is not to be confused with *māyā* (see below).

māyā In its earliest Vedic usage, "extraordinary, creative mental power" possessed particularly by the gods; in the Vedāntic and related contexts, the word means "mental fabrication, illusion, unreality." In Tantric philosophy, *māyā* is the differentiating power of supreme Consciousness. The word is not to be confused with *maya* (see above).

samyama In Patañjali's yoga, this is a "state of convergence" in which the yogī who concentrates one-pointedly on a particular quality takes on the nature of that quality.

PART IV

Fulfillment in Love

Chapter 12

In Love, the Path and the Goal are One

In the preceding chapters we have noted a number of characteristics associated with the state of spiritual love. We have also noted various ways we can open into and elevate our devotional yoga so that we may come closer to this state. These commitments, processes and spiritual practices are aspects of our yoga of devotional love.

Given this apparently instrumental relationship between practice (*sādhana*) and attainment (*sādhya*), one might say that the yoga of devotion brings bhaktas from one level of devotion to another as they move further along the path. Higher and purer forms of devotion are said to open bhaktas more and more fully to this highest or purest level of spiritual love. As we know, the *Bhakti Sūtra* opens with a defining characteristic of bhakti as of the nature of supreme devotional love, *paramapreman*. Following that initial definition, most of the sūtras in the text as a whole point their readers in various ways toward this highest level of devotion.

Throughout our discussions we have noted a number of the characteristics of this highest form of spiritual love, as it is understood in the larger devotional tradition of which this text is a part. We have also seen that it is described in many ways. It is *ahaitukī*, for example: love that is offered without ulterior motive, and *niṣkāma*: without self-centered desire. Spiritual devotion infused with such love is described as *śuddha bhakti*, *nirupādhi bhakti* and *nirguṇa bhakti*, all of which terms refer to pure devotion beyond the limitations of particular form and free of constraints arising from personal predilections or psychological predispositions. Similarly, it is *ananya bhakti*, *eka bhakti*, *ekānta bhakti*, and *kevala bhakti*, all of which refer to one-pointed devotion that is directed to and in service of God alone.

Ancient and classical texts have also used the word *parābhakti* and others similar to it to represent this supreme devotional love (the prefix *parā* means "supreme").[110] More recently Indian spiritual teachers such as Swami Vivekananda and Swami Chidvilasananda have similarly used the word *parābhakti* to represent this highest state of spiritual love.

As you have reflected on the nature of bhakti as a yogic sādhana, a question may have arisen in your mind: once this supreme love has been known and experienced, is there any need for devotional practices?

As a way to focus my comments in this regard, I refer now to sūtra 30. It reads:

स्वयम् फलरूपतेति ब्रह्मकुमारः ॥३०॥

svayaṁ phalarūpateti brahmakumāraḥ

"According to the son of Brahmā, it is of the nature of its own fruit."

— Sūtra 30

"According to the son of Brahmā"

This is a reference to Nārada himself. Brahmā is one of the great gods of classical India, one who is particularly associated with creation and creativity. Traditionally, the figure of Nārada is understood to have been born from Brahmā's mind and is thus sometimes referred to as Brahmakumāra, the child or son of Brahmā. With this phrase Nārada is therefore referring to himself and thus to his own understanding of the nature of devotional love.

"It is of the nature of its own fruit"

With the reference here to fruit, *phala*, our text also implies the idea of a seed. This brings to mind two related points. First, just as a seed will become a fruit, so too a cause will have an effect. Similarly, just as anytime there is a fruit there must first be a seed, so too whenever there is an effect, there must necessarily be a cause. In other words, our text is speaking here of the relationship between spiritual practices as a seed and the state to which those practices lead as the fruit that results from that seed.

This sūtra comes in the middle of a group, sūtras 25-33, which tell of the relationship between the path of devotional love and other spiritual paths. In those other sūtras, our text mentions some other teachers in India who defined or characterized bhakti in various ways. One such figure thought that bhakti results from the disciplined cultivation of discriminating knowledge and insight into the nature of God. Another felt that it comes as a result of one's conscious dedication to acting in the world in a sacred manner. Another thought it comes as a result of the practice of yogic austerities, and still another saw that it is the product of one's emotions. In these cases, spiritual love would be the fruit that comes from the seed of clear knowledge, or from performing certain rituals properly, or from undertaking diligent asceticism, or of intensifying one's feelings.

However, by saying in sūtra 30 that the highest spiritual love "is of the nature of its own fruit," Nārada tells us that it is ultimately not the product of anything but love itself. This point is worth expanding.

The Goal is Revealed in the Path

Love is of the divine Heart's own eternal and unconditioned nature. Being eternal, this Love is uncreated. Accordingly, the Love that supports each of us at the core of our being is not produced as the effect of any cause. Therefore, the Love we experience is not finally the result of our actions in the world, not the product of our disciplined knowledge, not the consequence of our austerities, not the effect of our emotions. Its presence and expression within us is not the fruit of anything but Itself.

Think about this for a moment. If Love were the result of some cause, then it would disappear if that cause were to disappear. It would be contingent on that cause. But Love is not contingent on anything whatsoever. Love is an aspect of God's nature, and God is not conditioned by anything. Dwelling within us as the Source of being, God inwardly shares Love with the human spirit. Thus, the Love that stands in the true Heart, which is our own highest nature, is not dependent on anything. It is completely free. It is spontaneous. The essence of such Love is the essence of God's own love. It is not created; it is revealed.

While it may feel as if our devotional perspectives and spiritual disciplines were creating this love in our lives, what is really happening is that those sensibilities and actions are inwardly clearing the way so that the Love that is already the Self's nature can shine forth.

The state of love is revealed in practices of love. The path and the goal are one and the same. Love is the means, and love is the end.

Understood and experienced in this way, the devotional love that drives your spiritual life is the very same as the Love in which you can find your completion. Ultimately, in their essence, there is no difference between the two. The *Jñāneśvarī* expresses similar sentiments. In one set of verses Kṛṣṇa says that a true bhakta is "my greatest joy, my very life" and that "to such a person, worship, the worshiper, and the object of worship are always Me, through the experience of union."[111]

There are several important ramifications of this identity of means and end in the practice of devotional yoga. I will mention three.

The first is that even when one experiences the expansive fullness and perfection of Love, even to a small degree, one also experiences deep joy in continuing to perform one's spiritual practices. The more we taste the ambrosia of Love, the more we offer our love.

Second, when we dwell in the highest form of devotion, the whole of our life becomes an expression of this state. It is not that part of the time we do spiritual practices, and then the rest of the time we forget the divine Heart. We offer our love to God in everything we do and in every moment of our day, a point to which I will return in the following chapter.

Third, when our hearts are illumined by our love for the divine Beloved, the spontaneous and yet also sustained expression of this love becomes, itself, the highest purpose of our lives. Love is so foundational to human existence, so important to a sacred universe, so encompassing in its effect, that it embraces and fulfills all other forms of human yearning and fulfillment. True love has no purpose external to itself, and yet it also gives meaning to all forms of human endeavor.

Love is the Fulfillment of the Goals of Life

As a way to expand this third point I refer to the relationship, as the bhakti tradition in India sees it, between spiritual devotion and the four ways in which, according to Indian thought, people seek fulfillment in life.

Each of these is known as a *puruṣārtha*, a word literally meaning "goal of a person." Classical Indian thought regards the four puruṣārthas to be: *kāma*, understood in this context not as harmful desire but rather as sensual enjoyment and pleasure more broadly; *artha*, wealth and power; *dharma*, commitment to sustaining one's family, society and the world through one's responsible and supportive action; and *mokṣa*, freedom from the redundant and oppressive cycles of existence.

The bhakti tradition, however, holds that there is a fifth puruṣārtha that is the single and best way to attain all four of the other goals. This is the way of devotional love. The *Bhāgavata Purāṇa*, for example, tells us that loving service is "the one and only means to attain one's goal, whether that goal be kāma, artha, dharma, or mokṣa"[112] and similarly proclaims that "the supreme goal of human life is to cultivate one-pointed loving devotion to God and to honor his presence in all beings."[113]

The discovery, recovery and expression of Love is understood to fulfill all of one's highest hopes and noblest of desires in the world. In other words, genuine love fulfills all of one's best and worthiest intentions. Indeed, the *Bhāgavata Purāṇa* asserts the position that all of one's spiritual disciplines and modes of action on the path to God find unbreakable attainment (*acyutārtha*) by means of devotional love.[114]

When there is higher love, kāma shifts from self-centered sensual desire to selfless, refined and pure delight and appreciation of the divine beauty in the world.

When there is higher love, artha is transformed from egoistic pursuit of self-aggrandizement to selfless work in helping others in the world toward well-being so that humanity itself is uplifted. Outer wealth becomes a helpful tool to support one's loving endeavors toward others in addition to allowing the shelter and food one needs to protect and nourish the body. Love also brings inner wealth in the form of feelings, emotions and sensibilities that refine and elevate one's humane nature.

In a like manner, to act out of love for the divine Presence in all things is a human being's preeminent dharma in life. On this particular point, the *Bhāgavata Purāṇa* notes that "the highest dharma [*parādharma*] is that which leads to selfless and unwavering devotion to God" and, referring to the path of love in its entirety, says "to feel unbroken devotion to the Lord: this is one's highest dharma in the world."[115]

Finally, to dwell in love for that divine Presence is understood to be more compelling and fulfilling even than freedom from the cycles of existence. The particular devotional tradition of which the *Bhakti Sūtra* is a part holds that the longing for *mokṣa* can actually veil a subtle but powerful self-centeredness. The *Bhāgavata Purāṇa*, which is also part of that tradition, notes that there are five types of liberation — living in the same heaven as God, possessing the same supernatural powers as God, being near God, having a similar form as God's, and union with

God. According to this tradition, however, to live in love brings an even higher freedom. That text goes on to say that the highest lovers of God do not accept these types of mokṣa, for their only wish is to offer loving service to God. Those who are immersed in the highest form of devotion renounce all of these ulterior motives. As Kṛṣṇa says of devotees who have given up attachment to selfish fruits of their love, "the only thing they want is the opportunity to offer loving service to me. Such is the majesty and glory of this highest form of love."[116]

The point here, in part, is that the lover of God freely offers love for no other purpose than to love freely. Love is the means and love is the end, and in love there is true freedom.

Indeed, the *Bhāgavata Purāṇa* maintains the position that, without the cultivation and expression of love, the pursuit of all the other goals in life becomes a hollow show.[117] On the other hand, when there is genuine love there is really no other goal to attain. As Kṛṣṇa says to his disciple Uddhava elsewhere in that text, "to those who follow the teachings, I have given experience of deep love and devotion to me. They give themselves totally to me. What other purpose is there for them to fulfill?"[118]

To live in Love is to actualize the highest potential and truest nature of the human spirit. To love is to be authentic to the real Self, for to love deeply is to give oneself fully to that which is most worthy of love, namely, the One who is *parāsatya*: the fullest, most authentic and supreme state of truth.[119] To live in Love fulfills one's true nature. This fulfillment brings forth one's compassion, resolve and strength. It stands gently yet firmly in one's inner equanimity and serenity. As the *Bhāgavata Purāṇa* says, such Love "fills the soul with peace."[120] There is no greater joy, no greater freedom, no greater fulfillment, than to live each moment in this Love.

Terms appearing in Chapter 12

artha Literally, "purpose, goal." In traditional Indian concept of values, the word can be understood to be a "purpose" of one's life. See also *puruṣārtha*, below.

Brahmakumāra In the *Nārada Bhakti Sūtra*, a name for Nārada himself, who according to some traditions is regarded to have been born of the imagination of the creator god (Brahmā) and thus to have been a son or child (*kumāra*) of Brahmā.

dharma One's ethical responsibility or moral obligation; one's particular way of supporting the integrity of existence. See also *puruṣārtha* and *parādharma*, below.

mokṣa Freedom or release from entrapping, redundant cycles of existence, traditionally often put in terms of release from the cycle (*saṁsāra*) of birth and death. See also *puruṣārtha*, below.

parābhakti Supreme devotional love; love in which lover and Beloved are at one with each other in the Love they share; full inner communion with the Beloved in which boundaries separating the lover and Beloved dissolve; full immersion into divine Love within yet transcending all other forms of love.

parādharma The highest (*parā*) responsibility or moral obligation (*dharma*); in the devotional tradition, the highest set of moral sensibilities based on the reality of Love.

parāsatya Supreme (*parā*) truth (*satya*); in the devotional tradition, the supreme truth that is Love itself.

puruṣārtha A goal or purpose (*artha*) of a human existence (*puruṣa* meaning "person"), often said to consist of four aspects: *kāma*, physical pleasure; *artha*, material success; *dharma*, responsibility to others and to the world; and *mokṣa*, freedom, release from all forms of bondage due to ignorance of the true Self within all beings. Some devotional schools of thought add a fifth *puruṣārtha* that embraces and fulfills all other goals of life, namely: *bhakti* or *preman*, pure unconditional love for the divine Beloved.

Table X

Some Synonyms and Near-Synonyms Describing the Highest State of Devotional Love (*Parābhakti*)

ahaitukī bhakti	Devotional love offered without ulterior motive or purpose.
ananya bhakti	Devotional love offered to none other than the Beloved.
eka bhakti	One-pointed devotion; devotional love directed solely to the true Beloved.
ekānta bhakti	Devotional love directed to the true Beloved as its only object.
kevala bhakti	Devotional love that is not mixed or tied up with other motivations; pure, uncompounded devotion.
mukhya bhakti	The "top, foremost, eminent, principal" level of devotional love.
nirguṇa bhakti	Devotion without limiting qualities, devotional love unconstrained by delimiting predilections; love for the formless Beloved beyond all qualities and characteristics.
nirupādhi bhakti	Unmixed devotion, devotion that is not a deceptive substitute for another emotion, devotional love without attributes, absolute love.
niṣkāma bhakti	Love offered without seeking the fulfillment of a self-centered desire.
śuddha bhakti	Pure, untainted devotion.

Chapter 13

In Love, All is Love

At the level of parābhakti, supreme devotion, one remains immersed in love, both as a constant *way of being* and as an abiding *state of being*. Indian thought holds that this unity is itself embraced by the larger unconditional, unbounded, transcendent Love that is God's own nature. In a passage describing one who is in this state of parābhakti, Kṛṣṇa says that such a devotee "experiences only Me, the pure One, limitless, and beyond the distinction of the goal of life and the means to attain it."[121]

In this state of divine Love there is only God, who is Love itself. In our earlier consideration of sūtra 70 — "They are absorbed in that" — we reflected on the totality with which a lover of God lives in that Love. In a manner similar to Nārada's, Swami Chidvilasananda has said:

> There are many kinds of devotion,
> many stages in devotion,
> and the highest stage
> is called *parābhakti*.
> This is supreme devotion
> in which the Lord and the devotee
> merge into each other completely,
> and the devotee knows nothing else but the Lord.[122]

At the preparatory levels of devotion, one's love and attention may be directed to an outward object of some sort that is understood to be different from oneself. Here, God is thought of as "out there" somewhere, perhaps localized in a particular place or identified with a specific form, to which one offers one's reverence. This is a dualistic devotion based on the perceived difference between the subject and object of one's love.

As devotion deepens, this absorption also takes place inwardly through such practices as contemplation, prayer and meditation. Here one looks within one's heart to behold the Beloved. Outward words fade away as one becomes quiet in the Heart's embracing silence. As the mind calms, one sees more clearly the light of Consciousness pulsating within it in the form of one's own awareness. This is a less dualistic form of devotion. It is communion with God "in here," deep within one's own being.

Then, in parābhakti, this turn inward is accompanied by an outward absorption in the divine Self. One again opens one's eyes to behold and celebrate that sacred Presence in the whole of the universe. When there is this absorption in God, the boundary between internal communion and external setting dissolves. Grounded in Love, one lives in the unity of Love.

In supreme devotion, one lives a life of appreciative, responsible engagement with the world, for one knows that the world is the abode of the divine Self, the true Object of one's love. Here, the lover of God recognizes God in all others. Swami Chidvilasananda has made a similar point in these lines in which she is speaking particularly of the practice of meditation but which presumably would apply to devotional practices in general:

> The goal of meditation
> is *parābhakti*, supreme devotion:
> the purest love, the greatest love,
> the highest love.
> When you have this love,
> you feel the same toward everyone.
> Even though in the beginning
> this love is very one-pointed

you love God, you love the Guru,
you love your own inner Self
once the fountain of love
begins to flow in your being,
this love is for everyone.[123]

The *Bhāgavata Purāṇa* describes a lover of God in a comparable manner and refers to such a one as a *bhagavottama*, the "highest devotee:"

> One who, as a result of worshipping the Beloved,
> sees the Self in all beings
> and who sees all beings in the Self of the Beloved:
> that one is a *bhagavottama*.[124]

The *Jñāneśvarī* presents a similar description of those who are immersed in the highest form of devotion. We might note the humility and sense of reverence that characterizes one who lives in this state. The passage includes a number of poetic images and is worth quoting at length. Describing such bhaktas, Kṛṣṇa says:

> Just as there is one thread running through a piece of cloth from one end to the other, similarly, they recognize no one but Me in the whole universe.... Just as water pouring from a height flows downward without effort, in the same way, it is their nature to pay respect to every creature that they see. Just as the branches of a tree laden with fruit bend toward the earth, similarly, they humble themselves before all creatures. They are always free from conceit. Humility is their wealth, which they offer to Me with words of reverence. Since they are always humble, honor and dishonor do not exist for them, and they easily become united with Me. Always absorbed in Me, they worship Me. O Arjuna, I have described for you the highest form of devotion.[125]

In this final chapter we will look at one of Nārada's sūtras that makes a similar point regarding the all-embracing scope of love at the level of parābhakti. In sūtra 55 our text gives us another concise description of what life is like when one lives in this highest state of spiritual love. It reads:

> तत् प्राप्य तदेवावलोकयति
> तदेव शृनोति तदेव चिन्तयति ॥५५॥
>
> ***tat-prāpya tad-evāvalokayati tadeva śṛṇoti tadeva cintayati***
>
> Achieving that experience one sees only love, hears only love, speaks only love, and thinks of love alone.
>
> — Sūtra 55

You may recall from Chapter 10 that the sūtra that immediately precedes this one, sūtra 54, describes spiritual love as being free of limiting qualities, free of self-centered desire, continually expanding, uninterrupted, most subtle and of the nature of inner experience. So, the "that" throughout this translation of our current sūtra refers to this state of spiritual love.

"Attaining"

It may seem sometimes that the love of which our sūtra speaks is a rather ideal or even perhaps an impossible state to enter into fully. Please notice, though, that it does not say "*if* you attain that." The difference may seem insignificant at first, but the wording is important. In this simple phrase, our text implies that the experience of this love is indeed within reach.

In grammatical terms, the word here for "attaining" (*prāpya*) is a gerund. It thus suggests an action that has taken place in the past or is now taking place. The word could also be translated as "having attained." Accordingly, our sūtra is saying, in part, that when one experiences Love in the world one does so because in some way there is already space in one's heart for that Love. The inner reality of Love precedes and allows one's outward experience of it.

We do not really "attain" this love, for God has freely given it to us and thus it already dwells within us. However, we do need to discover it within us. This discovery of Love takes place through the awakening power of grace and our own spiritual practices. We recover it when we enter into our hearts. The Love uncovered within us then can flow outward from our hearts and reconfigure our experience of the world. We could say that we fall in love with life.

This English expression, "fall in love," is most interesting! Where do we "fall" when we fall in love? In a sense, we descend inward, into our hearts, where Love sits within and with us. Then, we bring that love outward, as if we were drawing sweet water from the depths of a deep well. So, what is really happening when we fall in love is that we have been touched by the divine Heart, the true Self that stands within our own hearts and within the heart of the one we love. You might remember the passage from the *Bṛhadāraṇyaka Upaniṣad* quoted earlier: "It is not for the love of a husband that a husband is dear, rather it is because of the love of the Self [within a husband] that a husband is dear. It is not for the love of a wife that a wife is dear, but rather it is for the love of the Self that a wife is dear. It is not for the love of children that children are dear, but for the love of the Self that children are dear."[126]

Absorbed in this Love — "attaining" this love — we can more fully honor God's presence in others, in ourselves and ultimately in the entirety of existence. When we discover God in this way, we respond with love for that Presence everywhere.

"Sees, hears, speaks, thinks"

We might notice that all the verbs here are in the active voice. Our sūtra thereby implies that love is not a static state of being; it is a dynamic and ever-fresh mode of awareness. Love is energetic and moving. It dwells in the deep silence of the heart, but it expresses itself in the heart's pulsating engagement with the mind, the body, the soul, the world, the hearts of others.

Furthermore, while the verb translated as "hears" in this sūtra is in the indicative mode, the other three verbs are in the causative mode. We don't really have this latter mode in English. We can suggest the causative, though, by shifting the translation from "one sees only that" to "one makes only that to be seen." Similarly, "speaks only that" would be "makes only that be spoken of" and "thinks only that" would be "makes only that be thought of."

Admittedly, the English in such translations would be rather awkward, but, once again, the grammar here is important. Nārada implies that a lover of God is not to be passive in his or her devotion. Love is to be expressed in one's way of being in the world. It is not merely to see that which one has become accustomed to seeing, but rather to see with the eyes of love and thus to behold the infinite Mystery that stands within all upon which one gazes. It is to shift one's way of speaking so that all one says expresses love. And it is to monitor and elevate one's thoughts so that the mind itself is turned constantly toward God. One who is immersed in parābhakti brings that devotion to all one sees, says and thinks.

Nārada keeps the verb for "hears" in the indicative mode. Perhaps this is to mark the importance of astute listening in the yoga of love. When one truly listens, with one's heart as well as one's ears, one opens oneself to the subtle as well as manifest sound of the Self's creative, guiding, transforming and perfecting words. You might try listening closely sometime to the sounds of nature, or to music, poetic speech, or the soft whimpers and giggles of babies. At that moment, listen with the understanding that you are listening to the voice of the Self. Then, listen attentively and closely to the silence within all manifest sounds, and you similarly may hear the presence of the Self.

The four verbs in our sūtra can also be divided in another way. On the one hand there are "sees" and "hears," and on the other hand there are "speaks" and "thinks." The first two verbs imply that love is a revelatory experience of God, while the latter two imply that love is a committed way of being with God. Said differently, the former two suggest ways of receiving God's presence while the latter two are ways of giving oneself to God.

When one enters into the highest state of love one recognizes everything in the world as an expression of that Love — in everything one sees, one sees the divine Self and in everything one hears, one hears the Self. Accordingly, the sūtra would also be saying that at the same time one truly experiences love for all things, one commits oneself to living in consonance with that love — one speaks only of that, and one thinks only of that. Everything one does would be in service of that love.

"Only that"

The vision of the divine Self in all people and in all things embraces all of existence. It is interesting to me that the verb *lokayati*, which is the word in this sūtra translated here as "sees," is related to the noun *loka*, the latter meaning "world." There are other verbs that Nārada could have chosen to signify the act of seeing. Perhaps, by choosing this one, he indicates that the vision of God is one that encompasses one's world, as it were: the totality of one's life. There is the outer world, and there is the inner world. Immersed in supreme devotion, all of one's world, both inner and outer, is illumined by the light of this love. Indeed, gazing onto this world in both its inner and outer totality, the lover beholds "only that." The lover beholds only Love.

When there is parābhakti, the lover is immersed in the Beloved's nature as Love. So, when there is supreme devotion, there is no alienation from the One who is Love. As Kṛṣṇa says in the *Bhagavad Gītā*,

> One who is disciplined in yoga
> sees the Self dwelling in all beings
> and all beings dwelling in the Self.
> One sees the same [Self], at all times.
> One who sees Me everywhere
> and sees everything in Me:
> I am not lost for him,
> and he is not lost for Me.[127]

Similarly, in the *Jñāneśvarī* Kṛṣṇa says to Arjuna:

Whoever worships Me as
the One existing in all beings
through his realization of unity,
who knows that despite the multiplicity of beings
there is no duality in their hearts,
and who knows that My essence
pervades everything everywhere: . . .
just as a lamp and its light are one,
so is he in Me and I in him.[128]

The absorption into Love at the level of parābhakti is the discovery of the highest nature of the human heart. It is the realization of just who we really are, or at least could be if we were to live always in love for God. When we are absorbed in love, we become courageous in taking responsibility for our lives, in being just in the face of injustice, and in allowing the light of compassion to illumine our vision of others. When we are absorbed in Love, we live in deep gratitude for God's presence, joyfully celebrate the wonder of our existence and see God in every face we meet. We are able to do this because of God's own love for all beings, a Love that we have discovered burns even within our own hearts.

The attitude that God's presence is to be seen in all beings does not mean that one does not also see suffering in the world, for people do indeed experience great sorrow that arises from many sources. Indeed, one who loves God will be increasingly touched by the extent and depth of this suffering. Yet, one's love can also help reduce that suffering, even in what might seem like small ways.

I remember a short conversation I had with a woman a few weeks after the horrors of September 11, 2001. Immense suffering had been brought to the world, this time by terrible, violent acts taken against innocent people and by the dehumanizing forces of many kinds in the world that have led people to perform those acts. There was, and still continues to be, great sorrow in many hearts as a result of that terrible event.

She told me that, earlier in the morning we met, she had taken a walk through a park. She noticed the bright light of the rising sun on the tops of the trees. She heard the shimmering of leaves blowing in the gentle autumn breeze. The cool air refreshed her cheeks. She stopped to savor the moment. As she did so, rising tenderly from deep within her, welled up a sense of the divine Presence within all things. Remaining mindful of the immense suffering in the world, she also looked at the beauty around her. She found herself thinking, "All of this beauty is made real by God's love. What a miracle existence is!" She looked into the pink and orange dawning sky that was turning ever more blue and she knew: the world itself is a revelation of Love.

She continued by telling me that she then went to sit in a temple to pray and to meditate. The light from the now fully risen morning sun played on the floor. Small candles burned softly, and the gentle fragrance of flowers infused the air. She felt that everything in that quiet space — *everything*, she said — had given itself to the moment in an offering of pure love. The dance of light and shadows was Love, the flames were Love, the scent from the candles was Love. Then, she looked at the people who were coming into the temple to pray and to offer their silent worship and she came to see and feel that their very lives in all of their variety and complexity emerge from Love. She felt fondness and affection for every one of them, and yet she did not even know their names.

She said that her eyes then filled with soft tears of appreciation and gratitude for these people who would otherwise be complete strangers to her. Struck by this, she noticed that underneath these feelings, she felt a soft and quiet yet very powerful sense of God's presence within each of them. They remained who they were as individuals, but she saw a divine affirmation in each of them. She quietly offered her blessings to each of them and sent them her best good will. I suspect that she would have found it very difficult to treat them poorly in any way while immersed in her heart in this manner.

Her story made me wonder: what would it be like if everybody were to look at the world and at others in this way all the time? Would people inflict pain and sorrow on each other? Would they do things that brought anger, hatred, misery and even death to others?

The answer, it seems to me, would be "no," for they would see God's presence deep within each other, and this vision would make it impossible for them to do so. The world would become a more radiant and more humane place, for people would be more compassionate, more generous, more grateful, more respectful of the beauty and integrity of life and would act outwardly in ways that were consonant with these inner forces. People would be less willing to allow others to suffer in poverty or injustice. More concern would be given to the health of the environment. There would be less close-minded and judgmental attitudes toward people of other cultures and faiths.

Lovers of the divine Beloved serving in the medical profession would see God's face in those for whom they give care. Teachers would see God in their students, merchants would see God in their customers, employers in their employees, bus drivers in their passengers and passengers in their bus drivers. Appreciation for others and gratitude for life would surge forth within us as we see that all beings, including ourselves, are held in God's love.

We are born of God's love, we are sustained by God's love throughout our lives, and we remain in God's love at our deaths. Since God is Love, then Love is the object of all our sacred knowledge. Love is the reason we perform our many responsibilities to the world. Love stands within us as our true nature. To live in love is therefore our completion; it is our wholeness and our perfection, and it is our truest freedom. Living life in love for the divine Beloved, we can more and more fully offer ourselves in gratitude to that which is the Source and Fulfillment of our being, and can extend our love to others in service of this same sacred Presence within them.

Revelation of Love can take place at any time, even in circumstances we would not normally expect it to happen. When we understand and experience the world through Love, though, we know that everything in our lives finds its definition and meaning in relationship to it. The journey into Love never ends, for the journey itself is the end.

I wish you well as you follow the path of spiritual love. Guided and inspired by sacred texts and by the compassionate words of spiritual masters throughout the centuries, and supported always by the benevolent power of grace, may you turn toward and become immersed in the divine Heart. As you move through your life, may you know that you are cherished always by the Dearest One. May you delight in God's fine, inner presence and may you look for God in all you meet. May your reverence, courage, gratitude and joy ever increase. May your life be infused with Exquisite Love.

Translation of the Nārada Bhakti Sūtra

Note: A guide to pronunciation of Sanskrit words appears at the beginning of this book.

1 अथातो भक्तिं व्याख्यास्यामः ॥

athāto bhaktiṁ vyākhyāsyāmaḥ

Now, therefore, we will speak of bhakti.

2 सा त्वस्मिन् परमप्रेमरूपा ॥

sā tvasmin paramapremarūpā

It, truly, is of the nature of the highest form of love in this.

3 अमृतस्वरूपा च ॥

amṛtasvarūpā ca

And it is of the nature of ambrosia.

4 यल्लब्ध्वा पुमान् सिद्धो भवत्यमृतो भवति तृप्तो भवति ॥

yal-labhvā pumān siddho bhavatyamṛto bhavati tṛpto bhavati

Attaining it, a person becomes perfected,
becomes immortal, becomes content.

5 यत् प्राप्य न किञ्चिद् वाञ्छति न शोचति
न द्वेष्टि न रमते नोत्साही भवति ॥

yat prāpya na kiñcid vāñchati na śocati na
dveṣṭi na ramate notsāhī bhavati

Having reached it, a person neither desires anything [else], nor grieves, nor hates, nor enjoys [anything else], nor is active [in pursuit of selfish ends].

6 यज्ज्ञात्वा मत्तो भवति स्तब्धो भवत्यात्मारामो भवति ॥

yaj-jñātvā matto bhavati stabdho bhavati ātmārāmo bhavati

Having known which, one becomes ecstatic, one becomes stunned, one comes to delight in the Self.

7 सा न कामयमाना निरोधरूपत्वात् ॥

sā na kāmayamānā nirodharūpatvāt

It does not arise from desire because it is of the nature of calming control.

8 निरोधस्तु लोकवेदव्यापारन्यासः ॥

nirodhastu lokavedavyāpāranyāsaḥ

This control is the consecration of worldly and sacred activity.

9 तस्मिन्ननन्यता तद्विरोधिषूदासिनता च ॥

tasminnananyatā tadvirodhiṣūdāsinatā ca

And, in this, there is non-otherness and disinterest in that which goes against it.

10 अन्याश्रयाणां त्यागोऽनन्यता ॥

anyāśrayāṇāṁ tyāgo'nanyatā

In this non-otherness there is relinquishment of [all other] refuges.

11 लोकवेदेषु तदनुकूलाचरणं ताद्विरोधिषूदासीनता ॥

lokavedeṣu tadanukūlācaraṇaṁ tadvirodhiṣūdāsīnatā

Disinterest in that which goes against it [refers] to the performance of worldly and sacred activities that are favorable to that [love].

12 भवतु निश्चयदार्ढ्याद्ऊर्ध्वं शास्त्ररक्षणम् ॥

bhavatu niścayadārḍhyādūrdhvaṁ śāstrarakṣaṇam

Even after [spiritual love arises in the heart], let there be a firm commitment to heeding the teachings.

13 अन्यथा पातित्यशङ्कया ॥

anyathā pātityaśaṅkayā

Otherwise, there is danger of a fall.

14 लोकोऽपि तावदेव भोजनादिव्यापारस्त्वाशरीरधारणावधि ॥

loko'pi tāvadeva bhojanādivyāpārastvāśarīradhāraṇāvadhi

Certainly, also, let there be the performance of worldly activities such as eating that are essential to supporting the life of the body until its end.

15 तल्लक्षणानि वाच्यन्ते नानामतभेदात् ॥

tal-lakṣaṇāni vācyante nānāmatabhedāt

There are different descriptions of the characteristics of that [love] because there are various ways of understanding it.

16 पूजादिष्वनुराग इति पाराशर्यः ॥

pūjādiṣvanurāga iti pārāśaryaḥ

According to the son of Parāsarya (that is to say, according to the sage Vyāsa) [bhakti] is an affectionate feeling in worship and other [practices].

17 कथादिष्विति गर्गः ॥

kathādiṣviti gargaḥ

According to Garga, [bhakti] is [expressed through the telling of sacred] stories and so forth.

18 आत्मरत्यविरोधेनेति शाण्डिल्यः ॥

ātmaratyavirodheneti śāṇḍilyaḥ

According to Śāṇḍilya, [bhakti] is consonant with delight in the Self.

19 नारदस्तु तदर्पिताखिलाचारता तद्विस्मरणे परमव्याकुलतेति ॥

nāradastu tadarpitākhilācāratā tadvismaraṇe paramavyākulateti

According to Nārada, however, it is when all of one's manner of action is of a consecrated nature and when there is supreme sense of being lost upon forgetting.

20 अस्त्येवमेवम् ॥

astyevamevam

It is in these various ways [that bhakti is understood].

21 यथा व्रजगोपिकानाम् ॥

yathā vrajagopikānām

An example [of bhaktas would be] the cowherd women of Vraja.

22 तत्रापि न माहात्म्यज्ञानविस्मृत्यपवादः ॥

tatrāpi na māhātmyajñānavismṛtyapavādaḥ

Even in this case, there can be no objection regarding their forgetfulness of the knowledge of [God's] magnificence.

23 तद्विहीनं जाराणामिव ॥

tadvihīnaṁ jārāṇāmiva

For without that [knowledge, passionate sentiments would be] like that of decadent lovers.

24 नास्त्येव तस्मिंस्तत्सुखित्वम् ॥

nāstyeva tasmiṁstatsukhitvam

The happiness in such [selfish passion] is not happiness in this [the Beloved].

25 सा तु कर्मज्ञानयोगेभ्योऽप्यधिकतरा ॥

sā tu karmajñānayogebhyo'pyadhikatarā

[The happiness of spiritual love] is greater even than [happiness derived from] action, knowledge and other forms of yoga.

26 फलरूपत्वात् ॥

phalarūpatvāt

This is because [spiritual love is] the essence of the fruit [of these other forms of spiritual practice].

27 ईश्वरस्याप्यभिमानिद्वेष्टाद्दैन्यप्रियत्वाच्च ॥

īśvarasyāpyabhimānidveṣṭvāddainyapriyatvāc-ca

Also, [this difference between devotional love and other sentiments is due to] the Lord's aversion to the arrogant and fondness for humility.

28 तस्या ज्ञानमेव साधनमित्येके ॥

tasyā jñānameva sādhanamityeke

According to some, knowledge alone is the means [to spiritual love].

29 अन्योन्याश्रयत्वमित्येके ॥

anyonyāśrayatvamityeke

According to some, there is an interdependence between the various [means].

30 स्वयम् फलरूपतेति ब्रह्मकुमारः ॥

svayam phalarūpateti brahmakumāraḥ

According to the son of Brahmā [that is to say, Nārada], it is of the nature of its own fruit.

31 राजगृहभोजनादिषु तथैव दृष्टत्वात् ॥

rājagṛhabhojanādiṣu tathaiva dṛṣṭatvāt

That this is so can be seen in the examples of a king, a home, eating, and so on.

32 न तेन राजपरितोषः क्षुच्छान्तिर् वा ॥

na tena rājaparitoṣaḥ kṣucchāntirvā

Not by this is a king satisfied or hunger appeased.

33 तस्मात् सैव ग्राह्य मुमुक्षुभिः ॥

tasmāt saiva grāhya mumukṣubhiḥ

Accordingly, those who yearn for liberation should embrace this [love] alone.

34 तस्याः साधनानि गायन्त्याचार्याः ॥

tasyāḥ sādhanāni gāyanty-ācāryāḥ

Spiritual teachers sing of the means of [developing] this.

35 तत्तु विषयत्यागात् सङ्गत्यागाच्च ॥

tat-tu viṣayatyāgāt saṅgatyāgāc-ca

One can attain that [spiritual love], however, from renunciation of sense objects and from the renunciation of attachment.

36 अव्यावृत्तभजनात् ॥

avyāvṛtta-bhajanāt

From unceasing worship.

37 लोकेऽपि भगवद्गुणश्रवणकीर्तनात्

loke 'pi bhagavad-guṇa-śravaṇa-kīrtanāt

Even while in the world, [spiritual love arises] from hearing and singing forth God's qualities.

38 मुख्यतस्तु महत्कृपयैव भगवद्कृपालेशाद्वा ॥

mukhyatastu mahat-kṛpayaiva bhagavad-kṛpā-leśād-vā

Indeed, it is primarily through the compassionate grace of a great one, or through a portion of the compassionate grace of God.

39 महत्सङ्गस्तु दुर्लभोऽगम्योऽमोघश्च ॥

mahat-saṅgas-tu durlabho 'gamyo 'moghaś-ca

Although companionship of a great one is difficult to attain, it is unfathomable, and it is unfailing.

40 लभ्यतेऽपि तत्कृपयैव ॥

labhyate 'pi tat-kṛpayaiva

It is only through grace that this companionship is gained.

41 तस्मिंस्तज्जने भेदाभावात् ॥

tasmiṁs-taj-jane bhedābhāvāt

Because there is no difference between
that and those arising from it.

42 तदेव साध्यतां तदेव साध्यताम् ॥

tadeva sādhyatāṁ tadeva sādhyatām

That alone is to be cultivated, that alone is to be cultivated.

43 दुःसङ्गः सर्वथैव त्याज्यः ॥

duḥsaṅgaḥ sarvathaiva tyājyaḥ

Harmful association in every respect is to be given up.

44 कामक्रोधमोहस्मृतिभ्रंशबुद्धिनाशसर्वनाशकारणत्वात् ॥

kāma-krodha-moha-smṛtibhraṁśa-buddhināśa-sarvanāśa-kāraṇatvāt

Harmful association is the cause of selfish desire, anger, delusion, lapse in remembrance, loss of clear wisdom and the ruin of all.

45 तरङ्गायिता अपीमे सङ्गात् समुद्रायन्ति ॥

taraṅgāyitā apīme saṅgāt samudrāyanti

From small ripples of attachment swell [waves on a wild] sea.

46 कस्तरति कस्तरति मायां यः सङ्गं त्यजति यो
महानुभावं सेवते निर्ममो भवति ॥

kas-tarati kas-tarati māyāṁ yaḥ saṅgaṁ tyajati yo
mahānubhāvaṁ sevate nirmamo bhavati

Who crosses, who rises above, the [ocean of] illusion? One who lets go of clinging [to harmful associations], who serves those [immersed in] the great sentiment [of sublime spiritual love], who is free from the sense of "mine" . . .

47 यो विविक्तस्थानं सेवते यो लोकबन्धमुन्मूलयति
निस्त्रैगुण्यो भवति यो योगक्षेमं त्यजति ॥

yo vivikta-sthānaṁ sevate yo lokabandham-unmūlayati
nistraiguṇyo bhavati yo yogakṣemaṁ tyajati

. . . who abides in solitude, who dissolves bondage to the world, who becomes free of the three guṇas, who relinquishes [dependence on worldly] acquisitions and security ...

48 यः कर्मफलं त्यजति कर्माणि संन्यस्यति ततो निर्द्वन्द्वो भवति ॥

yaḥ-karmaphalaṁ tyajati karmāṇi saṁnyasyati tato nirdvandvo bhavati

... who relinquishes the fruits of actions,
renounces actions, becomes free of dualism.

49 यो वेदानपि संन्यस्यति केवलमविच्छिन्नानुरागं लभते ॥

yo vedānapi saṁnyasyati kevalam-avicchinnānurāgaṁ labhate

Relinquishing even [rites enjoined by the] Vedas, a complete, unceasing, intense affection [for God] alone is attained.

50 स तरति स तरति लोकांस्तारायति ॥

sa tarati sa tarati lokāṁs-tārāyati

[The bhakta] crosses [the torrent], [the bhakta] crosses [the torrent]. [The bhakta] helps all in the world to cross.

51 अनिर्वचनीयं प्रेमस्वरूपम् ॥

anirvacanīyaṁ prema-svarūpam

The essential nature of love cannot be expressed in words.

52 मूकास्वादनवत् ॥

mūkāsvādanavat

It is like one who cannot speak [attempting to describe] flavor.

53 प्रकाश्यते क्वापि पात्रे ॥

prakāśyate kvāpi pātre

It reveals itself where there is an able vessel.

54 गुणरहितं कामनरहितं प्रतिक्षणवर्धमानम्
अविच्छिन्नं सूक्ष्मतरम् अनुभवरूपम् ॥

guṇarahitaṁ kāmanarahitaṁ pratikṣaṇavardhamānam
avicchinnaṁ sūkṣmataram anubhavarūpam

It is free of limiting qualities, free of self-centered desire, ever-expanding, uninterrupted, most subtle, of the nature of inner experience.

55 तत् प्राप्य तदेवावलोकयति तदेव शृनोति तदेव चिन्तयति ॥

tat-prāpya tad-evāvalokayati tadeva śṛṇoti tadeva cintayati

Achieving that experience one sees only love, hears only love, speaks only love, and thinks of love alone.

56 गौणी त्रिधा गुणभेदादर्तादिभेदाद्वा ॥

gauṇī tridhā guṇabhedād-artādi-bhedād-vā

Preparatory [bhakti] is of three kinds according to the difference in one's nature or to difference in distress and so on.

57 उत्तरस्मादुत्तरस्मात् पूर्वापूर्वा श्रेयाय भवति ॥

uttarasmād-uttarasmāt pūrvapūrvā śreyāya bhavati

Each succeeding one becomes more splendid than the preceding one.

58 अन्यस्मात् सौलभ्यं भक्तौ ॥

anyasmāt saulabhyaṁ bhaktau

The [more splendid] state of spiritual love is easier to attain than others.

59 प्रमाणान्तरस्यानपेक्षत्वात् स्वयं प्रमाणत्वात् ॥

pramāṇāntarasyānapekṣatvāt svayaṁ pramāṇatvāt

[It is easier to realize] because its proof is self-evident and because it does not need proof in another manner.

60 शान्तिरूपात् परमानन्दरूपाच्च ॥

śāntirūpāt paramānandarūpāc-ca

It is of the nature of peace, and it is of the nature of supreme joy.

61 लोकहानौ चिन्ता न कार्या निवेदितात्मलोकवेदत्वात् ॥

lokahānau cintā na kāryā niveditātmalokavedatvāt

There should be no anxiety in relinquishing [the ways of the] world because one dedicates the world, oneself and one's sacred activities [to God].

62 न सत्सिद्धौ लोकव्यवहारो हेयः किन्तु फलत्यागस्तत्साधनञ्च कार्यमेव ॥

na sat-siddhau loka-vyavahāro heyaḥ kintu phala-tyāgas-tat-sādhanañ-ca kāryam-eva

In the development of [spiritual love], it is not worldly activity that is to be renounced, but rather the fruit [of that activity]; and one should cultivate the spiritual disciplines for this.

63 स्त्रीधननास्तिकचरित्रं न श्रवणियम् ॥

strīdhananāstikacaritraṁ na śravaṇīyam

One should not listen to [others' conversations about] sexual relations, wealth and the deeds of faithless people.

64 अभिमानदम्भाधिकं त्याज्यम ॥

abhimāna-dambhādhikaṁ tyājyam

Arrogance, deceit and so forth are to be renounced.

65 तदर्पिताखिलाचारः सन् कामक्रोधाभिमानादिकं
तस्मिन्नेव करणीयम् ॥

tad-arpitākhilācāraḥ san kāma-krodhābhimānādikaṁ tasminn-eva karaṇīyam

Offering all of one's actions [to God], one should act on [self-centered] desire, anger, pride and so on only in [relation to one's offering] to God.

66 त्रिरूपभङ्गपूर्वकं नित्यदास्यनित्यकान्तभजनात्मकं
प्रेम कार्यं प्रेमैव कार्यम् ॥

tri-rūpa-bhaṅga-pūrvakaṁ nitya-dāsya-nitya-kānta-bhajanātmakaṁ prema kāryaṁ premaiva kāryam

The three forms of [conditional love] previously mentioned are surpassed when the self offers devotion [that is like that of] a constant servant or a constant lover. One should act out of love. Truly, one should act out of love.

67 भक्ता एकान्तिनो मुख्याः ॥

bhaktā ekāntino mukhyāḥ

The foremost bhaktas are those who are one-pointed.

68 कण्ठावरोधरोमाश्रुभिः परस्परं लपमानाः
पावयन्ति कुलानि पृथिवीञ्च ॥

kaṇṭhāvarodha-romāśrubhiḥ parasparaṁ lapamānāḥ pāvayanti kulāni pṛthivīñ-ca

Their voices choking when talking with each other, with physical exhilaration, and with tears flowing from their eyes, they purify their kulas [that is to say, their communities] and the earth.

69 तीर्थीकुर्वन्ति तीर्थानि सुकर्मीकुर्वन्ति कर्माणि
सच्छास्त्रीकुर्वन्ति शास्त्राणि ॥

tīrthī-kurvanti tīrthāni sukarmī-kurvanti karmāṇi
sac-chāstrī-kurvanti śāstrāṇi

They turn [all] places into sacred places.
They make [all] activities into beneficial activities.
They make teachings into true sacred guidance.

70 तन्मयाः ॥

tanmayāḥ

They are absorbed in that.

71 मोदन्ते पितरो नृत्यन्ति देवताः सनाथा देयं भूर्भवति ॥

modante pitaro nṛtyanti devatāḥ sanāthā ceyaṁ bhūr-bhavati

Ancestors rejoice, gods dance, and the earth becomes protected [by this love], as if by a master.

72 नास्ति तेषु जातिविद्यारूपकुलधनक्रियादिभेदः ॥

nāsti teṣu jāti-vidyā-rūpa-kula-dhana-kriyādibhedaḥ

Among them there are no distinctions based on birth, learning, beauty, family, wealth and so on.

73 यतस्तदीयः ॥

yatas-tadīyaḥ

Since they belong to Him.

74 वादो नावलम्ब्यः ॥

vādo nāvalambyaḥ

There should be no reliance on [contentious] doctrine.

75 बाहुल्यावकाशात्वादनियतत्वाच्च ॥

bāhulyāvakāśātvād-aniyatatvāc-ca

Because there is room for many arguments
and because they do not lead to certainty.

76 भक्तिशास्त्राणि मनननीयानि तद्बोधकर्माणि करणीयानि ॥

bhaktiśāstrāṇi manananīyāni tadbodhakarmmāṇi karaṇīyāni

Teachings on bhakti should be reflected on;
practices that awaken it should be undertaken.

77 सुखदुःखेच्छालाभादित्यक्ते काले प्रतीक्षमाणे
क्षणार्द्धमपि व्यर्थं न नेयम् ॥

sukha-duḥkheccā-lābhādityakte kāle pratīkṣamāṇe
kṣaṇārddham-api vyarthaṁ na neyam

Relinquishing happiness, dissatisfaction, self-centered willfulness, worldly gain, and so on, when there is attentive awareness in every moment, not even half an instant should be passed uselessly.

78 अहिंसासत्यशौचदयास्तिक्यादिचारित्र्याणि परिपालनीयानि ॥

ahiṁsā-satya-śauca-dayāstikyādi-cāritryāṇi paripālanīyāni

Unwillingness to do harm, truthfulness, purity, generous
compassion, the affirmation of Divinity and other such
beneficial modes of conduct are to be fully protected.

79 सर्वदा सर्वभावेन निश्चिन्तैर्भगवानेव भजनीयः ॥

sarvadā sarvabhāvena niścintair-bhagvān-eva bhajanīyaḥ

God alone is to be worshipped by those
without worry all the time with all the heart.

80 स कीर्त्यमानः शीघ्रमेवाविर्भवत्यनुभावयति भक्तान् ॥

sa kīrttyamānaḥ śīghram-evāvirbhavaty-anubhāvayati bhaktān

When there is singing [of God's qualities], then [God] immediately reveals his presence in the devotees' awareness.

81 त्रिसत्यस्य भक्तिरेव गरीयसी भक्तिरेव गरीयसी ॥

tri-satyasya bhaktir-eva garīyasī bhaktir-eva garīyasī

Within the three-fold reality, spiritual love alone is of the greatest significance. Spiritual love alone is of the greatest significance.

82 गुणमहात्म्यासाक्ति-रूपासक्ति-पूजासक्ति-
स्मरणासक्ति-दास्यासक्ति-सख्यासक्ति-वात्सल्यासाक्ति-
कान्तासाक्ति-आत्मनिवेदनासाक्ति-तन्मयासाक्ति-
परमविरहासाक्ति-रूपैकधाप्येकादशधा भवति ॥

guṇamahātmyāsakti-rūpāsakti-pūjāsakti-smaraṇāsakti-dāsyāsakti-sakhyāsakti-vātsalyāsakti-kāntāsakty-ātmanivedanāsakti-tanmayāsakti-paramavirahāsakti-rūpaikadhāpyekādaśadhā bhavati

Though it is one, [spiritual love] it takes eleven forms of loving attachment [to God]: loving attachment to the qualities of God's greatness, loving attachment to [God's] beauty, loving attachment through worship, loving attachment through remembrance, loving attachment through service, loving attachment through friendship [with God], loving attachment [that is like] a parent's [love for a child], loving attachment like that of a lover, loving attachment through offering the totality of oneself [to God], loving attachment by being absorbed [in God], and loving attachment in feeling separate from the Supreme.

83 इत्येवं वदन्ति जन-जल्प-निर्भया एकमताः कूमार-व्यास-शूक-शाण्दिल्य-गर्ग-विष्णु-कौण्डिल्य-शेष-ऊद्धव-आरुणी-बलि-हनुमाद्-विभीषण-आदयो भक्त्य-आचार्याः ॥

ity-evaṁ vadanti jana-jalpa-nirbhayā eka-matāḥ
kūmāra-vyāsa-śuka-śāṇḍilya-garga-viṣṇu-kauṇḍilya-śeṣa-
uddhavāruṇī-bali-hanumād-vibhīṣaṇa-ādayo bhakty-ācāryāḥ

In this very way great teachers of spiritual love have unanimously taught without worry of people's chatter: Kumāra, Vyāsa, Śuka, Śāṇḍīlya, Garga, Viṣṇu, Kauṇḍilya, Śeṣa, Uddhava, Āruṇi, Bali, Hanumān, Vibhīṣana and others.

84 य इदं नारदप्रोक्तं शिवानुशासनं विश्वसिति श्रद्धते स भक्तिमान्भवति स प्रेष्ठं लभते स प्रेष्ठं लभते एति ॥

ya idaṁ nārada-proktaṁ śivānuśāsanaṁ viśvasiti śraddhate sa
bhaktimān-bhavati sa preṣṭhaṁ labhate sa preṣṭhaṁ labhate iti

One who faithfully and confidently embraces these auspicious teachings spoken by Nārada becomes filled with devotional love. In this way, one obtains the Dearest One — One obtains the Dearest One.

List of Tables

Table I Some Types of Bhakti ... 33

Table II Some Forms of Grace (*Kṛpā*) ... 67

Table III A Classification of the Divine Power to be Its Own Nature (*Svarūpa Śakti*) .. 137

Table IV Some More Types of Bhakti ... 161

Table V Levels of Bhāva ... 185

Table VI Some Sectarian Classifications of Bhāva ... 186

Table VII Levels of Beneficial Dispassion (*Vairāgya*) ... 187

Table VIII Types of Rasa ... 188

Table IX Concentrically Layered Nature of One's Embodiment ... 223

Table X Some Synonyms and Near-Synonyms of *Parābhakti* ... 245

Notes

1 *Ṛg Veda* 10.129.1-4.

2 *Atharva Veda* 19.52.4-5.

3 *Bṛhadāraṇyaka Upaniṣad* 2.1.20.

4 *Śvetāśvatara Upaniṣad* 1.15.

5 *Brahmabindu Upaniṣad* 12.

6 *Chāndogya Upaniṣad* 6.8.7 repeated six times through 6.15.3.

7 *Chāndogya Upaniṣad* 3.14.3.

8 *Śvetāśvatara Upaniṣad* 4.17.

9 Abbreviation of *Śvetāśvatara Upaniṣad* 6.1-7.

10 *Śvetāśvatara Upaniṣad* 6.10-12, abridged.

11 *Bhagavad Gītā* 7.7ab.

12 *Bhagavad Gītā* 18.61ab.

13 *Īśā Upaniṣad* 1 and 6.

14 *Ṛg Veda* 8.13, 9.104, 9.105.

15 *Bhagavad Gītā* 10.13.

16 For the story of Nārada and Vyāsa, see for example *Bhāgavata Purāṇa* 1.4.14-1.7.6.

17 *Jñāneśvarī* 10.149. Unless otherwise noted, all quotations in this book from the *Jñāneśvarī* come from Swami Kripananda, *Jñaneshwar's Gita* (South Fallsburg: SYDA Foundation, 1999).

18 See Swami Tyagisananda, *Aphorisms on the Gospel of Divine Love* (Madras: Sri Ramakrishna Math, 1967), p. 50; Swami Prabhavananda, *Nārada's Way of Divine Love* (Madras: Sri Ramakrishna Math, 1971), p. 12.

[19] *Bhagavad Gītā* 18.55.

[20] *Tirumantiram* 257.

[21] Mariasusai Dhavamony, *Classical Hinduism* (Rome: Gregorian Press, 1982), p. 318.

[22] *Bhagavad Gītā* 4.11.

[23] For textual support regarding these forms of bhakti, see for example *Caitanya Caritāmṛta* 2.8.

[24] The "as" of *atas* turns into an "o" for reasons pertaining to Sanskrit pronunciation.

[25] See *The Brahma Sūtra: The Philosophy of Spiritual Life*, translated with an Introduction and Notes by S. Radhakrishnan (London: George Allen & Unwin, Ltd., 1960), pp. 227-234.

[26] See Swami Tyagisananda, *Aphorisms on the Gospel of Divine Love*, p. 36, and Swami Prabhavananda *Nārada's Way of Divine Love*, p. 8.

[27] See *Bṛhadāraṇyaka Upaniṣad* 2.4.

[28] *Bhagavad Gītā* 11. 38-40.

[29] Swami Tyagisananda, *Aphorisms on the Gospel of Divine Love*, p. 50.

[30] See Swami Tyagisananda, *Aphorisms on the Gospel of Divine Love*, p. 50; Swami Prabhavananda *Nārada's Way of Divine Love*, p. 12.

[31] *Taittirīya Upaniṣad* 2.7.

[32] In this paragraph I rework somewhat a story appearing in *Bhāgavata Purāṇa* 1.12.1-30.

[33] See *Bhāgavata Purāṇa* 11.22.10.

[34] See *Chāndogya Upaniṣad* 6.14.1-2.

[35] *Vivekacūḍāmaṇi* 37-38, abbreviated slightly.

[36] *Kaṭha Upaniṣad* 2.8.

[37] Both quotations in this paragraph come from Swami Chidvilasananda, "In This Ecstasy There is No Dependence," *Darshan*, Volume 5 (August 1987), p. 72.

[38] Gurumayi Chidvilasananda, *The Magic of the Heart: Reflections on Divine Love* (South Fallsburg, NY: SYDA Foundation, 1996), p. 187.

[39] See for example *Caitanya Caritāmṛta* 19.133-145 and *Bhaktirasasaṁbodhinī* 6.

40 *Bhagavad Gītā* 16.4.

41 *Vivekacūḍāmaṇi* 112.

42 Swami Chidvilasananda, *My Lord Loves a Pure Heart*, pp. 135-136.

43 *Śivastotrāvalī* 5.22. Translated here by Constantina Rhodes Bailly, in *Shaiva Devotional Songs of Kashmir: A Translation and Study of Utpaladeva's Shivastotravali* (Albany: State University of New York Press, 1987), p. 51.

44 Swami Tyagisananda makes a similar point in his *Aphorisms on the Gospel of Divine Love*, p. 236.

45 *Bhagavad Gītā* 16.1-3

46 See for example, *Dhamma-cakka-ppavattana-sutta* 4, 8. The Pali here would be *sammā diṭṭhi* (right view), *sammā sankappa* (right thought), *sammā vācā* (right speech), *sammā kammanta* (right action), *samyak ājīva* (right livelihood), *sammā vāyāya* (right effort), *sammā sati* (right mindfulness) and *sammā samādhi* (right concentration).

47 See *Yoga Sūtra* 2.30-2.32. The Sanskrit terms here are: *ahiṁsā* (not wishing harm), *satya*, (truthfulness), *asteya* (not stealing), *brahmancarya* (sexual propriety), *aparigraha* (nongreediness), *śauca* (cleanliness), *saṁtośa* (equanimity), *tapas* (asceticism), *svādhyāya* (self-study), and *īśvara-pranidhāna* (reverential attitude toward the Lord).

48 See *Bhāgavata Purāṇa* 2.1.5 and 2.3.36, which mention the practices of hearing about God, singing God's praise, and remembering God.

49 See *Bhāgavata Purāṇa* 1.2.14, which refers to listening to words about God, chanting God's name, meditating and offering worship.

50 See *Bhāgavata Purāṇa* 10.10.38: praising God through one's speech, listening with one's ears to stories and teachings about God; serving God with one's hands; fixing one's mind on the feet of God; remembering God at all times; and offering reverence to the whole world, which is the abode of God.

51 See *Bhāgavata Purāṇa* 3.27.21-23: the performance of one's responsibilities in the world without any motivation other than service to God, an intense longing for God, a desire for direct knowledge of the truth, dispassion with regards to material possessions and worldly ambitions, austerity, hearing the sacred scriptures, and immersing into the inward divine presence through meditation.

52 See for example, *Bhāgavata Purāṇa* 7.5.23. As a unit, this group is known generally as *navadhā bhakti*, the "nine-fold devotion," and it consists of chanting God's name, remembering God's qualities, offering worship to God, surrendering to the feet of God, bowing to God's presence, serving God in a selfless manner, cultivating a sense of friendship with God, and giving oneself completely to God.

53 See *Bhāgavata Purāṇa* 2.3.19-24, 7.7.29, 7.7.30-36, 11.29.9-16, 11.19.20-23, 3.27.6-11, 4.22.22-25, 3.29.15-19, 11.11.34-41, 3.28.2-6, 5.5.10-13, 7.11.8-12, 11.3.23-31.

54 See for example *Śāṇḍilya Bhakti Sūtra* prose under 2.44.

55 *Nārada Bhakti Sūtra* 82.

56 See *Śāṇḍilya Bhakti Sūtra* 2.44 and Svapneśvara's commentary on this verse.

57 Gurumayi Chidvilasananda, "Love: The Tenderness behind the Shield," in *Kindle My Heart*, Revised Edition (South Fallsburg: SYDA Foundation, 1996) p. 36.

58 *Saṅgīta Ratnākāra* 1.3.1-2.

59 Gurumayi Chidvilasanda, "The Fire Love," *Darshan Magazine*, Volume 2 (1987), p. 71.

60 *Śrī Bhāṣya* 1.1.1.

61 *Śāṇḍilya Bhakti Sūtra* 2.44. The compound *tad-artha-prāṇa-sthāna* can be broken down from back to front as: *sthāna* (remaining firm, supporting), *prāṇa* (vital breath, thus life itself), *artha* (purpose) and *tad* (this, him: referring here to God).

62 *Bhagavad Gītā* 9.27.

63 *Bhāgavata Purāṇa* 11.14.23-24.

64 See *Bhāgavata Purāṇa* 1.6.16-19.

65 *Bihārī: The Satasaī*, translated from the Hindi and with an introduction by Krishna P. Bahadur (London and New York: Penguin Books, 1990), p. 74.

66 For textual support, see *Caitanya Caritāmṛta* 2.8.118-119.

67 *Śivastotrāvalī* 13.14-15. Translated here by Constantina Rhodes Bailly, *Shaiva Devotional Songs of Kashmir*, p. 78.

68 *Śivastotrāvalī* 5.15-16, in Bailly, *Shaiva Devotional Songs of Kashmir*, p. 50.

69 From *Songs of Kabir*, translated by Rabindranath Tagore (New York: Samuel Wieser, 1915; paperback edition 1974), pp. 80-81.

70 My use of the word *enstasy* recalls Mircea Eliade's use of it to describe the yogic state of inward repose, integration and completion. As far as I know, Eliade coined the term, forming it from *en-stasis*, the opposite of *ex-stasis* and thus of *ecstasy*. See for example his *Yoga: Immortality and Freedom*, translated by Willard R. Trask. Bollingen Series 56. Second edition. Princeton: Princeton University Press, 1969, Index *s.v.* "enstasy."

71 *The Devotional Poems of Mirabai*, translated by A. J. Alston, reprint edition (Delhi: Motilal Banarsidass, 1998), p. 102.

72 Relevant Sanskrit terms here would be: *romāñca* (horripilation), *stambha* (the sense of being stunned), *kanthāvarodha* or *svarabheda* (a catch of the voice in the throat or stumbling of words), *aśru* or *aśrunipāta* (flow of tears), *sveda* (perspiration), *vepathu* or *kampa* (a trembling in the body); *vaivarṇya* (shift in skin tone) and *pralaya* (a sense of dissolution).

73 See sūtra 54, discussed in Chapter 10, below.

74 *Bhagavad Gītā* 7.16-18.

75 *Jñāñeśvarī* 7.73.

76 *Jñāñeśvarī* 7.94. This rendering by Swami Kripananda is modified slightly.

77 *Bhagavad Gītā* 17.2-3.

78 *Śiva Sūtra* 1.12: *vismayo yogabhūmikāḥ*.

79 See for example *Bhāgavata Purāṇa* 1.3.30, 8.3.12, and 8.3.18.

80 *Kaṭha Upaniṣad* 2.2.

81 *Vivekacuḍāmaṇi* 22-26. Sanskrit terms here are *sama, dama, titiksa, śraddhā* and *samādhāna*, respectively.

82 *Bhāgavata Purāṇa* 6.4.34.

83 For this story, see for example *Bhāgavata Purāṇa* 10.29.1-10.33.30.

84 *Bhāgavata Purāṇā* 10.47.6-8.

85 *Bhāgavata Purāṇā* 10.46.4-6.

86 *Bhāgavata Purāṇā* 10.44.15.

87 See for example *Bhāgavata Purāṇa* 3.32.37.

[88] David L. Haberman has a good discussion of the difference between *kāma* and *preman*, as presented here, in his *Journey through the Twelve Forests: An Encounter with Kṛṣṇa* (New York: Oxford University Press, 1994), pp.162-163.

[89] See *Yoga Sūtra* 1.2 and various English translations.

[90] *Bhagavad Gītā* 9.34.

[91] *Bhagavad Gītā* 6.7.

[92] *Bṛhadāraṇyaka Upaniṣad* 4.3.32.

[93] *Bṛhadāraṇyaka Upaniṣad* 4.3.21.

[94] *Chāndogya Upaniṣad* 7.25.2.

[95] *Taittirīya Upaniṣad* 3.6.1.

[96] *Taittirīya Upaniṣad* 2.1-2.5.

[97] *Taittirīya Upaniṣad* 2.4.1.

[98] Daniel P. Sheridan, *Loving God: Kṛṣṇa and Christ: A Christian Commentary on the Nārada Bhakti Sūtras* (Leiden: W. B. Eerdmans, 2007), p. 39.

[99] *Bhagavad Gītā* 11.54.

[100] See for example *Yoga Sūtra* 3.4.

[101] See *Yoga Sūtra* 3.24.

[102] *Bhagavad Gītā* 8.22.

[103] *Gītā Bhāṣya* 9.34.

[104] *Bhāgavata Purāṇa* 3.29.11-14.

[105] *Bhāgavata Purāṇa* 3.25.32-33.

[106] *Jñāneśvarī* 11.676-678, 11.682-684, modified slightly.

[107] *Śivasotrāvalī* 9.3. In Bailly, *Shaiva Devotional Songs of Kashmir*, p. 59.

[108] *Bhāgavata Purāṇa* 11.14.27-28.

[109] See *Bhāgavata Purāṇa* 10.29.8-11.

[110] *Śvetāśvatara Upaniṣad* 6.23 uses the phrase *parā bhakti* and *Bhagavad Gītā* 18.68 *bhaktim param*. Similarly, *Bhāgavata Purāṇa* 4.11.30 refers to *paramabhakti* and says in 3.24.45 that one who expresses this devotion is immersed in *parābhakti-bhāva*, the refined sentiment of supreme spiritual devotion.

[111] *Jñāneśvarī* 6.480-481. This rendering by Swami Kripananda is modified slightly.

[112] *Bhāgavata Purāṇa* 4.8.41.

[113] *Bhāgavata Purāṇa* 7.7.55.

[114] *Bhāgavata Purāṇa* 1.5.22.

[115] *Bhāgavata Purāṇa* 6.3.22.

[116] See *Bhāgavata Purāṇa* 3.29.13-14.

[117] *Bhāgavata Purāṇa* 7.7.52.

[118] *Bhāgavata Purāṇa* 11.19.24.

[119] See *Bhāgavata Purāṇa* 1.1.1.

[120] See *Bhāgavata Purāṇa* 1.2.6.

[121] *Jñāneśvarī* 18.1135.

[122] Swami Chidvilasananda, *The Magic of the Heart*, p. 89.

[123] Swami Chidvilasananda, *The Magic of the Heart*, p. 212.

[124] *Bhāgavata Purāṇa* 11.2.45.

[125] *Jñāneśvarī* 9.219-227.

[126] See *Bṛhadāraṇyaka Upaniṣad* 2.4.

[127] *Bhagavad Gītā* 6.29-30.

[128] *Jñāneśvarī* 6.392-395.

Index

A

abhyāsa 148, 159
acyutārtha 242
adbhūta rasa 188
ahaitukī 143, 161, 237, 245
ahaitukī bhakti 143, 161, 245
ahiṁsā 79, 80, 81, 89, 272, 278
akhila 63, 66
akhilācāratā 63
ālambhana vibhāva 180, 183
amṛta 46, 47, 48, 49
anādyavidyā 55, 66
ānanda 82, 90, 127, 136, 137, 168, 218, 219, 221, 223, 234
ānanda-maya kośa 219, 223, 234
ananya 58, 59, 66, 143, 161, 228, 231, 234, 238, 245
ananya bhakti 66, 143, 161, 228, 231, 234, 238, 245
ananyatā 226, 227, 231
añjali mudrā 102, 116
anna 218, 219, 223
anna-maya kośa 218, 223
āntara śauca 82, 89
anubhava 208, 221
anubhavarūpa 208, 221
anubhāva 183, 208, 221
aparāvairāgya 187
arcana 101
arpita 63
artha 241, 242, 244, 279
āsakti 33, 101, 103, 114, 115, 116, 119
  ātmanivedana āsakti 114, 116
  dāsya āsakti 33, 103, 116
  sākhya āsakti 33
  smaraṇa āsakti 101, 119
āsana 11, 19, 106, 107, 116
āstikya 85, 86, 87, 89
aśuddha bhakti 161
Atharva Veda 5, 276
Ātmabodha 218, 223
ātma-kṛpā 60, 67
ātman 60, 67, 84, 106, 116, 126, 136, 152, 159, 221
ātmānanda 218
ātmanivedana āsakti 114, 116
ātmaniveśana 152, 159
ātmārāma 126, 128, 136
ātma-sammāna 106, 116
ātmavicāra 152, 159
avicchina 221
avidyā 54, 66, 152, 159

B

bahumāna 102, 116
bāhya śauca 82, 89
bhaga 7, 8, 19
Bhagavad Gītā vii, 10, 14, 26, 27, 32, 40, 74, 87, 94, 115, 141, 142, 144, 146, 201, 216, 227, 228, 253, 276, 277, 278, 279, 280, 281, 282
bhagavad-kṛpā 57, 60, 61, 67, 265
Bhagavān 7, 8, 15, 19, 26, 32, 108, 126, 151, 166, 167, 170

Bhāgavata 14, 17, 19, 20, 26, 55, 94, 99, 124, 125, 126, 151, 167, 190, 229, 232, 241, 242, 243, 249, 276, 277, 278, 279, 280, 281, 282
Bhāgavata Purāṇa 14, 55, 94, 99, 124, 125, 151, 167, 190, 229, 232, 241, 242, 243, 249, 276, 277, 278, 279, 280, 281, 282
bhagavottama 249
bhajana 101, 116, 166, 183
bhakta 27, 28, 29, 32, 35, 78, 101, 102, 103, 111, 140, 167, 169, 171, 175, 189, 201, 209, 217, 230, 240, 267
bhakti i, iii, iv, v, vi, vii, viii, ix, xi, 3, 7, 10, 13, 15, 16, 17, 19, 21, 24, 25, 26, 27, 28, 29, 30, 31, 32, 33, 35, 36, 40, 41, 45, 46, 51, 53, 62, 63, 66, 69, 70, 71, 72, 75, 78, 85, 86, 87, 91, 93, 94, 98, 100, 101, 103, 104, 105, 114, 115, 116, 121, 123, 124, 126, 139, 140, 142, 143, 147, 148, 149, 153, 154, 155, 157, 158, 161, 163, 164, 165, 166, 167, 168, 169, 170, 174, 181, 182, 188, 189, 191, 193, 194, 195, 205, 206, 208, 210, 212, 213, 220, 222, 226, 227, 228, 229, 231, 234, 237, 238, 239, 241, 242, 244, 245, 259, 261, 262, 268, 272, 275, 277, 279, 281
  ahaitukī bhakti 143, 161, 245
  ananya bhakti 66, 143, 161, 228, 231, 234, 238, 245
  bhāva bhakti 28, 33
  dāsya bhakti 28, 33
  eka bhakti 143, 161, 238, 245
  ekānta bhakti 238, 245
  haitukī bhakti 143, 161
  kevala bhakti 143, 161, 238, 245
  mādhurya bhakti 28, 33
  mukhya bhakti 245
  navadhā bhakti 279
  nirguṇa bhakti 157, 158, 161, 238, 245
  nirupādhi bhakti 143, 161, 238, 245
  niṣkāma bhakti 194, 205, 206, 245
  prema-bhakti 28, 33
  saguṇa bhakti 157, 158, 161
  sakāma bhakti 194, 205, 206
  sākhya bhakti 28, 33
  śānta bhakti 28, 33
  sopādhi bhakti 143, 161
  śuddha bhakti 157, 161, 212, 222, 238, 245
  vātsalya bhakti 28, 33
  viraha bhakti 28, 33
bhakti rasa 174, 188, 189
Bhaktirasasaṁbodhinī 277
bhakti sādhana 62, 66
bhakti śāstra 93, 98, 116
bhāva 28, 33, 118, 134, 136, 163, 169, 170, 171, 173, 174, 176, 179, 183, 184, 186, 199, 200, 206, 275, 281
  brahma bhāva 186
  dāsya bhāva 33, 186
  dhyāna bhāva 186
  divya bhāva 186
  mādhurya bhāva 186
  paśu bhāva 186
  pūjā bhāva 186
  sākhya bhāva 33, 186
  sākṣī bhāva 199, 200, 206
  śānta bhāva 186
  stava bhāva 186
  vātsalya bhāva 186
  vīra bhāva 186
bhāva bhakti 28, 33
bhavati 124, 140, 150, 259, 260, 266, 267, 268, 271, 273, 274
bhāyanaka rasa 188
bībhatsa rasa 188
bodha 92
brahma bhāva 186
Brahmakumāra 238, 244
Brahman 30, 109, 110, 112, 116, 117
Brahma Sūtra 30, 31, 277
Bṛhadāraṇyaka Upaniṣad 8, 38, 217, 251, 276, 277, 281, 282

C

cāritrya 79, 89
Chāndogya Upaniṣad 9, 57, 218, 276, 277, 281

D

dāsya āsakti 33, 103, 116
dāsya bhakti 28, 33
dāsya bhāva 33, 186
dayā 84, 89
devarṣi 14, 19

dharma 14, 19, 70, 89, 90, 241, 242, 244
dhūmāyita 134
dhyāna bhāva 186
dīpita 134
divya bhāva 186
duḥkha 203, 205
duḥsaṅga 71, 73, 89, 90

E

eka bhakti 143, 161, 238, 245
ekāgrata 227, 234
ekānta bhakti 238, 245
eka rasa 183
ekendriya vairāgya 178, 187

G

gauṇī 140, 159, 212, 268
guṇa 140, 144, 145, 147, 151, 156, 157, 159, 211, 221, 265
guṇarahita 211, 212, 221
guru/Guru 58, 59, 60, 66, 67, 95, 103, 116, 249
guru kṛpā 67
guru seva 103, 116

H

haitukī bhakti 143, 161
Hari 24, 32
hāsa 174, 183
hāsa sthāyibhāva 174
hāsya rasa 174, 188
haṭha yoga 11, 19, 116
hlādinī śakti 127

I

icchā 203, 205
Īśā Upaniṣad 11, 276

J

japa 111, 116, 117, 181
japājapa 111, 116, 117
japa mālā 111, 117
jñāna 92, 133, 136
Jñāneśvarī 144, 240, 249, 254, 276, 281, 282
jvalita 134

K

kāla 205
kāma 192, 193, 194, 195, 205, 212, 241, 242, 244, 266, 270, 281
kāmanarahita 212, 221
karma 145, 159
karuṇā 84, 89, 176, 188, 202
karuṇā rasa 176, 188, 202
Kaṭha Upaniṣad 58, 153, 277, 280
kevala bhakti 143, 161, 238, 245
kīrtana 107
kośa 218, 221, 223
  ānanda-maya kośa 223
  anna-maya kośa 223
  mano-maya kośa 223
  prāṇa-maya kośa 223
  vijñāna-maya kośa 223
krodha 176, 183, 266
kṛpā 56, 57, 60, 61, 66, 67, 93, 119, 265, 275
  ātma-kṛpā 60, 67
  bhagavad-kṛpā 57, 60, 61, 67, 265
  guru kṛpā 67
  mahat-kṛpā 57, 60, 61, 67
  śāstra kṛpā 67, 93, 119
Kṛṣṇa 15, 19, 20, 26, 27, 32, 54, 108, 115, 124, 125, 127, 131, 132, 133, 141, 142, 144, 151, 167, 190, 201, 227, 228, 229, 232, 233, 240, 243, 247, 249, 253, 254, 281

L

lābha 203, 205
leśa 60, 66
loka 253, 269

M

mādhurya bhakti 28, 33
mādhurya bhāva 186
mahābhāva 171, 174, 176, 177, 183, 185
mahānubhāva 174, 183
mahāśunya 117, 159
mahat-kṛpā 57, 60, 61, 67
mālā 111, 117
manana 96, 97, 117
manas 220, 221, 223
mano-maya kośa 218, 223

mantra 111, 116, 117, 181
matta 128
maya 218, 219, 223, 232, 234
  ānanda-maya 219, 223, 234
  anna-maya 218, 223
  mano-maya 218, 223
  prāṇa-maya 218, 223
  vijñāna-maya 219, 223
māyā 232, 234
mettā 84, 89
mokṣa 241, 242, 243, 244
mudrā
  añjali mudrā 102, 116
mukhya bhakti 245
mukhyatā 60

N

nāda 109, 117
Nāda Brahman 109, 110, 112, 117
nāman 107, 117
nāma-saṅkīrtana 107, 108, 117
navadhā bhakti 279
nididhyāsana 96, 97, 117
niḥsvārtha seva 103, 118
nirguṇa 151, 156, 157, 158, 159, 161, 238, 245
nirguṇa bhakti 157, 158, 161, 238, 245
nirodha 195, 205
nirupādhi bhakti 143, 161, 238, 245
niścinta 168
niṣkāma 194, 205, 206, 238, 245
niṣkāma bhakti 194, 205, 206, 245
niṣkriya 98, 118
nivedana 115, 116, 118
niyama 88, 89

O

oṁ 24, 32

P

parābhakti 28, 238, 244, 245, 247, 248, 250, 252, 253, 254, 275, 281
parādharma 242, 244
paramānanda 217, 220, 221
paramānanda-svarūpa 217, 221
paramapreman xi, 55, 60, 66, 139, 159, 194, 195, 208, 237
paramapremarūpa 35, 41, 49, 215, 259, 269
Paramātman 215, 221, 233
paramavyākula 64, 66
parāsatya 243, 244
parāvairāgya 179, 187
paśu bhāva 186
phala 239, 269
prāṇa 218, 219, 221, 223, 279
pranāma 102, 118
prāṇa-maya kośa 218, 223
praṇava 24, 32
prāṇāyāma 11, 20
prāpya 250, 260, 268
pratīkṣa 196, 205, 206
pratīkṣamāna 196, 200, 205, 206
pratikṣana 214
pratikṣana-vardhamāna 214
pratyāhāra 133, 136
prema-bhakti 28, 33
preman 33, 41, 49, 55, 66, 194, 212, 244, 281
preyas 153, 159
prīti 102, 118
pūjā 101, 118, 186
pūjā āsakti 273
pūjā bhāva 186
puruṣārtha 241, 244

R

rajas 144, 145, 146, 148, 150, 159, 212
rasa 48, 49, 174, 176, 177, 183, 185, 188, 189, 202, 275
  adbhūta rasa 188
  bhakti rasa 174, 188, 189
  bhāyanaka rasa 188
  bībhatsa rasa 188
  eka rasa 183
  hāsya rasa 174, 188
  karuṇā rasa 176, 188, 202
  raudra rasa 177, 188
  śānta rasa 188
  śṛngāra rasa 188
  vīra rasa 174, 188
raudra rasa 177, 188
Ṛg Veda 3, 14, 192, 276
rūpa 41, 46, 49, 208, 270, 271
rūpa āsakti 273

S

sādhana viii, ix, 53, 62, 66, 67, 69, 70, 75, 87, 88, 139, 148, 151, 152, 154, 158, 160, 164, 171, 177, 207, 209, 212, 217, 219, 230, 237, 238
sādhya 237
saguṇa bhakti 157, 158, 161
Śaiva 89, 90, 130, 186
sakāma bhakti 194, 205, 206
sākhya 28, 33, 186
sākhya āsakti 33
sākhya bhakti 28, 33
sākhya bhāva 33, 186
sakriya 98, 118
sākṣī bhāva 199, 200, 206
śakti 127, 136, 137
  hlādinī śakti 127
  saṁvit śakti 127, 137
  sandhinī śakti 127, 137
  svarūpa śakti 127, 137, 275
saṁgha 29, 32, 70, 90
Sāṁkhya 17, 20, 144, 145
sammāna 102, 106, 116, 118
saṁnyāsa 155, 160
saṁskāra 43, 49
saṁvit śakti 127, 137
samyama 228, 234
sandhinī śakti 127, 137
saṅga 70, 90, 105, 119
Saṅgīta Ratnākāra 110, 279
saṅgīta yoga 109, 118
saṅkīrtana 107, 108, 117, 118
  nāma-saṅkīrtana 107, 108, 117
śānta bhakti 28, 33
śānta bhāva 186
śānta rasa 188
śānti 33, 215, 217, 221
śāntirūpa 216
śāntirūpāt 215, 269
śarīra 210, 221, 222
  sthūla śarīra 221, 222
  sūkṣma śarīra 221, 222
sarva 169, 170
sarvadā 166, 169, 170, 272
sarvatadbhāva 118
śāstra 67, 93, 94, 98, 116, 119
śāstra kṛpā 67, 93, 119
sat 8, 20, 39, 82, 90, 105, 119, 125, 127, 132, 136, 137, 180, 269
Satasaī xii, 279
sat-cit-ānanda 82, 90, 127, 136
satsaṅga 105, 119
sattva 144, 145, 146, 149, 150, 159, 160, 212
sāttvikabhāva 125, 134, 136
satya 79, 82, 90, 244, 272, 278
śauca 79, 82, 83, 84, 89, 90, 272, 278
  āntara śauca 82, 89
  bāhya śauca 82, 89
seva 103, 116, 118, 119
  niḥsvārtha seva 103, 118
sevana 103, 119
Śiva 78, 89, 90, 110, 130, 150, 280
Śivastotrāvalī 278, 279
Śiva Sūtras 150
smaraṇa 64, 67, 100, 101, 119
smaraṇa āsakti 101, 119
śoka 175, 176, 183
śoka sthāyibhāva 176
sopādhi bhakti 143, 161
śravana 96, 117
śreyas 140, 149, 153, 160
śrī 140, 149, 160
śṛṅgāra rasa 188
stabdha 131
stava bhāva 186
sthāyibhāva 171, 173, 174, 176, 184, 185
  hāsa sthāyibhāva 174
  śoka sthāyibhāva 176
  vīra sthāyibhāva 174
sthūla śarīra 210, 221, 222
śuddha bhakti 157, 161, 212, 222, 238, 245
sūkṣma 210, 211, 221, 222
sūkṣma śarīra 210, 221, 222
sūkṣmatara 211, 222
sūtra 13, 15, 16, 20, 25, 30, 36, 41, 45, 46, 55, 56, 57, 58, 60, 62, 63, 64, 65, 70, 71, 72, 74, 75, 78, 79, 80, 84, 85, 86, 87, 88, 90, 91, 92, 93, 96, 101, 103, 107, 114, 124, 125, 126, 128, 131, 135, 140, 144, 149, 150, 153, 163, 164, 166, 167, 170, 171, 189, 190, 191, 192, 193, 194, 195, 196, 200, 201, 202, 203, 204, 207, 208, 211, 213, 214, 215, 217, 226, 230, 231, 232, 233, 238, 239, 247, 250, 251, 252, 253, 280

svarūpa 46, 49, 127, 137, 217, 221
paramānanda-svarūpa 217, 221
svarūpa śakti 127, 137, 275
Śvetāśvatara Upaniṣad 8, 10, 276, 281

T

tadarthaprāṇasthāna 115
Taittirīya Upaniṣad 218, 223, 277, 281
tamas 144, 145, 146, 147, 148, 150, 159, 160, 212
tanmaya 232
tyāga 75, 76, 90
tyājya 75, 90

U

udāsinatā 230
udbodha 92
uddīpana vibhāva 180, 184
uddīpita 134
utsāha 174, 184

V

vairāgya 154, 155, 160, 178, 184, 187, 275
ekendriya vairāgya 178, 187
vaśīkara vairāgya 178, 184, 187
vyatireka vairāgya 178, 187
yatamāna vairāgya 178, 187
Vaiṣṇava 20, 186
vandana 102, 118
vardhamāna 214
pratikṣana-vardhamāna 214
vāsanā 43, 49
vaśīkara vairāgya 178, 184, 187
vātsalya bhakti 28, 33
vātsalya bhāva 186
vibhāva 180, 183, 184
ālambhana vibhāva 180, 183
uddīpana vibhāva 180, 184
vijñāna 219, 220, 223
vijñāna-maya kośa 219, 223
vīnā 14, 20
vīra 174, 186, 188
vīra bhāva 186
viraha bhakti 28, 33
vīra rasa 174, 188
vīra sthāyibhāva 174
virodha 230
virodhiṣu 230
vismaraṇa 64, 67
Viṣṇu 15, 19, 20, 110, 274
viveka 153, 154, 160
vṛtti 119
vyabhicārabhāva 171, 184, 185
vyākula 64, 66, 67
vyatireka vairāgya 178, 187

Y

yajña 76, 90
yama 88, 89, 90
yatamāna vairāgya 178, 187
yoga vii, viii, ix, 11, 12, 19, 20, 30, 71, 77, 81, 83, 86, 87, 88, 91, 99, 100, 105, 109, 112, 113, 116, 118, 123, 148, 149, 150, 165, 170, 181, 182, 195, 201, 212, 225, 234, 237, 240, 252, 253, 263
haṭha yoga 11, 19, 116
saṅgīta yoga 109, 118
Yoga Sūtra 13, 30, 88, 89, 90, 228, 278, 281
yogī/yoginī viii, 12, 13, 20, 23, 53, 76, 96, 112, 125, 133, 170, 177, 203, 234

Contact Information

For more on William K. Mahony, including information on his workshops and retreats, please go to his website:

www.wkmahony.com

For more information on books published by Anusara Press, please contact us:

Anusara Press™
9400 Grogan's Mill Road, Suite 240
The Woodlands, TX 77380
(888)398-9642
(281)367-2744 (fax)
www.anusara.com